ALWAYS RED

ALSO BY LEN McCLUSKEY

Why You Should Be A Trade Unionist

ALWAYS RED

LEN McCLUSKEY

OR Books
New York · London

© 2021 Len McCluskey

Published by OR Books, New York and London
Visit our website at www.orbooks.com

All rights information: rights@orbooks.com

First printing 2021

Library of Congress Cataloging-in-Publication Data: A catalog record for this book is available from the Library of Congress.
British Library Cataloging in Publication Data: A catalog record for this book is available from the British Library.

Typeset by Lapiz Digital. Printed by CPI in the United Kingdom.

hardcover ISBN 978-1-68219-272-6 • ebook ISBN 978-1-68219-276-4

Dedicated to

The City of Liverpool

CONTENTS

FOREWORD

I knew of Len McCluskey years ago, long before I met him. I knew of his leadership abilities and of the role he played alongside the Liverpool dockers in their disputes. He has always shown his upfront support for the working class and the victimised.

Len tells it like it is and, in my experience, is not frightened of getting his hands dirty. His support for the Shrewsbury 24 Campaign—in which, of course, he was campaigning for me and the other 23 building workers unjustly prosecuted after picketing in 1972—was second to none and he spoke out about it on many, many occasions. He has never wavered in his support for the pickets.

Another personal experience I had with Len was one Saturday morning in a church in Liverpool. The rain was torrential that day. Len was filling bags at a food bank and giving them to people who were struggling. Apart from handing out the food bags he made time to have a word with everyone who came in. Helping out in the foodbank was an incredibly moving experience for me as it was obvious some of the people who came for the food were working and couldn't manage on the pittance they were being paid in their employment. We stayed until everybody had been sorted out before calling it a day and making our separate ways home.

One thing that stands out to me about Len happened in the CASA club in Liverpool. I don't know the origins of the club, only that it was known as the dockers' club (I think it may have been purchased by dock workers with their redundancy payments). I was sitting listening to a group of dockers talking about some dispute taking place and Len's name was mentioned. When they stopped for a break, I asked one of them what Len McCluskey was like and, to a person, they all chipped in: "He's one of us."

There can be no greater accolade from one worker to another than to be acknowledged as "one of us."

I have always enjoyed Len's confrontations with members of the establishment in TV debates and with the employers whose only aim in life is to put profit before people. I know he is passionate about many things: the struggles of the working class, the Hillsborough campaign, the NHS and many other causes.

The authenticity of his story comes across in these pages. It is told with passion and humour but often touched with a poignant sadness. In reading it, as I urge you to do, you will discover the real Len McCluskey.

—Ricky Tomlinson

April 2021

INTRODUCTION

This is the story of a class fighter. The story of a workers' representative. The fight for my class runs through the tapestry of my life like a bright red thread, from the quaysides of Liverpool docks to the prime minister's office in 10 Downing Street.

The history I have witnessed along the way has been dramatic. The power of organised labour was reaching its height when I was elected as a trade union shop steward at the age of 19. But it wasn't to last—in the 1980s, as a union officer, I felt the blows as Margaret Thatcher's government beat working people back. I played my part in the trade unions' great move left after the disappointment of New Labour. And as the general secretary of the most powerful union in the country I was at the centre of national politics during a tumultuous time, as a golden opportunity for the left was dashed on the rocks of Brexit.

Through it all, I have embraced a 'fighting back' culture. My trade union, Unite, is a 'fighting back' union—we don't go looking for trouble, but we never walk away from a fight if our members are attacked. The same 'fighting back' instinct has shaped my politics—a refusal to accept that the status quo is good enough for our people. That has led me to take risks and adopt positions that are not the norm for a trade union leader, from refusing to ever repudiate a strike, to throwing Unite's support behind social movements and direct-action groups, to sustaining Jeremy Corbyn as Labour leader. Controversy and criticism have never been in short supply—but every decision I have taken has been for a purpose, and I stand by them all.

I have no sympathy with the idea that trade unions should confine themselves to workplace issues, although of course representing our members at work is our first duty. We should never be shy about raising our voice in the political arena. But for me it goes deeper than that: trade unions are built on the working-class values of solidarity and community spirit—the impulse to help each other out and stand together in the face of adversity. Our members don't leave those values behind when they clock off work; they carry them into the communities in which they live. So I believe trade unions must be part of those communities too, and part of wider society, concerned with the full range of issues that confront working people.

That outlook was formed by my experiences growing up in Liverpool surrounded by a strong and proud working-class community. Liverpool, of course, is a red city, and although it has both a red and a blue football team, I was always red. On the terraces at Anfield, watching my Liverpool heroes, I felt the power of togetherness—a community spirit so strong it later sustained a 30-year campaign to get justice for the 96 killed at Hillsborough, a tragedy I witnessed firsthand. At work, as a young man on the Liverpool docks, solidarity was a way of life. Working-class values anchored me as I rose up through my trade union and then guided me as I moulded Unite into the powerhouse it has become.

Those experiences are recounted in part one of this book, 'From Cradle to Brave.' They have made me the trade unionist I am today. Despite my years as an official, I still think like a shop steward—insisting the bureaucracy in a union should serve the workers, not the other way around—and I always back workers in struggle. But I am acutely aware that the circumstances of that struggle, and just how hard workers have to fight to win the dignity and respect they deserve, are determined by politics.

It was a political decision to make the lives of working-class people harsher and harder by attacking their trade unions in the 1980s. As a result of that class warfare, inequality widened, wealth became more concentrated at the top, and the share of national income that found its way into the pockets of workers shrank dramatically. This happened because organised labour was shackled, while unbridled capitalism was allowed to lay waste to our communities. This is the world in which trade unions have had to operate ever since.

So I make no apology for the prominent political role I have played to try to right those wrongs. Although my involvement in politics has taken up only a fraction of my time since becoming Unite's general secretary in 2011, my account of those experiences makes up the majority of this book due to the extraordinary rollercoaster ride it has been and the importance of the events I have witnessed. The main thrust of this story is reflected in the title of part two, 'From Falkirk to Finsbury Park.' A phoney 'scandal' in the Scottish constituency of Falkirk was used by Ed Miliband's Labour Party to mount an outrageous attack on my union that led directly, astonishingly, to the rise of Jeremy Corbyn, the unassuming MP from Finsbury Park in Islington. It was a spectacular example of the law of unintended consequences—an attempt to neuter the trade unions and the left had the opposite result. But from Unite's point of view, that outcome was not entirely accidental. We were instrumental in securing the democratic changes to the party that opened the way for Corbyn, and it was our backing once he emerged as a leadership contender that gave him the legitimacy and resources to succeed.

I don't back away from my part in that history. I know that had there been a different general secretary of Unite, Corbyn might never have become leader in 2015 and wouldn't have survived the coup against him nine months later by the spineless bullies of the Parliamentary Labour Party. It was Unite that rallied trade union support behind him and commissioned the legal advice to ensure he would be on the ballot in a second leadership contest, and I was the one working to buy him time in negotiations with Labour's deputy leader Tom Watson. But while I'm proud of the role I played, the real credit belongs to Corbyn for taking the fight to the establishment and to his shadow chancellor John McDonnell for turning the tide against austerity.

Having spent the Miliband years trying to work out—as general secretaries always do—how to influence a Labour leader, I suddenly found myself in a very different position. I was part of the 'Corbyn Project' and that made me public enemy number two. Those behind the failed coup against Corbyn soon turned their attention to unseating me as general secretary, with a campaign of smears and negativity that was alien to the trade union movement.

So the result of the snap general election in June 2017 came as sweet vindication. Against all expectations, Corbyn's Labour recorded the biggest increase in its share of the vote since 1945, deprived the Tories of their majority, and came within touching distance of power. If not for a campaign of sabotage from within his own party, Corbyn would have been in Number 10. That general election proved it is possible to win support for a left-wing programme, contrary to all the naysayers and doom-mongers. It gave hope to future generations.

But it's a historical tragedy that just at this moment of breakthrough for the left, British politics became consumed by a constitutional issue that undermined the class appeal of the slogan 'For the many, not the few.' Brexit dealt Corbyn a terrible hand. Labour was split from top to bottom. It would be difficult to invent an issue less suited to Corbyn's style of leadership or more destructive of his insurgent, outsider credentials. Every Labour MP had promised to respect the referendum result in the 2017 election, but now shadow Brexit secretary Keir Starmer led the charge for a second vote, and for Labour to become a 'Remain party.' That made no sense to me—nearly all the seats Labour needed to gain to win an election, and those it had to hold to avoid defeat, were in Leave-voting areas.

I favoured breaking free of this horrible, divisive issue by allowing a deal to pass so long as it accommodated Labour's priorities of protecting jobs and rights. I knew there was a deal to be done because I was engaged in secret negotiations with Theresa May's government. But within the Labour leadership, the pro-Remain faction, which came to include Jeremy's two closest political friends, Diane Abbott and John McDonnell, gained the upper hand. The once tight-knit team around Jeremy pulled apart and the Corbyn Project unravelled. As Labour descended into incoherence, the Tories reinvented themselves under Boris Johnson with a single-minded mission to get Brexit done. It was like watching a slow-motion car crash as we headed for an inevitable general election. That contest—a Brexit election, be in no doubt—confirmed my worst fears, and the greatest chance the British left ever had slipped through our fingers.

I was angry that my unheeded advice had been proved right in the worst possible way. But I didn't expect Keir Starmer, of all people, to agree. Corbyn's successor quickly reversed his position on Brexit, insisting Labour had to appeal to the Leave-voting 'red wall' constituencies that had switched to the Tories. Labour's dalliance with a second referendum had served him well, if not the party.

I initially got on well with Keir, speaking to him more regularly than I had to Jeremy. But though our conversations were positive, I found he would regularly do the opposite of what we had discussed. He had won the leadership standing on 10 Corbyn-esque policy pledges and a promise of party unity, yet soon began abandoning those positions and hounding out the left, employing bureaucratic tricks that would have made even Tony Blair blush.

This all culminated in the extraordinary, appalling and destructive decision to suspend Jeremy Corbyn—Keir's decision, he told me on the phone shortly after taking it, despite his public insistence that Labour's general secretary had made the call. As Keir saw it, Jeremy had contradicted a line in his speech on the Equality and Human Rights Commission's report into antisemitism in the Labour Party. I'm sure it was a kneejerk reaction, a fit of temper, because the very next day I was sat opposite Keir for a secret meeting on how Jeremy could be readmitted to the party. As I reveal in this book, a deal was struck to lift the suspension on the basis of a statement in Jeremy's name co-authored by Keir's office.

Although things proceeded as planned, with Jeremy publishing the statement and a panel of the party's ruling body readmitting him, Keir then reneged on our deal by withdrawing the whip, leaving Jeremy as a party member but not a Labour MP. It was a dishonourable and shoddy way to behave with potentially disastrous consequences for Labour and his own leadership. I didn't speak to Keir after that. The trust I had placed in him had proved to be misguided.

Once again, the left has found itself down but not out. The conditions that led to its resurgence have not gone away, but it is time to go back to first principles. I believe the left must never lose sight of class politics. The main lesson I draw from a lifetime of experience is that hope lies in organised labour. It's the struggle of working people to secure what they are due that fuels the forward motion of history. So this book ends with a return to the industrial sphere to address the future of trade unionism and how Unite is pioneering new ways to strengthen collective action in the face of formidable challenges, from the Covid pandemic to the automation of millions of jobs.

Perhaps unexpectedly, the dramatic ups and downs of a turbulent era have only bolstered my faith in the future. The left has demonstrated that our radical policies are popular and our antiestablishment convictions are shared by millions. The times demand solutions that only the left and the labour movement are offering. Provided our confidence is unshaken and we keep the flame of hope burning, I know our time will come. That's why I will be always red.

PART ONE

FROM CRADLE TO BRAVE

CHAPTER 1

A LIVERPOOL UPBRINGING

Margaret and Leonard McCluskey didn't think they would have another son. Six years had passed since their three-year-old boy, John, died of consumption—that terrible disease that killed so many working-class people. Leonard, because he was at war, only saw young John on five occasions—the sixth was to bury him.

Margaret (Peggy) and Leonard (Len) were a typical working-class couple, strong in character and kind of heart. Born in Liverpool in 1915 and 1912 respectively, they had endured all the hardship of the '20s and '30s followed by the fear and stress of war. They had a daughter, Kathleen, whom they loved very much. But by 1950, once things had finally settled down, they were 35 and 38—an unremarkable time of life to have children nowadays but considered old back then. No wonder they regarded it as a "miracle" when, on Sunday, 23 July, at Oxford Street Hospital in Liverpool, they welcomed a new baby boy into the world. They named me after my dad.

> *I was born in Liverpool, down by the docks,*
> *Me religion was Catholic, occupation hard knocks.*
> *At stealing from lorries I was adept,*
> *And under old overcoats each night I slept.*

The opening lines of the famous song 'In My Liverpool Home' could almost describe my start—I'm not so sure about the hard knocks, and the overcoats weren't needed every night, but still. That kid from the back streets of Liverpool feels a world away from this man described by the journalist Owen Jones:

"McCluskey is the most powerful trade union leader, dominating the industrial and political scene for more than a decade. Without him, Corbynism simply wouldn't exist." The question is: how did one become the other?

———————

Every family has stories passed down from one generation to the next that define their identity and place in the world. Here is one of mine. My maternal grandma died in her early forties leaving my granddad to look after one son and four daughters. He was a big, powerful man, a stoker on ships. He was on the Carpathia when it arrived to pick up survivors from the Titanic. At times he would fall out of work and there would be no money. My Aunty Lil told me of an occasion when the family was huddled in the kitchen in the winter cold, with no heat and no light. Lil, Aunty Sue, Aunty Mary, and the youngest, Uncle Larry, were crying while my granddad tried to keep them warm with coats. "Don't worry, now," he said, "our Maggie will be home soon and it's pay day, she'll have some pennies for the gas." Maggie—my mum—was 14 years old at the time, working in a bakery. Here was this proud, hardworking man having to rely on his young daughter to keep his family warm. I can imagine how his dignity must have been shattered. That is the heritage that defines me. I am sometimes accused of being a class fighter—damn right I am. There are families suffering the same miseries today and I'll go on fighting for my class for as long as I can.

I can thank my mum for the security that comes from always having someone on my side. Throughout my life she has had my back. I could never do any wrong, even when I did. She was strong and fiercely protective, yet every bit as tender as her beautiful singing voice. Ours was a large family with plenty of aunts, uncles and cousins. My mum was at the centre of it. It was only after she had gone at the age of 96 that I realised how important she had been in holding the family together.

Unsurprisingly, given her teenage experiences, my mum was the matriarch of my family when I was growing up. Whenever I wanted to buy something my dad would refer me to her, saying: "You should see the Chancellor." She was brilliant at balancing the finances, which was quite a feat because while she had a steady job in a medium-sized clothes shop owned by the Thompsons family, my dad, as a ship repairer, would be in and out of work moving from one job to the next. Her budgeting meant my sister and I never wanted for anything. In fact, while this was not true of Kathleen, I would go so far as to admit that I was a spoiled child.

My dad spent his life in the shipyards and on the docks chasing work. He prided himself on his work ethic—"an honest day's work for an honest day's pay." He was the loveliest man I have ever met. He saw the good in everyone, very rarely said a bad word about those he knew, and would always put himself out for others. Like so many of his generation, the War took its toll on his health and in later life he suffered heart attacks and strokes. He died in 1984 aged 72. One of my great regrets is that I never told him I loved him. I've asked myself why a thousand times over. Maybe it was some working-class macho thing.

If my dad was the loveliest man I have ever met, our Kath is the loveliest person I have ever met—my big sister, who even today still wants to know if her little brother is OK. She has always been the calmest, gentlest of souls, kindness personified, ready to help anyone in need. When she speaks I hear my dad.

Growing up at 9 Iris Street in Kirkdale was a happy experience. It was a home full of love and warmth, despite the fact our two-up-two-down terraced house was long past its demolition date. Most of those Coronation Street-style houses had a lean-to shed in the small back yard constructed by the tenants. That became the kitchen, with the original kitchen serving as the 'living room,' and the front room converted into a 'parlour.' In our house my dad added a vestibule so you didn't step directly in from the street. There wasn't a toilet inside; it was in the small back yard, which was also home to the tin bath that hung by a nail on the whitewashed wall. Those terraces, because of their age, were subject to infestations by rats, mice and, to my horror, cockroaches, provoking a dislike I am not over to this day. I slept in my mum and dad's bedroom until I was 10, when Kath, who was 10 years older than me, got married and left home.

Having lost one son, my parents took no chances with me. I was wrapped in cotton wool, especially by my dad. As a result, I contracted every childhood disease you could name, from measles to chickenpox and whooping cough. I even had pneumonia. My mum would later say she should have thrown me out on the street more often to harden me up.

What I remember most about my childhood is a close sense of community on our street and those surrounding it. There were 40 houses on our road, 20 on either side, with the obligatory corner shop. If someone was in trouble, neighbours would rally around. I don't want to paint an idyllic picture because there were plenty of fights and arguments, normally about children, but all in all people pulled together. I can recall the vibrancy of the street whenever a 7-year-old made their Holy Communion and the unbridled joy, excitement and chaos of the send-off for the annual charabanc trip to the Blackpool Illuminations. I remember the street party for the Queen's coronation in 1953 and the celebrations when the local priest, Father Taylor, became a canon. Weeks were spent making wooden trellises to go around the front doors, which were then covered with homemade paper roses. The edges of the curbs were painted with whitewash ready for the procession. Everyone joined in, even if they weren't Catholic.

On Saturday nights my mum, dad, aunts, uncles and their friends would go to the Miranda pub or St Richard's Club. When time was called they would gather in each other's houses for a singsong and a few more drinks while us kids tried to sneak a sip of alcohol. On New Year's Eve everyone came out into the street to hear the ships in the Mersey sound their horns to herald the New Year. Sometimes 40 or 50 ships would join in—it was quite a sound. Then we would dance, arm in arm, through the other streets. The joy was palpable—it feels as if I could reach out and touch it.

As kids we played in the street from morning until night—typical children's games like Kick the Can and Knock Down Ginger, as well as every kind of sport, especially football and cricket with imaginary wickets or stumps chalked on the wall. When Wimbledon was on we would play tennis with an invisible net and homemade rackets. A gang of us would sometimes go to Stanley Park to play our games, especially on a Friday after confession in St Richard's Church.

I had a strange experience at confession when I was 11 years old. I found myself having a conversation with the priest that was way beyond my comprehension.

He asked if I liked the feel of velvet, to which I replied, "Yes." Did I stroke it (the velvet)? "Yes." Did I do it with other boys? By this time I had no idea what he was talking about, but I could sense that he liked me to answer yes. The inquisition came to a sudden stop and he absolved me from whatever sin I had committed, giving me five Our Fathers and 20 Hail Marys. The normal penance was about one Our Father and five Hail Marys. Afterwards my mates wanted to know what I had received. I was reluctant, not to say scared, to tell them in case I really had transgressed. When they eventually got it out of me they were aghast and asked what I had done wrong. Of course, I didn't know, so I fended them off with, "That's privileged between me and the priest." My street cred soared and I became very popular. Looking back, maybe that was the moment I developed a taste for controversy.

When it came to politics, ours was a Labour household in a Labour area. My mum and dad were Labour through and through—they said they would sooner cut off their right arm than vote Tory—but they were not political activists. They were in awe of the National Health Service—with my childhood sicknesses it seemed I was forever at the GP surgery. They used to tell me how it was before the NHS, when young women with sick children would beg for the pennies needed to see the doctor. "Whatever you do in life, son, always fight to defend the NHS," my dad told me.

I can also vividly remember my dad relating experiences of the liberation of the Nazi death camps that had been relayed to him. He had a photo album that depicted the horrors of the Holocaust and explained the evil nature of the Nazi creed. Those stories and images have stayed with me and guided me all my life. I can still feel the disgust and anger that gripped me, and the sense of sorrow for all those murdered, but in particular the Jewish people. As a result, I have been a passionate fighter against antisemitism since I was 12.

Around the age of 13 my dad gave me the novel 'The Ragged-Trousered Philanthropists' and told me it was one reason, so they said, that Labour had won the 1945 election because it had been passed between soldiers during the War. The central character, Owen, is like my dad—a very talented painter and decorator whose skill was not appreciated. The book was a big influence on me as I became politically aware, but in particular it was the need to recognise the skill of workers, whatever their job, that stayed with me. I have visited many hundreds of factories and workplaces since and I have always been struck by the pride people take in their work.

The novel's author, Robert Tressell (real name Noonan), died in Liverpool aged 40, before his book was published. He was buried in a pauper's grave with 12 other poor, unfortunate souls. Thanks to the work of volunteers, his burial site was discovered opposite Walton Gaol in 1970 and a beautiful headstone was laid in 1977 (there is a replica in Unite's offices in Liverpool). On the day of the ceremony, my dad and I joined a march of trade unionists, banners flying, to Walton Trades and Labour Club where a local theatre group treated us to an enactment of the famous 'money trick' scene from the novel.

My dad was a solid trade unionist but never an activist. He believed everyone should be in a trade union and I now realise that in his own quiet way he instilled his values in me. His first union was the National Amalgamated Society of Operative, House and Ship Painters and Decorators (what a mouthful), which eventually became part of the Union of Construction, Allied Trades and Technicians (UCATT). Later on, he would constantly tell me that UCATT and my original union, the Transport and General Workers' Union (T&G)—which subsequently became Unite—should come together. I told this story to the UCATT executive in 2017 when I was trying to persuade them to merge with Unite, and got a little emotional about it. (I don't know if it helped convince them but they did decide to merge.) At a gathering in Scotland the following year, Steve Dillon, who had been a regional secretary in UCATT, presented me with a beautifully framed poster advertising my dad's first union (I won't write out the name again) with the inscription: "Presented to Len McCluskey in memory of his father, Leonard McCluskey, Snr." If I had been emotional at the UCATT executive, it was nothing compared to my reaction at receiving this gift, which brought me to tears. I took it to Liverpool to show my sister Kath, my niece Karen and my son Ian, and there was more crying. My dad would have been proud.

I was educated in Catholic schools—I say educated, but it wasn't particularly educational. My schooling was strict, not very stimulating, and remembered primarily for priests and nuns trying to get money out of me for one religious cause or another. There were 40 to a class at St Alexander primary school. We had senseless fights with the pupils from St Paul's Protestant school in the same road, even though some of them were mates from my street with whom I got on fine when playing games. The experience incubated doubts in my mind about religion that grew into a full-blown rejection later in life. I'm not an atheist; I'm agnostic—or a fence sitter according to my nephew Mark, who is more like my younger brother. I see religion as a force that seeks to divide people, and anything that divides workers is, I believe, bad.

From St Alex's I went first to Major Street school, which was being demolished around our ears before it fell down, and then to the brand new Pope Pius X school at the Rotunda, the junction of Stanley Road and the infamous Scottie (Scotland) Road. Having failed my 11-plus (I can't remember a thing about it), I passed the 13-plus—an exam for 'late developers'—and went off to Cardinal Godfrey school where I spent five eventful years.

The headmaster was Brother Moran, a Christian brother who was also a psychopath. He would regularly appear from the headmaster's study, cane in hand (the cane was almost as big as him), and in true Errol Flynn-style he would charge up the corridor slashing from side to side at any unfortunate boys in the way. He would time his sorties to coincide with the change of class, when the corridor would be heaving with easy targets. Panic would spread. Boys would desperately try to get back into the classroom they had just left, often to find their teacher had quietly stepped inside and locked the door. As quickly as it started the terror would be over as the 'Gaffer' returned to his lair and schooling resumed with boys nursing cuts and bruises. Of course, had we reported these outrages to our parents we would have received another blow on the grounds that we "must have deserved it." How things have changed since, probably for the best—probably.

The sixth form at Cardinal Godfrey was split into arts and sciences—I was in arts. There were only six of us and we thought we were the bee's knees—flamboyant and controversial, unlike our opposite numbers in science who were far more serious and studious. Our free lessons were spent playing poker (at which I became quite proficient) and making spliffs. I forged friendships that have endured to this day with Peter Walsh, John Foley and George McCain. The family of another friend in our class, Paul Georgeson, owned a garage (which is still there) on Breck Road. Regularly, Paul would come into school in a classic car he had borrowed. On Fridays the whole school would walk down the road to attend Mass at St Michael's Church. We would jump in whichever car Paul had that day and slowly drive past the students and staff, giving a royal wave. The best times were when he had a Rolls-Royce or a Bentley. Understandably, the teachers regarded us with contempt, but to some of the younger boys we were rebels and heroes.

On the whole, I enjoyed school, especially for the camaraderie of friends and the sport—football, basketball and volleyball. We had a typical physically strong PE teacher who was credited with introducing volleyball to Merseyside schools. He was also an avid basketball player, although I think his enjoyment mainly came from being able to out-muscle and intimidate 16 and 17-year-old boys (basketball is a very physical game). However, on one occasion when the sixth form played the teachers at football, one of my teammates scythed him down and he collapsed in a heap. I can still hear the raucous cheers from the boys around the pitch ringing in my ears (I am sure I detected a smile on some of the teachers' faces too). The sense of togetherness among the pupils was palpable. Being part of a collective has always appealed to me. To allow individuals to flourish is vital, but there is something noble about a group having a common goal—even if it is just to bring down the PE teacher.

In the upper sixth we were all made prefects. We took to our new status with relish, strutting around the building instructing younger boys to do chores, but we soon got fed up with that, especially as more and more of them would tell us to fuck off. I realised then that a little badge on your lapel doesn't bring you respect; you have to earn it by your actions. We got our chance when we were put in charge of the tuck shop. Unbeknown to the headmaster, we hit upon an incentive scheme. Long before it became a common retail slogan, we introduced buy-one-get-one-free (BOGOF). It was a raging success. Every day the boys would excitedly ask us what was on offer. We had to control the queues in the corridor. The Gaffer was delighted as the pennies piled up into pounds (there's nothing quite like money to keep the Church happy). This went on for 12 glorious weeks. We were loved by everyone.

Then came the dreadful day of reckoning. It was a lovely afternoon, we were on a free lesson sitting in our small classroom playing cards, smoking, the sun was streaming through the open window, the birds were singing in the trees and God was in his heaven. All was well with the world, when suddenly the serene peace was broken by a piercing sound, much like a banshee caught in a bear trap. The quizzical looks on our faces turned to fear and panic when someone mentioned the words "stock take." There was no mistaking the Gaffer's screams as he discovered that the profit he thought was accruing was in fact a serious loss. We needed to make ourselves scarce and quick about it, but his anger propelled him with such speed that he caught us as we were trying to escape. As he lashed us with his cane he repeated in his broad Irish accent, "Youse Liverpool boys, youse Liverpool boys are teeves, teeves, get out of my school."

We stayed away for about a week, enough time for our cuts to heal, and then quietly slipped back into class to complete our A-levels. My only foray into being an entrepreneur had ended in ignominy. I've had a sneaking admiration for businesspeople ever since—but don't tell anyone.

———————

Throughout my teens, politics seemed to be all around, but there was no single, eye-opening moment that made me political. I remember coming home from school and switching on the TV to hear that JFK had been assassinated. I was 13 and I cried. I didn't know the true significance but I felt something bad had happened. TV brought into our living room the horror and futility of the Vietnam War and allowed us to see the police brutality against those fighting for Black civil rights in America (as I write the appalling murder of George Floyd has sparked protests under the banner 'Black Lives Matter' across the US and the world, demonstrating that too little has changed). Catholics began demanding civil rights in Northern Ireland, a cause closely followed in Liverpool. I was also aware of the attacks on the Cuban people for having the audacity to overthrow a corrupt dictator in hock to the pimps and the Mafia of the US. The romantic image of Che Guevara began to appear on posters and T-shirts everywhere—the face of youthful revolution against the establishment.

Harold Wilson was elected prime minister in 1964, ending 13 years of Conservative government. The result was greeted with great joy in our house and throughout our neighbourhood. Wilson, whose constituency was in Liverpool (Huyton), had a distinctive image, with his Gannex Macintosh and a pipe. My dad smoked a pipe; I remember taking a collection of his pipes into our sixth form general studies discussions for my mates to display when we were in debate. Our teacher, Brother Cowan, was not amused.

The infectious politics of the 1960s went hand-in-hand with the social revolution tearing up the rules—all set to a soundtrack of pop music, with Liverpool its beating heart. My cousin Vinny (I always smile when I see the Joe Pesci film) was a good guitarist and our friend Keith was brilliant on his Gibson. I wasn't a bad singer so, along with a mate, Ian, on drums, like thousands of Liverpool boys we formed a pop group. Our first gig was at the Derby Arms in Derby Road, Bootle, where one of our uncles knew the manager. The excitement, anticipation and fear we felt as we rehearsed our 'set' was enough to give a real adrenalin rush. It's fair to say that the punters in the Derby Arms that night weren't as excited by our performance and, sadly, our first gig doubled as our last. Fame would need to come from another source.

Holidays were spent in North Wales—Butlins as a child and, when I was a teenager, the caravans and chalets of holiday camps with names like Happy Days and Robin Hood in Rhyl and Towyn. We would go with aunts, uncles and cousins. By day I would play football, cricket and other games, then later enjoy what nightlife there was in the pubs and clubs before ending up by the sea playing guitars and experimenting with cannabis and other drugs as the dawn broke. As Gladys Knight asked in the classic song 'The Way We Were,' "Can it be that it was all so simple then, or has time rewritten every line?" Either way, I remember those as happy times, especially on the beach where love was in the air and the music was loud and intoxicating—or was that the drugs?

My first holiday abroad was not a typical experience. I planned to go with my school friend Peter Walsh and his mate, Steve. Our friend John Foley was doing the Hokey Cokey—in one minute, not so sure the next. They all wanted to go to Spain where sea, sand, sex and sangria was the order of the day for a few pesos. I would not go to Spain because it was ruled by the fascist dictator General Franco—a sign of how politically committed I was becoming. Having dug my heels in, we eventually settled on Austria, of all places, and the most expensive resort of Seefeld in Tirol. God knows why. Three of us booked while John wrestled with his indecision. By the time he had declared he wanted to come, the excursion package was full and we couldn't get our deposits back. We met in one of Liverpool's famous pubs, Rigby's, to mull our dilemma. After a few drinks we decided to 'bunk' John onto our trip—four for the price of three.

The journey comprised a train from London to Dover, ferry to Calais, overnight train to Innsbruck, and a coach to our hotel in Seefeld. Getting an additional passenger from London to Calais didn't present us with too difficult a task but the rest of the journey was more challenging. Our designated carriage on the train to Innsbruck had three seats either side—plenty of room for the four of us until we were joined by a couple and their 11-year-old son whose name I can still remember: Simon. The man, an Oxford don, said: "Oh, there seems to be a mistake, I'll get the guard."

"No, no," I interrupted, "you and your wife and son sit down, I'll go and get the guard."

I waited until the train had departed before returning to report that the guard could do nothing but the don and his wife shouldn't worry because the four of us could squeeze into the three seats opposite. When the guard came to inspect the tickets one of us disappeared to the toilet, then we were safe until he returned to release the beds (couchettes) at night. We employed a rotation system for the three beds, with the fourth person sitting on an eight-pint can of bitter in the corridor.

It was a relief to depart the train in Innsbruck and head for the coach. Once on board a young woman called a register, ticking off names before asking if she had missed anyone. The don watched with puzzlement as one of our number said nothing. Here was a man used to studying the origins of Pythagoras' theorem who was clearly struggling with this modern mathematical conundrum. As the coach dropped off passengers at various hotels along the way our stress levels began to ease. We were almost home and dry. But our delight turned to shock when our stop arrived and the don's family got off with us—they were staying in the same hotel.

We had no trouble sneaking a fourth person in. The waitress got used to seeing different faces at breakfast each morning. We would smuggle out some bread, ham, cheese and pastries and link up with the fourth musketeer in the town square. We had a good time in Austria, although it was very expensive. That became less of a problem when we befriended the local DJ, Gerhard, who also worked in the casino and would let us have free drinks in his club.

When the time came to head home, you guessed it—the don and his family were travelling back with us. On the train I played travel chess with the precocious Simon and let him win (at least that's what I told myself). By this time, the don had figured out the conundrum, but he was not going to shop us—on one occasion he came back from the toilet to advise us the guard was close and one of us should disappear. Despite the ultimate success of our plan, my mates never tired of telling me we should have gone to Spain instead. It was 20 years before I finally visited the country and fell in love with it. I have been many times since.

On leaving college all of us entered the world of work. How different it was then compared with what young people face today. We had lots of options— big decisions that would determine how our lives unfolded. I had been accepted by Cardinal Newman Teaching College in Birmingham along with John Foley.

He won some money on the football pools and decided to ta
before a gap year was heard of). He told me to go ahead, sayir
year later. I replied I wasn't going by myself (so much for the l
instead, I would get a job for a year. So, along with Peter Walsn, I applied to go
into the insurance sector. We both got accepted by Sun Life Assurance and were
given a start date. Meanwhile, I was also offered a job working on the docks for
the Port of Liverpool Stevedore Company, with the same start date. I only made
my decision on the Sunday night before my Monday morning start.

John went on to be a brilliant teacher for 40 years, ending up as a highly
respected headmaster. Peter was successful in the financial sector, reaching the
dizzy heights of chief executive. I chose the docks, a path less trodden, and the
rest is history.

CHAPTER 2

THE DOCKS

When I walked through the dock gate on that sunny Monday morning in 1968 the first words said to me were: "You join the union here, son." Unlike millions of workers today, I didn't have to fight to have a union. The men and women who went before me had fought and won that battle. Some had lost their lives doing so. I was eager to sign up.

It wasn't long before I became actively involved in the union. As young men (there were no women), my coworkers and I were paid a youth rate. Despite doing the same jobs as the older men, we had to wait until we were 23 before getting the full rate. That didn't seem fair to me, so I organised a meeting of about 150 young members working for different companies on the docks and we set about campaigning for parity of pay—a single "rate for the job."

The port employers knocked us back, of course, but our own union branch wasn't keen on the idea either. It was run by older men who thought we were cheeky young beggars (or was it bastards?). But we persisted—even threatened to strike—and, incredibly, we won. I remember it as though it was yesterday—my wage went from £21 a week to £42, a 100 per cent increase.

On the back of that victory I was persuaded to stand for election to be a shop steward. I was successful, and so began, at 19 years of age, my life as a workers' representative—a role I would relish for more than 50 years.

———————

The docks were a world of excitement and fascination. No two days were the same. There were seafarers from around the globe; hundreds of lorry drivers delivering and collecting cargo; and thousands of men moving from ship to ship. I was instantly hooked and spent 11 of the happiest years of my life working there.

I entered the docks as a young know-it-all with a few A-levels and quickly realised I knew nothing of any importance. There's an old saying "never judge a book by its cover"—anyone who sees dockers as unskilled labourers with little education would do well to remember it because I met men who were humorous and kind with a wealth of knowledge on diverse subjects from the American Civil War to opera and all things in between.

I was a planman. It was my job to produce a plan showing where the cargo for each port was stored on the ship. The plan would sail with the ship and be used to determine how many gangs of dockers were needed to discharge the cargo in the ports it visited. The ships I worked on primarily ran to the west coast of South America—the PSNC Line and the National Chilean Line—where there were 26 major ports in various countries. Planmen were counted among the white-collar workers who worked on the quayside and in the offices and cabins—but the term white-collar gives the wrong impression. We were not Registered Dock Workers but were very close to the dockers, working alongside them daily on the ships and cargo. When they were on strike, we were on strike. The bond between us was unbreakable.

When I started on the docks the power of the workers was greater than ever. The pendulum had swung towards us after the findings of the Devlin Committee in 1965, through which dockers shook off the last vestiges of casual work practices. The bosses didn't like it one bit. There were often skirmishes and strikes, which resulted in Liverpool docks getting a reputation for being too militant and strike happy. Now, it's true that Liverpool is a city that is not afraid to stand up for itself—I love it for that—but a significant proportion of the strikes in the 1970s were due to the employers being unhappy they could no longer treat the dockers as they had in the '50s and '60s.

At the same time, the union for dock workers, the Transport and General Workers' Union (T&G)—the biggest union in the country with 1.5 million members when I joined, rising to 2 million by 1977—was moving to the left. Having been under right-wing control in the 1950s when Arthur Deakin was general secretary, the T&G became a more democratic union thanks to Frank Cousins and, in particular, Jack Jones from 1968 (Jack was one of my heroes, a true giant who I later befriended). As a result, shop stewards began to wield more power. Remnants of the old guard still filled the bureaucracy among the officer ranks, but it was the shop stewards who held sway with the rank and file. Men like Jimmy Symes, Jimmy Nolan, Dennis Kelly and others had the task of holding the dockers together, both locally and nationally, through the National Dock Shop Stewards' Committee.

The heyday of workers' power on the docks was not to last. Defending the dockers' terms and conditions became increasingly difficult with the arrival of containerisation—the method of transporting goods in standard-sized containers that could be easily loaded onto ships—which meant an inevitable decline in the number of men employed. A typical ship I worked on would bring in 20,000 tonnes of cargo—mainly iron-ore and other natural minerals as well as general goods—that would take two weeks to unload. Meanwhile, lorries would be delivering 20,000 tonnes of general cargo into the sheds in North 1 Canada. When the ship had been discharged, it would move its berth across the dock and the general cargo would be loaded on board, taking another two weeks. Once the same goods were containerised it would take just 24 hours to unload 20,000 tonnes from a ship sailing into Seaforth Container Terminal and a further 24 hours to load it up again—a 48-hour turnaround compared to four weeks before containerisation. You can see the almost impossible situation the dockers' leaders had to deal with.

The resulting tensions exploded in 1972. Five London dockers were sent to Pentonville Prison for contempt of court after defying a court order not to picket companies 'stuffing' containers close to the docks using cheap casual labour. A campaign to free the Pentonville Five was launched, which included a national dock strike and even a Trades Union Congress call for a general strike. The show of force led to the men being released after only six days following an intervention by the official solicitor—a mysterious post that had been taken out of the cupboard, dusted down and tasked with saving the government's blushes by reversing the court's decision. My friend Geoff Shears, a great socialist now well known in the labour movement for having headed up the largest and most radical trade union solicitors, Thompsons, remembers arriving in Fleet Street that morning as a young articled clerk to do some work for the NGA print union only to be confronted by thousands of workers streaming out of the newspaper buildings to march to Pentonville Prison to greet the men's release. He joined them, but dressed in his suit, collar and tie, and with a briefcase by his side, everyone wanted to know if he was the official solicitor.

Thousands of dockers and trade unionists had gathered outside the prison by the time the men were freed. They were carried shoulder-high into Caledonian Road. I was in the crowd. I had been involved in the campaign and was, of course, out on strike (Liverpool stayed out for six weeks due to another issue). The feeling of joy and solidarity was incredible. The release of the Pentonville Five demonstrated the power of organised labour and how effective it could be when given bold leadership, free from clammy bureaucratic hands.

Solidarity was embedded in dock life. Workers in dispute would often send delegations from near and far to ask the dockers for help if the goods their industry produced went through the docks. Inevitably those goods would be blocked—either officially or, more likely, unofficially—until their dispute was resolved. I recall one-day stoppages in support of the nurses and the building workers known as the Shrewsbury Pickets. (I later befriended one of the unjustly gaoled men of the Shrewsbury Pickets, the great socialist actor and comedian Ricky Tomlinson, and was proud, as general secretary of Unite, to give continued support for their fight for truth and justice.)

This was a heroic period; a time when class solidarity across different sectors of the economy was something we lived and breathed. When the shipyards of Glasgow came under threat in 1971 with the collapse of Upper Clyde

Shipbuilders and the refusal of the Conservative government to intervene, the workers organised a "work-in" and continued to fulfil the orders the company had taken. Their spokesman, shop steward Jimmy Reid, became famous for his incredible oratory. I remember his visit to the Liverpool docks to speak to us. I've heard many great speeches over the years but listening to Jimmy when I was young and full of fire was electrifying and inspirational—the hairs stood up on the back of my neck. Much later, when I was general secretary, I had the privilege of delivering the 2013 Jimmy Reid Memorial Lecture in Govan and meeting his family.

Hearing so many stories from Liverpool, the UK and the world taught me that workers are workers whatever city or country they come from. The realisation that all workers have the same problems and concerns was the beginning of my true understanding of class politics.

All seaports have a physical link to the wider world but none more so than Liverpool. Many nationalities have visited and settled in the city, enriching the culture and generating interest in the politics of various countries and causes. On the docks, our sense of solidarity extended well beyond our own shores. I well remember the debates in the shop stewards' committee about supporting the Anti-Apartheid Movement and boycotting South African goods, and we supported the Chile Solidarity Campaign following the overthrow of the democratically elected president Salvador Allende by the CIA-backed General Augusto Pinochet in 1973.

I worked on the ships that serviced Chile and became actively involved in the solidarity movement after learning from Chilean seafarers about the atrocities being committed. We would take leaflets onto the ships and hide them inside the cargo going to Valparaiso for distribution throughout Chile. The leaflets would tell the oppressed Chilean workers they were not alone—their brothers and sisters from around the world were fighting for them. We would daub with paint the word *Venceremos* (we will overcome) on the inside of the ships' hulls as well as on hundreds of cartons and cases. Many Chileans used to jump ship and seek asylum—to this day there is a strong Chilean community in

Liverpool. Unfortunately, Pinochet remained in power until 1990, but few today would doubt we were on the right side of history.

The docks were such a vibrant place. The characters who worked there were unforgettable. Humour is often associated with Liverpudlians—there's an old saying that you have to be a comedian to live in Liverpool—and we have certainly produced many comedy greats, although some of the better-known ones have been Tories! Still, we have Alexei Sayle and Ricky Tomlinson to fall back on. Quick wit and a sharp tongue are part of the culture of the city and on the docks that was magnified. The nicknames given to some dockers became legendary:

Angry Cat—was forever shouting down the ship's hatch, "Is meowl man down there?"

The Destroyer—was always looking for a sub.

The Judge and *the Lazy Lawyer*—could be found sitting on a case when there was work to be done.

The Balloon—a foreman whose saying was "Don't let me down, lads."

The Eleccy Mouse—because he drove a three-wheeled Robin Reliant.

Tarmac—would order a pint and one for the road.

The Lone Sailor—would always be in the Atlantic pub (opposite the Huskisson Dock, my last place of work).

Compo Johnny—knew every trick in the book to get compensation.

I had occasion to appreciate Compo Johnny's talents firsthand. One lunchtime, when I was about 20 years old, I was playing football in an empty dock shed when I was viciously cut down by a tackle. No quarter was asked or given in those days. Clearly an ambulance was needed, but instead one of my mates announced that Compo Johnny was in the next berth. While he was sent for, I was left writhing in agony (my pain threshold has always been low). After what felt like forever, but was probably 10 minutes, Compo arrived, surveyed the scene, and instructed my mates to move me to where some groundwork was being done in the avenue outside the shed. The story would be that I had stumbled on the unprotected hole.

Against my protests, I was picked up and laid (it felt like dumped) beside the hole. I heard the word "ambulance" mentioned but, to my dismay, Compo declared that we had to wait until after one o'clock. The time the ambulance was called would be recorded and the 'accident' had to be in work hours in order to protect my job and sick pay. My friends stood about chatting, completely ignoring my whimpering pleas. "Stop crying like a fucking baby, you'll be fine," was the only comfort I got from my mate, Tony Corrigan.

When I finally got to hospital it was confirmed I had broken a bone in my left elbow—coincidentally, the exact same bone my dad broke in a motorbike crash during the war while delivering messages around Hastings, which stopped him joining his comrades heading out to Dunkirk; fate is indeed strange. For my broken bone I received an £18 industrial injury payment, which was fine, but I appealed anyway.

I decided to represent myself before the Medical Appeal Tribunal, to the surprise of the three people on the panel, given my young age (I would be back there many times representing others in the years to come). I explained that my left arm had not returned to normal, which had affected my golf, my piano playing and any other activity that came to mind. I was taken by one of the panel, a doctor, into a side room to be examined. "Stretch out your left arm and no trickery," he demanded. "That looks perfectly OK," he said. He then asked me to stretch out my right arm, to which he exclaimed to his surprise and mine, "You have women's arms!" I assured him in as gruff a voice as I could that it was only the way I was standing. But it turned out that while men's arms curve slightly upwards when outstretched, women's arms curve slightly downwards. This relatively unknown medical phenomenon revealed that while my left arm had been shifted by the injury into a male position, it had not fully recovered to its original female position. To my delight, this meant I was awarded £250 compensation. I've been close to my feminine side ever since.

Tony Corrigan, the friend who showed so little sympathy when I was calling out in pain, was like a brother to me. We shared many escapades, especially while we worked on the docks. We were both planmen, both young revolutionaries, and both what you might call a pair of scallies. The air of revolution was everywhere in '60s Liverpool—music, clothes, hair, and politics. The times they were a'changing, as Bob Dylan had told us. In 1968 a revolution broke out in Paris—led by students, but with 10 million workers occupying factories. Tony and I were out one Friday night when he announced we should be with the real revolutionaries in Paris, not drinking and enjoying ourselves in Liverpool. I agreed. The following morning there was a knock at the door while I was still in bed. "Lennie," my mum shouted, "it's Tony." I staggered down the stairs and there he was with a little sack over his shoulder. I was slightly taken aback as he demanded it was time to join the Paris Commune. After some words, off we went. "Mum, I'm going out."

We hitchhiked to London with some difficulty and arrived in Shepherd's Bush late at night, exhausted. The only thing to do was head for the nearest pub, not knowing where to sleep or what our next move should be. As luck would have it, two Australian girls befriended us and when they found out we were from Liverpool and went to school with the Beatles (well, didn't everybody from Liverpool go to school with the Beatles?) they offered us food, comfort and shelter.

Four days later, Tony burst into the bedroom angrily declaring: "It's over, the revolution is over. Fucking French, you can't rely on them for anything." And that was it. After fond farewells it was back to Liverpool. I've been looking for a revolution ever since.

On the hitchhike home we worried about what to tell our mates. How could we admit we only got as far as London? I suggested we say we got injured on the barricades and couldn't remember much. "Brilliant," said Tony, which quietened him for a while, and then 'whack'—I felt a crack on my head and went stumbling down a grass verge. When I looked up, Tony was holding a piece of wood. I scrambled back up the bank, blood running down my face, cursing and swearing, but when I got to the top he just gave me the piece of wood and told me to hit him. I threw it down and stormed off. His logic was that we needed scars to show we'd been injured. He mithered me to do it, saying he had done me a favour but I was letting him down. Eventually, if only to shut him up, I took the piece of wood and hit him. "Thanks, Lennie," he said as he slumped to the ground.

Back in Liverpool we dined out on our story for a few weeks until our mates became more sceptical, asking detailed questions that threatened to make us look ridiculous. We decided to drop the story and never talk about it again to anyone.

Nineteen sixty-eight was also the year Tony and I formed the Che Guevara Appreciation Society (CGAS) on the first anniversary of his death. Membership was conditional on taking an oath made up of five pledges:

1. To renounce capitalism;
2. To seek ways of overthrowing the establishment;
3. To pledge allegiance to worldwide revolution;
4. To support the call for armed militia in any struggle;
5. To never cross a picket line.

Tony and I were chair and secretary of the society but we used to alternate the roles. We produced leaflets and circulated them around the docks. At our monthly meetings the first order of business would be:

"Comrade Secretary, any applications for membership?"

"No, Comrade Chair."

We would then adjourn across the dock road to the Dominion pub for refreshments. After a number of months of the same process—"Comrade Secretary, any applications?"; "No, Comrade Chair"—I ventured to suggest over a pint that we might consider watering down some of the pledges to see if it helped attract more members. Tony was furious, calling me a revisionist. He would hear no more backsliding. The Society continued for several months without a single application and, without us saying a word to each other, quietly slipped into oblivion.

Tony and I would be involved in many struggles together, both industrial and political—whether in the Chile Solidarity Campaign and the Anti-Apartheid

Movement or stencilling on walls in the dead of the night messages such as "Keep Labour Left" (I've been trying to do that all my life).

Tony had three brothers, all of whom had a genetic fault, and all of whom died before they were 40 years of age. Tony died aged 42 but not before he met the love of his life, Barbara. They had three beautiful girls—Janet, Susan and Katie. Tragically, Susan died of leukaemia when she was only eight-and-a-half. Tony asked me to see her in her coffin—she was the first dead child I had seen.

When Tony contracted cancer I would visit in order to 'cheer him up.' Barbara would open the door and tell me to be strong and positive. Within 10 minutes it would be Tony comforting me as I broke down. When leaving, Barbara used to hug me and say maybe next time would be better. It never was. I still miss him and often drift back nostalgically, remembering the two young lads who wanted to change the world.

The bonds forged in a workplace can be very strong and last a lifetime. As a young worker I was often inspired by those I worked with and I relied on their support, as representing people in a trade union role can bring pressure and stress. When you speak for a collective, you need to know they are there for you when you need them. It was my regional official, Eddie Roberts, a committed socialist and brilliant orator, who was my mentor in those early years. There was also a group of friends who used to guide me—mates like Tony Nelson, Terry Teague, Kevin Robinson, Dave Williams, Bobby Morton, Geoff Bayley and my great friend Mike Carden, whose son Dan would later be my personal assistant for five years before becoming an MP for Liverpool Walton. Dan joined Jeremy Corbyn's shadow cabinet and has shown himself to be a highly talented and presentable person destined for high office.

In the mid-1970s I met Jim Mowatt, who over the years became one of my closest friends. He had come down from Glasgow to be the head of education for the North West TUC. He was (and remains, as director of education in Unite) simply the best educationalist in the labour movement, as borne out by the testimonies of thousands of shop stewards, many of whom have gone on to higher positions in their respective unions. Jim also served as the T&G's national officer for engineering. Funny, flamboyant, generous, loyal and, on occasion, controversial, he has always been a brilliant raconteur. If he ever wrote an autobiography it would be very colourful. However, Jim has developed a habit of merging fiction with fact over his lifetime and often says he would need me by his side to explain what was real and what was not, as in his own mind he can no longer distinguish the difference. I would, in any case, need to be by his side to make certain he didn't divulge some of the escapades we got up to together.

The solidarity on the docks led to a natural alliance with road transport haulage lorry drivers. One of the most powerful branches in the whole of the T&G was the Merseyside lorry drivers' 541 branch with which I had a particularly strong relationship. These were trade unionists from the old school with an abundance of characters. I struck up a close friendship with one of them, Tony Woodhouse, in the 1970s, and he has since walked every step of my journey with me. Despite always being supportive and fiercely protective of me, his own journey has been just as remarkable, rising to become the chair (president) of Unite from its inception, the highest position a lay member can hold in the union. Tony always gets embarrassed when I tell conferences he is the finest trade unionist I've ever met, but it's true—while I've been fortunate to know many inspiring trade unionists there is nobody who embodies the very essence of solidarity like he does. The chair of 541, Wally Nugent, was very supportive and caring towards me. Tony, Dave Williams—another great trade unionist—and I were like three protégés learning from Wally's complicated (to say the least) strategic brain. Wally died but there was a lovely reunion at Christmas in 2010 when the three of us visited his grave with cans of mild, his preferred drink. I had been elected general secretary, Tony had been elected Unite's chair and Dave had been elected to represent the road transport sector on the union's executive. Wally would have been very proud. Pouring one can over the grave and drinking the rest we remembered with fondness our wise old sage. It was a nice moment.

———————

In 1979, aged 28, I left employment in the docks to become a T&G official. My involvement in union work had already become all-consuming when I was asked by Eddie Roberts and Jimmy Symes (two very experienced and respected regional officials) to consider applying for an empty post: the official for ACTSS, the white-collar section of the T&G. After discussing it with my wife, Ann, I decided to give it a go. Within a fortnight I was interviewed by an executive panel headed up by Deputy General Secretary Harry Urwin.

I remember being in a shop stewards' meeting in Transport House in Liverpool when I was called up to the office of Dick Palmer, the divisional officer. The regional secretary, Dougie Farrar, was also there. "Well, I suppose you've heard on the grapevine that you got the job?" he said. I had. "If it had been left to me you wouldn't have got it, you weren't the best."

"It's lucky for me," I replied, "that you haven't got much influence."

It was not the best way to begin with a new boss. When I started a week later, Palmer took me to meet my secretary, showed me a room in which there was a desk piled up with files (the post had been vacant for six months), and said, "There you go." I was thrown in at the deep end, but I set about the task of catch-up with excitement as well as a little trepidation.

Having good friends who could keep my feet on the ground was very important in my new role. Without them, it would have been too easy to lose a sense of proportion when I moved away from the shop floor. That was brought home to me early on. Just a few weeks into the job I was involved in wage negotiations on behalf of cashiers working in betting shops run by Stanley Racing, a bookmaker chain based on Merseyside, later taken over by Ladbrokes. They were on £36.75 a week. The company offered an insulting 25p pay rise. I thought it was a joke and told them so. The shop stewards, who were used to the company treating them this way, were delighted at my indignant reaction. After a day arguing with the bosses we accepted a £2.50 increase. I still thought it was miserly but the negotiating committee were happy.

I left the meeting to go down to the docks—which were part of my allocation as an officer—where the workers were in dispute with the employer over pay for weekend night work. The Mersey Docks and Harbour Company had offered £50 a night; our shop stewards were demanding £70. I thought that was a mistake. During a break I had a blazing row with the shop stewards, all of whom were my friends. As we left for an overnight adjournment, Tony Corrigan asked me to go for a drink with him. "Didn't take you long to change," he said in the pub. I asked him what he meant and he berated me for the position I'd taken. I told him the story of Stanley Racing; that we'd just spent all day securing a pay rise of £2.50 a week, while on the docks the shop stewards were complaining at being offered £50 a night. Tony told me that was irrelevant; it was up to the men who worked on the docks to determine what they would accept for their labour. I suddenly realised I was wrong—I had been subconsciously influenced by the relative difference in pay between the two disputes.

It was a salutary lesson that I never forgot. It is only the workers and shop stewards in any company who should decide what is right for them. That is why, down the years, I have often told shop stewards that they should never rely on union officials to make major decisions because those officials will be subject to all kinds of different pressures and influences. Workers must have the confidence to make the final call themselves. That became a core principle of my trade unionism.

I remained a member of my dock branch, for which I had previously been a senior shop steward, covering 1,000 white-collar workers. Although we had always been tight with the dockers, we had gradually become known as the most militant branch on the docks as we argued, often with the dockers' leaders, for our right to fair treatment. One of our major campaigns had been to have our workers registered under the National Dock Labour Scheme. Introduced by the post-war Labour government, the scheme regulated employment on the docks, ending many of the chronically insecure arrangements that dock work had previously been renowned for. Extending it to white-collar dock workers would require an Act of Parliament. In the mid-1970s we reached agreement with the employment secretary, Michael Foot, to make that happen, but the

Labour government had a narrow majority and was defeated when three right-wing Labour MPs voted with the Tories (some things never change).

One of the great advantages of the scheme was that when a company went bust, other employers in the port were required to absorb the dockers who had lost their jobs. Despite failing to get it established in law, my branch adopted a policy saying we expected our members to be treated the same as the dockers in that situation. Our philosophy was simple: as Dennis Kelly, the chairman of the Liverpool Docks Shop Stewards' Committee had said, we were "dockers without books"—dock workers who didn't carry the registration books handed out under the National Dock Labour Scheme.

This policy position was tested in 1980, soon after I became an officer, when the company T.G. Harrisons announced it was leaving the port. The dockers were taken on by other companies but 40 members of our branch were facing redundancy. We argued for them to be absorbed by the Mersey Docks and Harbour Company, which was the Port Authority, but this was refused, meaning a major strike was on the cards.

This led to one of the most extraordinary initiatives of my working life. T.G. Harrisons gave no help in trying to persuade Mersey Docks to take on its employees; in fact, I'm sure the company actively worked against it. The managing director was a pompous man known as Captain Johnson who harboured a vindictive desire to see our branch's redeployment policy broken. Under that policy, any member who decided to take redundancy money would forfeit their right to be redeployed and would have to leave the docks. In the final few days before closure, Captain Johnson smiled at me as he said, "On Friday, I will personally hand over the redundancy cheques to each individual at 5 p.m." I replied that at 5.05 p.m., each of those individuals would hand over their cheque to the union branch and on Monday they would start with the Mersey Docks and Harbour Company. He laughed, but that's exactly what happened. Facing a dock strike by my members, after a full weekend of discussions Mersey Docks blinked first and on Monday morning all 40 of our members started work with their new employer.

However, there were complications. Mersey Docks would only employ these men as new starters with no back service. That meant they would have to work two years before receiving holiday or sick pay, and those with long service would lose the benefit of those years in any future severance calculations. Fortunately, under the company's redundancy and severance scheme everyone received the same after two years, so our T.G. Harrisons members would only be disadvantaged for a short period.

Our solution was to take matters into our own hands. The union branch would pay holiday and sick pay for those two years. The branch had a healthy fund that members paid into over and above their union dues. At one point each member's contribution was £1 a week—nearly as much as the union membership fee. We used the fund to make donations to good causes and to send delegations to meet politicians and join picket lines (I was a member of every such delegation including the one to the famous dispute at Grunwick, which was the first time anyone had experienced 'kettling' by police). The 'redundancy' payments swelled the branch fund considerably and meant that the redeployed workers were not punished because a company had gone bust through no fault of their own.

Two years later, when another company, West Coast Stevedore, left the port, 83 of our members found themselves in the same situation. This time there was no argument and the transfer to Mersey Docks was made on the same terms. Again, all the workers handed over their redundancy cheques, which were quite substantial for some as this workforce was older. By now, the branch fund had ballooned to more than £200,000. The same happened again when the Isle of Man Steamship Company left the port, although this time the resolution came after a strike which involved 'capturing' the ship by welding the back end roll-on/roll-off ramp to the quayside.

We had established a great tradition of protecting members' jobs, but the rug was pulled from under us in 1989 when Mersey Docks changed its formula for severance payments to one based on years of service. That disadvantaged all the workers who had been absorbed as new starters, so the branch decided to return their redundancy pay, with appropriate deductions for any holiday and sick pay they had received in their first two years.

That episode stands out as one of the finest examples I have seen of workers standing together to defend jobs and ensure no one loses out. By pooling resources and acting collectively instead of for themselves, those workers found they had the financial and industrial power—as well as the determination—to secure fair treatment for all. It was the kind of solidarity that, for me, defined the docks.

CHAPTER 3

MILITANCY AND MISERY

It was a revelatory moment for me. The convenor—a decent, hardworking man all his life—looked me in the eye and told me the stomach for the fight was gone. The factory where he worked in Wavertree, Liverpool, had never had an industrial stoppage in its 25-year history and was the most productive of the six facilities owned by Britvic, the drinks company. But Britvic had decided to close it anyway.

It was the early 1980s. Manufacturing industry was being destroyed everywhere you looked. Unemployment was rocketing. It was carnage. The labour movement was taking a sustained battering while the Thatcher government seemed to relish the suffering it was inflicting.

Facing any closure, the union's mantra to the workers was: "We are only the caretakers of the work—we have to defend the jobs for our young people." Most workers understood and embraced that philosophy but as defeat after defeat piled up, confidence collapsed.

The Britvic workers had initially been up for a fight but on this visit I detected a change of mood. That's why I spoke to the convenor. I was surprised to hear him say we should cut a deal to get what we could. I pointed out that in his mid-50s, he would never work again. He said, "Lennie, in my street in Kirby, I'm the only one working, everyone has lost their job, but everyone is surviving. I'll be OK."

That was when I knew life was changing. The stigma of unemployment was lifting. People were becoming anaesthetised to job losses. Our collective fight was ebbing away. I wondered what kind of future was in store for the next generation.

When a group of workers is beaten it affects the confidence of all workers and, likewise, when some workers win a battle, all workers feel stronger. In the 1980s we weren't winning any battles.

The 1980s was a time of terrible hardship and reversals for working people, but in the popular imagination it is the 1970s that are seen as the dark days—a notion that was allowed to take hold without challenge by the Labour Party or trade union leaders. The fact is that working people made significant gains in the 1970s. Workers' pay peaked as a share of national income. The Health and Safety at Work Act was passed in 1974, giving reps statutory rights to make their workplaces safe, saving the lives of tens of thousands of workers in the years since. Then in 1975 the Equal Pay Act was introduced, acknowledging for the first time in law that women should receive the same pay as men doing the same or similar jobs.

Of course, there were also industrial problems, including in the nationalised industries—primarily because of appalling management and unions not being sufficiently skilled to deal with the inevitable economic pressures brought about by the oil crisis of 1973 and the subsequent capitulation by the centre-right Labour government, which went cap-in-hand to the International Monetary Fund for help. That led to the so-called 'winter of discontent' in 1978, paving the way for the election of the Thatcher government in May 1979.

That is when the real dark days began, as Margaret Thatcher's laissez-faire economic policies were let loose, inflicting damage on the economy so severe it is still being felt today. Large swathes of manufacturing were wiped out. Communities were laid to waste, never to recover. The country was turned into a giant car boot sale with a big sign saying, 'UK FOR SALE.' The speculators and spivs flooded in, buying up companies and then closing them down because it was easier and cheaper to sack British workers.

Five pieces of legislation were introduced to make it difficult for trade unions to fight back and defend their members. Millions of good people were thrown on the scrap heap. Thatcher's mouthpieces in the right-wing media crowed that it was a price worth paying. 'Get on your bike and look for work' was the response from Norman Tebbit to those whose lives and families had been destroyed. It was vandalism, pure and simple.

In the three-year period from 1979-1982, Merseyside was brutalised by job losses as factory after factory closed down. I remember vividly the T&G membership was almost halved on Merseyside from 108,000 to 57,000 due to these closures. I was involved in lots of campaigns and industrial struggles to try to defend jobs, including the occupation of the Meccano factory in Binns Road and civil disobedience when the Dunlop factory in Speke was closed. All of these brave struggles ended in defeat. From each one I learned lessons on how best to fight back.

This onslaught had huge repercussions for the left. In the 1970s, the left had gained strength. My hero Jack Jones was in charge of the T&G and formed a powerful alliance with Hugh Scanlon, leader of the AEU engineering union. In the Labour Party impetus was growing behind Tony Benn and the Campaign for Labour Party Democracy, of which I was a supporter as a confirmed Bennite. That movement peaked with Tony's attempt to replace Denis Healey as deputy leader in 1981. He failed by the smallest of margins after Neil Kinnock, then thought of as a leftist, switched his vote (a sign of things to come). From there on it was downhill.

The right did what the right does best and split the party with the defection of the 'Gang of Four' (Roy Jenkins, Shirley Williams, David Owen and Bill Rodgers—all high-profile Labour MPs) to form a new party, the SDP, in 1982. Labour leader Michael Foot was vilified by the media and stabbed in the back by his own MPs (a foretaste of what Corbyn would encounter three decades later). These events, together with Thatcher's popularity after the Falklands War, helped the Tories to a landslide victory in the 1983 election. Of course, the blame was pinned on the left while the treachery and divisiveness of the right wing of the party was overlooked (it's funny how history repeats). Under Kinnock, elected as a unifier, the party moved to the right—influenced by so-called 'modernisers,' the precursors of the Blairites. Meanwhile, those of us on the left were fighting brutal battles on all fronts, often internally in our own movement, allowing Thatcher to go almost unchecked.

During this time I was heavily involved in the creation and development of the National Broad Left in the T&G. Groups of people with similar political objectives, both of the left and the right, have always been a feature within any organisation in the labour movement. So it might come as a surprise that, despite the T&G having been for some time the left-wing standard bearer of the movement, there was no sophisticated left organisation and network within the union. That changed in the early 1980s. I was given time off from my job by my regional secretary, Bobby Owens, to effectively become the secretariat to a small group that had been elected or chosen to act as the executive of a new National Broad Left, putting me right at the heart of the political action. The Broad Left soon became a major power within the union. It has been likened by the academic Monica Clua Losada to a jellyfish—"invisible, quiet and with the ability to sting before victims knew it was there." I preferred to describe it as "shambolic but effective." The T&G left was also boosted by the emergence of two excellent young orators within its ranks in the form of Alan Quinn from Liverpool and Peter Hagger from London, who were elected to the union's executive council.

Of course, amid all the industrial and political despair there were nice moments in my day job, particularly when I was involved in successful pay negotiations or, better still, when I helped an individual member with a grievance or a disciplinary issue. But on many occasions I was unable to get a good result and it hurt, especially when an outcome was grossly unfair. Sometimes there were legal routes that could be tried, but the law has never been on the side of workers and is heavily biased towards bosses.

———————

I didn't learn my politics from books or in a student union. My politics were formed by the circumstances of the world around me—life on the docks, in my trade union, and in the battles my class fought with the establishment, often successfully in the 1970s, and disastrously in the 1980s.

Much of my early political education came from talented shop stewards on the docks who were members of the Communist Party. There was an ironic context to this. At the beginning of the Cold War, during Arthur Deakin's right-wing leadership of the T&G, the union adopted a policy of "bans and prescription." Members of the Communist Party were not allowed to become full-time union officials (this remained the case until 1968). The unintended consequence was that Communist Party members were driven into the rank and file and emerged as highly motivated and effective shop stewards, with great influence among the workers and younger trade unionists. It was such men who introduced me to the Communist Party's programme, 'The British Road to Socialism.' I was thinking of joining the Communist Party in 1969, but I couldn't get the previous year's Soviet invasion of Czechoslovakia out of my mind. Without being fully aware of the political ideology involved, I felt distinctly uncomfortable about it.

As I became more knowledgeable over the years my opposition to Stalinism grew, despite an encounter in the late 1970s with one of our movement's giants, Scottish miners' leader Mick McGahey. After a march in Glasgow I went into the Communist Party's Red Star Club for a drink with other marchers. Mick must have been told I was an up-and-coming fighter from Liverpool who was "a bit of a Trot." He put his arm around my shoulder at the bar and said, "Always remember, son, Uncle Joe wasn't all bad."

I should say at this point that it's easy to cast criticism on an individual or an ideology from the safe distance that history affords, and to judge them by standards that have developed in our own democracies, warts and all. It's easy to forget the terrible conditions that workers in Russia endured leading up to the 1917 revolution; hard to recreate what it was like when 14 nations (you would struggle to name that many) invaded Russia to reinstate the Tsar; difficult to imagine the scale of devastation inflicted by the Nazis in World War II when 20 million Soviet citizens lost their lives. But my anti-Stalinism comes from a mature analysis that tells me the crushing of opposition leads to corruption and the kind of tyranny that defies everything I believe in.

So I never did join the Communist Party. Instead, I became a member of the Labour Party. It was hearing Tony Benn speak when I lived in Wigan in 1970 that convinced me. His eloquence and ability to draw together different strands was awe-inspiring. He became my political hero. I never dreamed that he would later become my friend when I moved to London and, in particular, when I became General Secretary.

However, I suddenly found myself the centre of attention for every conceivable Trotskyist group—the Workers' Revolutionary Party, Workers' Socialist League, Socialist Workers' Party. There I was, a young working-class lad and a shop steward on the docks. They were like bees around honey. While I found the Trotskyists to be decent, committed individuals, they seemed most times to be on a different planet. I had no empathy with them and fended them off.

Over the years I came to realise that the sectarian nature of such groups is what fuels ultra-leftism. In my experience, ultra-leftism is as much an enemy of socialism and the advance of workers as the right-wing establishment. It seeks to undermine and divide workers during any struggle for the sake of recruiting a few members to a particular sect. While it is always important to guard against a bureaucracy that can too easily sell workers out, ultra-leftism tends to put its own short-term gains before the long-term interests of the working class. Lenin called it the politics of purity.

But then along came the Militant Tendency who seemed to me completely different. Here were people who lived in my community, worked in real jobs, and spoke a language that dealt with issues that mattered in a realistic and understandable way. It was said the Militant Tendency gave respectability to Trotskyism and there was an element of truth in that. Although they are still around today as the Socialist Party, Militant were successful back then because they were a force within Labour. Though best known as a phenomenon of the 1980s, they were active in the Labour Party, and in Liverpool, from much earlier. It was the 1970s when I first encountered them.

Contrary to popular belief, I was never a member of the Militant Tendency, although I was attracted to many of their policies and developed friendships with several of them that have stood the test of time, including Tony Mulhearn, a highly respected figure in Liverpool politics who sadly died in 2019, and the flamboyant 'face' of Militant, Derek Hatton, still a close friend. When the cock crowed in the late '80s and Militant were expelled from the Labour Party and debarred from office, many sought to distance themselves from them and deny any past association. I was not one of the deniers.

I had lived through the heroic battles between Liverpool City Council, heavily influenced by Militant from 1983, and the Thatcher government. These were incredible, heady days. District Labour Party meetings would have attendances of 700-800 members. Democratic argument raged. The city was alive with debate. It was so intoxicating it almost had the feel of the Smolny Institute in the 1917 October Revolution.

I was 'stood down' from all my industrial work for the T&G to assist the City Council in their fight against cuts to jobs and services. They went toe-to-toe with a government whose Thatcherite free-market ideology was wreaking havoc on Merseyside. The city's grant from central government had been slashed, meaning the only way to manage the council's budget was to shed 5,000 jobs, make massive cuts in services, and impose dramatic increases in rents and rates. The leadership of the council had been elected on a promise to resist all of that.

The council instead passed a "needs budget," funding social programmes including the construction of 5,000 homes (twice as many as every other local authority put together). These were not your run of the mill council properties built with the cheapest materials. These were brick-built, semi-detached houses with front and back gardens on small estates. They were beautiful. I still have the image in my mind of driving into those estates at election time and seeing 'Vote Labour' posters plastered everywhere. It gladdened the heart and raised the spirits.

The councillor who drove the housing programme, Tony Byrne, was not actually a member of Militant. Housing was his raison d'être and his Jesuit priest training made him ultra-disciplined to the point where he dismissed any issues that got in the way of his programme. He had little time for trade unions or any organisation that could impact his housing budget. This caused many a potential explosion and it was left to Derek Hatton to try to 'fix' the problems. Derek and Tony had a good relationship but were an odd couple! Tony was scruffy and uninterested in his appearance, while the Armani-clad Derek always looked as though he'd stepped out of a fashion magazine. He's still the same to this day.

As a result of their defiance, the council came into confrontation not just with Margaret Thatcher, but with Neil Kinnock too, culminating in the Labour leader's famous 1985 conference speech that described "a Labour council, *a Labour council,* hiring taxis to scuttle round the city handing out redundancy notices to its own workers." It was a disingenuous claim, or a lie, as Derek Hatton was seen to mouth on TV. The council had already spoken to trade union leaders, of which I was one, to explain they had no intention of implementing any redundancies; it was purely a legal tactic as part of a strategy. Kinnock's deception was why Eric Heffer, a highly respected Liverpool MP, walked off the stage in disgust during the speech.

Kinnock was praised by the right-wing establishment for disowning the council. But in Liverpool the bravery of the 47 councillors who were eventually debarred—most of them not actually members of Militant—is still remembered. The title of the 1988 book by Tony Mulhearn and Peter Taffe, 'Liverpool: A City that Dared to Fight,' is apt (and it's a good read).

Liverpool is today thought of as a solid Labour city but it's worth recalling it wasn't always that way. It was only in 1983, under radical leadership, that Labour regained control of the City Council from a Liberal-Conservative coalition, and then continued to win elections despite unprecedented attacks, not only from the media, Tories and Liberals, but also from the national leadership of the Labour Party and most of the trade union general secretaries.

It's not stretching the truth to say that Labour's continued dominance of Liverpool politics (in 2020 there was not a single Conservative councillor on the 90-seat council and all six MPs in Liverpool, Bootle and Knowsley were Labour) owes much to the legacy of that time. It's why, during the challenge to Jeremy Corbyn's leadership of the Labour Party in 2016, 10,000 people turned out in the rain to hear him speak on St George's Plateau. Corbyn may subsequently have lost support in other cities and towns but in Liverpool he is still loved. That's because of something I found when knocking on doors during elections in the 1980s: people just wanted someone to fight for them, to be on their side. That's what they saw in the so-called Militant years, and that's what they liked about Corbyn—someone brave enough to fight on their behalf.

It's that indomitable character that defines my city. Its people look adversity in the eye and spit back in its face. Fighting back is in our nature—it's the umbilical cord that links politics, music, football and the arts. That spirit shone through the dark clouds of the 1980s. The city saw an explosion of musical talents—Frankie Goes to Hollywood, Echo and the Bunnymen, The Teardrop Explodes, The Farm, OMD, China Crisis, The Mighty Wah!, Dead or Alive, A Flock of Seagulls, The La's, The Wild Swans, and The Christians to name a handful. The writings of Alan Bleasdale, Jimmy McGovern and Willy Russell kept our spirits high. And, of course, we had the two best football teams in England—Everton and Liverpool.

They may have taken our jobs; they may have tried to demonise us; they may have skitted us with their crude caricatures—but they never, never, never broke us.

CHAPTER 4

THE PRAETORIAN GUARDS

There was a sense of jubilation in Smith Square, where the dockers had just voted yes to a national strike. I had driven down from Liverpool to London for the conference, excited by the idea of solidarity action to support the steelworkers, who had already been out on strike for three months. It was high stakes—a national dock strike would bring the country to a standstill.

It was April 1980. The steelworkers were first in the sights of new prime minister Margaret Thatcher. A derisory pay offer and the threat of closures in the publicly-owned steel industry had provoked the first national steel strike for half a century. The steelworkers had stood firm for 13 weeks; now, suddenly, they had a real chance of winning with the help of the dockers.

The dockers' vote to strike felt like a momentous decision. We were on a high. But soon we soon got news that brought us down to earth with a bang. That same day, the executive committee of the steelworkers' union, the Iron and Steel Trades Confederation (ISTC), was meeting a couple of miles away in King's Cross. They would have known about the dockers' conference. But the ISTC had a right-wing general secretary, Bill Sirs, who chose this moment to let down his members. The executive called off the steel strike. As the news filtered through, we felt totally deflated. There was no point us striking in support of the steelworkers if their leaders had thrown in the towel.

The settlement the ISTC reached with the government was described as an honourable draw at the time, but by the following year the number of people working in the steel industry had been cut in half.

Looking back, that was a pivotal yet little noted moment in British history. At the time, Thatcher was a deeply unpopular prime minister (before the Falklands War boosted her standing). She had plunged the country into a sharp recession. It's not far-fetched to think that dockers joining a national strike by steelworkers, with the possibility of other workers taking similar action, could have brought her down. It was an opportunity missed.

––––––––––––

The Thatcher government's assault on the labour movement was vicious and premeditated. She went for us where we were strongest, taking on four power-houses of organised labour in turn—the steelworkers, the miners, the printers and the dockers.

Having dispatched the steelworkers in her first term, a strengthened prime minister moved on to the main fight, the pinnacle of her confrontation with the organised working class: the Great Miners' Strike of 1984-5. It is one of those historical events that will be studied and argued over long into the future. The strike witnessed the Labour leader Neil Kinnock attacking the miners' leader Arthur Scargill, effectively siding with the Tory government against the very workers who had been the backbone of our party and our movement for generations—the Praetorian Guard, if you like.

Those miners came up against the full force of the state. The scale of the assault unleashed against them was daunting and the tactics the state employed were deeply sinister, as captured in Seumas Milne's seminal work, 'The Enemy Within.' In the face of such devastating might, the miners could only rely on the solidarity of the working class. I was overwhelmed by the support they received from the public. Seeing old women and young kids donate food at collection points in Liverpool, even if it was just an odd can of soup from their own shopping, was moving and for me epitomised what my class stood for—compassion, community and solidarity. My own union branch 'adopted' Armthorpe Colliery, just outside Doncaster, and would take them van-loads of supplies. At Christmas in 1984 we called for kids' presents to be donated and got an extraordinary response.

I remember the 1984 TUC Congress—the atmosphere was electric. Eric Hammond, the right-wing general secretary of the electricians and plumbers' union EETPU and a practitioner of so-called business unionism (which involved trade unions being compliant and complicit with employers), attacked Scargill, saying the miners were "lions led by donkeys." There was uproar in the hall. Ron Todd, the general secretary of the T&G, stood up waving his papers to attract the attention of the chair, who seemed to be deliberately ignoring him until a chant went up from the delegates: "Ron Todd, Ron Todd." When he was eventually called, Ron delivered a stinging rebuke to Hammond, saying: "I'm an animal lover, but I tell you what, I'd rather be a donkey than a jackal." There was rapturous applause and cheering. It made me proud to be T&G.

It was devastating when the miners went down to a defeat that was felt by all workers, with repercussions that changed the country. The sadness felt by ordinary people who had willed them to win was stark. There was also anger at the betrayal by the leaders of our movement. Kinnock had attacked the miners throughout, condemning them and Scargill for violence by the pickets without raising a word of censure against the police for the brutality we all witnessed on our televisions. The trade union leaders were the same: the TUC showed just how impotent it was with no real stomach for any fight, and individual trade unions were either complicit with Thatcher or incapable of developing a strategy to give the miners the support they needed. In the years that followed, Scargill's claim that the Tories intended to close all the pits—which had been denounced as scaremongering—came to pass, leaving scores of once-proud mining villages destroyed.

Thatcher and her henchmen crushed the National Union of Mineworkers but they did not break the spirit of the mining communities. That spirit still shines like the brightest of stars every year at the 200,000-strong Durham Miners Gala, the biggest and greatest working-class celebration in Europe. I have had the privilege of speaking at the event on a number of occasions. My speech in 2019 included the following passage:

> In the biggest act of industrial sabotage ever seen, she closed the pits here and across the country, but she never destroyed the spirit of the miners—I see it in every one of you. And while Thatcher is pushing up daises, here we are in glorious Technicolor, celebrating our solidarity and our community spirit; celebrating our past and preparing for our future.

Learning from the miners' defeat is, I believe, essential. Their experience has informed me, as general secretary, how to prepare for what our enemies may throw at us. There is no question that the establishment learns from such episodes too. Ted Heath's 1970-74 government—remembered only for the three-day week—was brought down by the miners, something that was neither forgiven nor forgotten. I had a feeling, when celebrating that victory in 1974, that they would come back for the miners and the rest of us if they ever got the opportunity. They learned their lesson, prepared well, and got their chance. We didn't learn our lesson and didn't prepare—and that became the sorry story of the 1980s.

That pattern was repeated by the print unions in one of the other great industrial battles of the decade. They failed to develop a strategy to deal with the coming threat of new technology. In 1983, local newspaper publisher Eddie Shah launched an all-out attack on the NGA union at his print works in Warrington. I was on the picket line. The strike was memorable for the aggressive tactics deployed by police, making themselves willing players on the side of the employer. They would block exits from the M6 and M62 motorways to stop pickets reaching the Warrington site. On one occasion I found a number of different exits blocked and only got to the picket line because I knew the geography of the area. I remember thinking this new form of policing was more militaristic than the norm. Once again the TUC showed its customary spinelessness by repudiating the NGA's action, whose funds had been sequestrated. The EEPTU demonstrated what a scab union it was under Hammond, signing a single-union 'no strike' deal with Shah's company.

All of this was a prelude to the big one three years later—the print strike at Wapping, home of Rupert Murdoch's News International. Again, the police acted like a paramilitary force for the employer; again, the EEPTU signed a 'no strike' deal, this time with Murdoch; again, the dispute was bitter and the defeat felt by many.

Watching this play out, I thought it inevitable that the Thatcher government would sooner or later come for the dockers. Along with my 6/567 branch on the docks in Liverpool, I had been urging the dock leaders locally and at the highest level of the union's leadership to prepare for what seemed a certain attack on the National Dock Labour Scheme. The dockers themselves were reliant on the National Dock Shop Stewards Committee to make sure any strike would be effective by locking all ports around the UK, but given we knew the government had been making sophisticated preparations for this battle for nearly a decade, I was not optimistic that my union had devoted sufficient thought and imagination to how it would respond.

When the attack finally came with the abolition of the scheme in 1989—a century after the Great Dock Strike of 1889—I'm afraid my fears were realised. The strike faltered and eventually collapsed, resulting in the T&G being derecognised in all registered ports with the exception of Liverpool, from where the dispute had effectively been run. I can still see the coaches leaving at midnight from Pepper's Pub opposite Transport House (now Jack Jones House), going to various non-registered ports around the country in order to picket. But it was all in vain. The defeat meant many dockers were singled out and sacked by the various port employers. You can always rely on bosses to be vindictive when the boot is on their foot. The casualties in London's Tilbury docks included two great socialists and friends of mine, Colin Coughlin and Kevin Hussey.

As well as retaining its trade union recognition, Liverpool also retained its dignity as the men marched back into work. But the bosses on the Liverpool docks would bide their time until another opportunity arose in the mid-1990s.

Margaret Thatcher sought to permanently alter Britain by breaking the labour movement. Her success, though not complete, was substantial. But the prize was a harsher country, in which the creed of looking after number one displaced the working-class community spirit of helping each other out.

Thatcher's biggest achievement was not destroying this or that trade union, but getting inside people's heads and changing attitudes—for the worse. Before Thatcher, the idea of one group of workers sacrificing in support of another—something I consider one of the highest moral virtues—was ingrained. She made it illegal. Today, "secondary action"—when one group of workers strikes in solidarity with another with a different employer—is anathema even within the labour movement. I don't mind hearing workers say they can't strike in solidarity because it will get them into trouble, but too many have accepted they can't do it because it's somehow wrong.

Or take the closed shop, only spoken of today as an embarrassing reminder of the bad old days. In fact, it was an important part of collectivism, giving workers real power over their work lives. It's still good enough for barristers, I notice.

The erosion of our sense of class solidarity dates from the 1980s. Thatcherites may regard that as vindication, but what was the result? Millions of people lost their pride, their sense of purpose, their communities, and even their way of life. Much of the pleasure and camaraderie of life was replaced by insecurity and stress. Society fragmented and inequality widened. I don't call that progress.

CHAPTER 5

FAMILY

Autobiographies are expected to embrace every aspect of the author's life, including their personal life, but to do so impacts on others. When it comes to those with whom I have had relationships, I do not intend to expose them to public gaze or scrutiny. I have been lucky in my life to have been loved by special women and shared incredible moments of happiness with them that will forever live in my heart. The truth, though, is that they deserved more than I was able to give. You often hear people say they have no regrets in life. Well, while it is true that I have no regrets about any industrial or political decisions I have taken, I have many in my personal life.

When relationships break down it's always sad for those directly involved, but there is further sadness at losing touch with the wider family. Joe Doyle, my father-in-law from my first marriage to Ann Doyle, was a lovely man who died far too early. Billy and Doris Forde, my in-laws from my second marriage to Alicia Forde, are wonderful people. Billy is a socialist and a great trade unionist—which is why he was blacklisted in the construction industry for many years—as well as being simply the funniest person I have ever met. I could happily spend hours laughing in his company, especially with Doris. I miss them.

I am sorry for hurting people who simply didn't deserve to be hurt. I wish I could turn back the clock—but as I can't, I have no intention of making them relive such times.

I am, however, happy to share my pride in my children, Ian, Calum, Frankie and Victoria. They are all extraordinary people and while each has different mothers who should take the credit, I'd like to think I have influenced them in their journeys through life.

Ian, my eldest son, is a regional officer in Unite, having previously been a Unite organiser. He carries my passion for representing workers. It's not easy having the same surname as the general secretary but he handles it well and I'm so very proud when shop stewards and members tell me how good he is. I smile when he rings, excited to tell me he achieved a good outcome for one of our members, whether saving their job at a disciplinary or resolving a grievance. It takes me back to the days when I was a regional officer. Ian holds the distinction of being the first McCluskey to go to university—to Leeds, where his degree was in business and media studies. He is also a mad follower of Liverpool Football Club and has a huge knowledge of its history. One of the great sorrows of our lives was the death of Ian's son Joe, my grandson. He died in his mum's womb and had to be delivered at 36 weeks. He is remembered each year on the anniversary of that sad day.

Calum is also a Liverpool fan. He is brilliant at maths, holding a degree in pure mathematics from the prestigious Kings College, University of London. He taught himself 'coding.' Although he has spent some time trying to explain it to me, I still haven't a clue. I'm told by others how important it is and I once heard a discussion on TV in which someone said, "There will be a time when the world is divided into two—those that know coding and those that don't." Calum is into eating healthily with organic vegetables and understanding his body, something I suspect he gets from his mother, Jennie Formby, the former general secretary of the Labour Party.

Frankie is a very talented design engineer, and it seems a lot of the time he is engaged with companies who are trying to headhunt him—he's that good. He hardly has time to settle in one firm before another tries to entice him away. He's also an excellent amateur footballer and not a bad boxer. He is a decent and caring lad, qualities he has inherited from his mother, Alicia Forde, who is an NHS nurse. He is, however, an Evertonian. He's the reason I sometimes want Everton to win—only sometimes you understand, and never when they play Liverpool.

From the moment my daughter Victoria was born she had me wrapped around her little finger, and nothing has changed since. She gained a first-class degree from the University of York in politics, philosophy and economics and then received a distinction in her master's at the London School of Economics. She passed the civil service fast track examination and is currently working in the Department for Work and Pensions in London. She has a strong urge to travel and took a gap year to explore Australia, Vietnam, Laos, Thailand and Cambodia. She has travelled extensively in Europe and the US. She gets the travel bug from her mother, Paula Williams, an ex-T&G activist and a retired Unison official.

I often ask our activists to say thank you to their families for lending them to our movement. Every minute they spend carrying out work for the union is a minute away from their loved ones. I certainly didn't spend as much time with my children as I should have done when they were young. I only hope they can forgive me. Watching children grow up is one of the joys of life and, unfortunately, given my chequered personal history I did not enjoy those pleasures as fully as I would have liked. However, I still have many wonderful moments to treasure from their birth to their adulthood. I could, like any parent, write a book about each of them, but that would also entail unfolding their lives to comment and question. It will suffice for me to say I love them very much.

My sister Kath has three children, Mark, Karen and Ian (yes, the same name I later gave my son, which just shows how much imagination I had back then—although in my defence I was intent on naming my first boy after my first football hero, Ian St John). My niece Karen, who is also my goddaughter, is more like a younger sister to me, a close confidante in my life. She has a myriad of knowledge of all the names of the brood of cousins from Huyton, a rough area of Liverpool, and she keeps me right at family gatherings. Kath's husband Ted is, unfortunately, a Tory, although as a river pilot he always reminds me that he has been a member of my union longer than I have. We've had lots of clashes over the years, but despite his politics he is a good man who adores his family and who treated my mum (who used to call him by his full name, Eddie Douglas) like his own. In fact, whenever my mum, in her later years, would talk about winning the lottery and I would say, jokingly, that as the first son she should give it all to me to look after and share out, she would retort: "Not likely, you're far too easy with money, I'd give it to Eddie Douglas, he'd know what to do."

She was a fabulous person, my mum. There's a saying that you live on in the people you leave behind; there's something comforting about that. It gives me solace knowing that my mum will never be dead while our Karen, who displays all the same, wonderful characteristics, is alive.

CHAPTER 6

ANFIELD, HEYSEL AND HILLSBOROUGH

The Boys' Pen in the top corner of the Kop was exactly what its name suggests—a cage. I was nine years old when I first watched my heroes, Liverpool Football Club, play on the hallowed turf of Anfield from that animal enclosure. I remember the scraps as some trainee criminals tried to extort the other boys.

When I was a kid, paying a few pence to get into the Boys' Pen was the only way my mum would let me go to the match. She and my dad, who was never a football-goer but was a red, thought it was the safest place to be. Little did they realise it was bedlam.

My mates and I soon learned that the first order of business upon getting into the Boys' Pen was to get out of it. The railings were very high, topped with barbed wire, but for our own safety we would scale the heights and drop down into the Kop, a stand with one of the most fearsome reputations in football, but a haven by comparison.

So began one of the great loves of my life: football.

———————

Liverpool Football Club has affected every element of my life and still dominates it today. Going to the match with your mates, kicking and heading every ball during the game, is an experience that gradually seeps into your blood and becomes part of who you are. If you aren't a football fan, it's difficult to explain how it feels to be part of the tribe. It can become all-consuming and make you behave in a completely illogical way.

Liverpool is a football city. You are either a blue (Everton) or a red (Liverpool). I was **always red**. I've been so lucky to live the best part of the history of Liverpool Football Club—from the Boys' Pen watching them play Leyton Orient on a cold and rainy Tuesday night in 1959 to Madrid's sparkling Estadio Metropolitano as they beat Spurs to lift the European Cup for the sixth time in 2019.

The road in between has had massive ups and downs. It has involved some of the best times in my life and two of the worst tragedies. But there are so many wonderful memories that I could fill a book. In fact, many of the moments that have been so important to me have been captured in Brian Reade's brilliant book, '43 Years with the Same Bird,' which truly encapsulates the nature of Liverpool fans. I had a permanent smile on my face as I relived the excursions to all parts of Britain and Europe.

Let me take you on a short journey. When I first started going to games Liverpool weren't very good. We were in the old Second Division and Anfield stadium was a second-rate heap. My attendance at matches coincided with the arrival of Bill Shankly as Liverpool manager in 1959 and the transformation of the club into one of the most feared teams in Europe. Shankly established a dynasty built on solidarity and community spirit, capturing the very essence of Scouse humour and determination in the face of adversity—that never-say-die attitude.

I remember the day in 1962 when we beat Southampton 2-0 to be promoted into the First Division (today's Premier League). Along with thousands, I got onto the sacred turf at the end of the game. It was a very muddy pitch and it ruined my shoes. I got a clip from my mum, but it was worth it.

Into the big time we went and so began the great roller-coaster ride that I'm still enjoying, white knuckles gripped to the rails. I climbed on board as a kid and hung on as I grew through my teenage years into a man. At school my long-term friends were all reds fans—my best mates Peter Walsh, John Foley and my minder Larry Gallagher (Gally). We would persuade the headmaster to let us commandeer the old rickety school bus to take us to away games. You can imagine the camaraderie that was forged on those trips. It stills holds strong when we meet today—sadly without Gally who passed away far too early. I still see his younger brother, John, in an executive box these days, with my good friends Paul, John and Julian Flanagan. Such friendships exemplify the quality of togetherness that has been important to me all my life.

My early teenage years were largely spent at my Aunty Lil and Uncle Billy's prefab house in Bootle. As well as their children, Lawrence and Monica, my cousin Vinny and other friends would be there. Nobody was allowed to walk on the front garden (opposite the Merton Pub), leaving it lush and green, but the back garden didn't have a single blade of grass—a casualty of football, cricket and tennis. Occasionally Aunty Lil would decide to reseed the back garden, but would always relent at the sight of so many long faces—my Uncle Billy being the worst, he was the biggest kid of us all. If we weren't in the garden we'd be playing Subbuteo, which was all the rage at the time. Everybody was a mad Liverpudlian, including one of our great friends Johnny Nixon, nicknamed Yash, who, along with my Uncle Bill, used to know Shankly and would often be invited into his house for tea and a chat when they went to see him, normally to ask for tickets.

Our Monica was my favourite cousin. She was about 15 months older than me, as were her friends who all went to the matches. I was delighted to be told I could join them on away games. They used to get the coach at the Crown Pub on Walton Hall Avenue to travel all over. If it was an away game in London the coach would leave at midnight, arriving about 6 a.m. The girls used to tease me. As a 14 or 15-year-old I was suitably embarrassed, but I loved every minute. They were all, in my eyes, very attractive and desirable.

It was with Monica that I travelled by train to Glasgow—standing all the way—for the European Cup Winners' Cup final in 1966. With us was Monica's boyfriend at the time, Rory Storm, the rock star (Ringo Starr had been the drummer in his band the Hurricanes)—symbolic for me of how football and music were synonymous with Liverpool in the '60s. It was a cold and miserable night in Hampden Park and we lost 2-1 to Borussia Dortmund. That was the first time

I watched Liverpool lose a final. There have been 14 other occasions since—a fact that shocked me when I tallied them up.

Each defeat was painful, but the 25 finals we have won have more than compensated. There have been unbelievable times and wonderful adventures along the way. There was a period in the '70s and '80s when, as a group of friends, we would hire a 12-seater minibus to take us to Wembley every season (well it felt like that—Liverpool were always either in the Charity Shield, the FA Cup final or the League Cup final). Our trips would be so regular that Liverpudlians used to refer to Wembley as Anfield South. We would set off from the Old Roan Pub close to the M57 at 6.30 a.m. on the Friday and the first noise would be 'psst'—the opening of cans of lager. We used to stay in Harrow on the Hill with one of our mates, Alan, a teacher at Harrow School. He had a small terraced cottage that belonged to the school, as did everything on the Hill, including the pubs the Castle—which was opposite the cottage about eight feet away—and the White Horse further down the road. What nights we had in them. We would crash out in the cottage sleeping on couches, chairs and the floor—until Alan got married and children arrived, when he would open up Harrow's gym where we would play five-a-side and drink wine and beer until the early hours of the morning with portraits of Lord Palmerston and Winston Churchill looking down disapprovingly.

Cup finals weren't the only big days. Some of the biggest were the games against Everton, Liverpool's local rivals. The fixture is often called the friendly derby. There's no doubt the bitterness that characterises other derbies is missing in the main. Many families count both blues and reds among their number. Fans even travel together when the two sides play each other outside Liverpool, as they did in a string of cup finals in the '80s. But I remember there being plenty of arguments and fights that challenge the friendly image. Indeed, come derby day when I was working on the docks, I would have vicious rows with my friend Tony Corrigan, an Evertonian. As close as we were, there were occasions when we wouldn't speak for days on end, sometimes weeks, after a match.

The biggest Liverpool victories of all have been the 13 league titles, including, after a 30-year wait, the incredible 2019-20 Premier League triumph. That team simply couldn't be stopped—not even by the Covid-19 virus. The celebrations were wild.

———————

Liverpool fans are renowned for their songs and banners. Over the years, both have evolved to become very sophisticated. I have lived through that evolution.

Liverpool, of course, was the heart of a music revolution in the '60s. Merseybeat was engulfing the world. All the songs of the day by the Beatles, Cilla Black, and Gerry and the Pacemakers would flow down from the Kop. It was somewhat surreal to behold 30,000 people singing and swaying to Cilla's 'Anyone Who Had a Heart.' It was the Kop that made 'You'll Never Walk Alone' known throughout the world, a theme always identified with Liverpool but now sung by clubs all over Europe. I know supporters of Celtic, a team I also love, will try to say they sang it first, but I'm afraid their claims do not stand up to scrutiny. It was Gerry and the Kop that made the song famous. But I will forever be grateful to Celtic fans for their rendition of 'You'll Never Walk Alone' at Liverpool's first match after the Hillsborough disaster in 1989. The sound of it ringing out in Parkhead, Glasgow brought tears to my eyes.

It was Liverpool fans who began adapting popular tunes with new words full of humour and passion. We had normal chants like any other team's fans, but adapted songs became increasingly dominant and grew in inventiveness as the years rolled by. Each generation took it upon itself to create new songs— its contribution to the rich tapestry of sound woven into the fabric of the Club. Some songs were tailored to whichever city in Europe Liverpool were playing in, especially at European Cup finals. Others reflected the nationality of the club's manager. When it was the Frenchman, Gerard Houllier, the Marseillaise would ring out, but with different words. When Rafa Benítez arrived we all became Spanish with a twist of Scouse. The songs were invented by ordinary fans and practised at away games and in the pubs surrounding Anfield—The Albert, The Twelfth Man, The Arkle, The Sandon, The Park, The Halfway House—until the entire ground knew the words. An example, to the tune of 'You Are My Sunshine' is:

Luis Garcia,
He drinks sangria,
He came from Barca,
To bring us joy.
He's five foot seven,
He's football heaven,
So please don't take our Luis away.

The sophistication rose to a new level with the advent of BOSS Night in 2011. It started with the Liverpool fanzine *BOSS Mag* putting on gigs after games, first in Duke Street and Oscars, then in District—a much larger venue in the Baltic district of the city by the Albert Dock—and ultimately expanding to organise events at big games abroad, such as in Shevchenko Park, Kiev for the 2018 Champions League Final. Even though Liverpool lost, those of us who were there will forever talk about a fantastic day. A year later, in Madrid's Salvador Dali Square, an estimated 70,000 Liverpool fans witnessed another unforgettable BOSS show—only bettered by our 2-0 victory over Spurs. BOSS performers have included established stars like Peter Hooton of The Farm and John Power of The La's and Cast, and up and coming artists like Jamie Webster, who has built a loyal following and is hopefully destined for greater fame. BOSS Night has been a factory for new songs and words—it was at BOSS Night that Jamie Webster popularised one of Liverpool's most famous new chants, 'Allez Allez Allez.' Peter Hooton says when he went to a few BOSS sessions in the Baltic he felt uncomfortable because everyone was so young—so you can imagine how I felt when I sneaked into one of the gigs. If only for an hour, it was good to feel young again.

The creativity of Liverpool fans is not only heard in our songs but seen in our banners and flags. As the introduction to a wonderful collection of photographs, 'Liverpool FC Banners,' proclaims: "They've been proudly displayed all over the world and are part of the unique DNA of a Kopite. They've hailed heroes and mocked rivals, adapted poetry and songs, been philosophical and funny, proclaimed and protested and made opinions and beliefs abundantly clear." Banners adorn Anfield at every home game and redecorate each away stadium Liverpool visits. A fan's ritual at any major final is to walk around and view the banners displayed usually in some designated public square. It's like visiting a gallery because each banner really is an individual work of art, painstakingly thought out in its message, design and production. I've stood in amazement at some of the more political and philosophical creations. Collectively they embody the spirit of the club.

Just like the songs, the banners have evolved over time, from the simple painted words "Shankly Lives" on a white sheet to the elaborate image of Stevie G as a gladiator. Each new generation adds its contribution. At only 15 years old my great nephew, Adam, came up with the message: "The most difficult part of attaining perfection is finding something to do for an encore." Where did that come from, I ask myself? The answer is, it's in our blood. Adam's creation made page 79 of the book of banners.

One flag you won't find draped around a Liverpool fan is the Saint George's Cross. The same applies to the Union Jack. A well-known Liverpool banner provides the best explanation why: "WE'RE NOT ENGLISH WE ARE SCOUSE." This encapsulates the distinctive identity of Liverpool—the sense of an outsider city. Perhaps it has its roots in Irish immigration that made Liverpool Catholic. But you won't see many Irish tricolours either. This is why the word "unique," used in the book of banners, is so apt to describe Liverpool's culture—and is undoubtedly reflected in its politics.

Trying to choose which banner I like the best is almost impossible; like picking a favourite Monet or Turner or deciding on just one Dylan or Beatles song. All of them have given me joy, happiness and laughter and made me feel better. (See the photographs section for a selection of good ones.)

Liverpool supporters' songs and banners tell the history of the club with all its joy and sorrow. They have long since escaped the confines of Anfield and become part of the fabric of life in our city. As reds, we carry them in our souls. A recent slogan delivered by manager Jurgen Klopp on LFC TV says it all:

"WE ARE LIVERPOOL—THIS MEANS MORE."

———————

The highs of life as a Liverpool supporter have been accompanied by two of the darkest incidents in football history—the Heysel and Hillsborough disasters. I was present at both tragedies and witnessed first-hand the utter disregard the authorities had for ordinary football fans. The memories of those events anger and sadden me in equal measure today.

In the early 1980s the two top clubs in Europe, Liverpool and Juventus, had managed to miss each other in competition draws. They were finally due to meet in the 1985 European Cup final. These were two of the best-supported clubs in Europe, but their fans were known to be volatile. So where did UEFA, the governing body, decide to hold the game? At Heysel, a dilapidated stadium in Brussels that wouldn't have passed safety standards in the Beazer Homes League. Terraces made of packed soil; insufficient toilet facilities; and little to stop people getting in without a ticket—the ground was an utter disgrace and so was the decision to use it. I understand that Peter Robinson (secretary of Liverpool FC 1965-2000) raised concerns when the club visited the ground for the first time weeks before the match. He was assured that every safety precaution was in place. All I can say is: he had eyes. The club should have refused to play on safety grounds.

As thousands of fans crammed into the stadium on match day, they found the authorities had allocated a third of the 'Liverpool end' to neutral Belgian fans. Only they weren't neutral—it later emerged from the inquiry into the disaster that Italian travel firms had snapped up the tickets within minutes of them going on sale (it's likely someone received a healthy backhander). The result was the Liverpool section, taking up two-thirds of the stand behind the goal, was overcrowded (remember how easy it was to get in without a ticket), while the remaining space was half-empty, and those who were there were Juventus fans. Only chicken wire and a handful of police separated the two sets of fans. It was a recipe for disaster, and that's precisely what unfolded once mindless morons among the Liverpool fans, fuelled by drink in the heat, decided they had to retake the 'territory' that belonged to them.

What followed made me ashamed to be a Liverpool fan. I was there with my son, Ian. It was a frightening experience but at least we came home. Thirty-nine

Italian fans were crushed to death when, in their panic to get to safety, one of the decaying walls collapsed.

Brussels Police were useless. They had no experience of dealing with a match of this nature—something that didn't seem to have crossed the minds of UEFA officials. Yet no one in UEFA or the Belgian authorities was ever held to account for creating the conditions for the tragedy. While Liverpool Football Club and individual fans were punished, those in charge got off scot-free. Heysel Stadium was demolished in 1995 to wipe away its infamy, but the horror and sorrow of the families of those 39 souls can never be wiped away.

Four years later, on 15 April 1989, I was present at Hillsborough Stadium in Sheffield to see Liverpool play Nottingham Forest in the semi-final of the FA Cup. I was sitting in the stand adjacent to the Leppings Lane end as a scene of utter dread unfolded before my eyes. Recalling it 30 years later, tears still roll down my cheeks.

At first it was difficult to see what was happening but very quickly it became clear that something serious was wrong. A wave of foreboding came over me as I realised that my son, Ian, had tickets with his mates for the Leppings Lane end. In those days football grounds had terraces—standing areas without seats, leaving fans vulnerable to crushing if the space became overcrowded, which is precisely what happened at Hillsborough. While police appeared to stand and do nothing, fans were placing bodies on makeshift stretchers made from advertising hoardings and carrying them the full length of the pitch to the access way because ambulances were being stopped from entering the stadium.

I came out of the stand and walked to the troubled end of the ground. There was a line of police standing shoulder-to-shoulder blocking the way. I pushed my way past them and beheld a scene every bit as bad as I had feared. Fans who had died were being laid out alongside each other, their faces covered. I found myself lifting the coverings to see if any of the dead was Ian, even though I could see from each body that it wasn't him.

In a daze I walked back through the line of police. Turning to face them I unleashed the rage that was welling up like a volcano. It was like an out-of-body experience. These innocent, ordinary, mostly young PCs and WPCs just stood there, suffering my tirade. Out of the corner of my eye I saw an inspector coming towards me. I was ready to blast him with all I had when suddenly, from nowhere, I felt a vice-like grip around my arms, shoulders and body. It was an older sergeant who said, "You're alright son, you're alright." The rage inside dissipated. When he released his hold, I felt utterly spent. "Go home now," he said as he shepherded me away.

You may wonder why I was immediately so angry at the police. My answer is that instinct told me they were to blame. What is sometimes forgotten is that the previous year the same fixture, Liverpool vs Nottingham Forest in the semi-final of the FA Cup, had taken place at the same stadium, and the police handling was similarly amateurish. There was chaos at the Leppings Lane end. I was amazed that nobody was hurt. But no lessons had been learned. This was a time when the Tory government and the media preferred to demonise football fans, who were treated, if not like animals, then certainly without respect or dignity.

I eventually learned that Ian was safe. He and his four mates had been caught up in the pen behind the goal. It took them an hour and a half to get free but one of them was missing. They searched for hours until they found him. He had been taken to hospital but was OK. At that time, before mobile phones, it was agony for everyone waiting to find out if their loved ones and friends had got out. Ian was a big, strong lad. He said to me: "You wouldn't have made it, dad, if you'd been in there." It was horrific.

Ninety-six fans who went to a football match on a sunny day never came home; their families never received the call to say they were safe. There followed one of the most shameful episodes in British history, a cover up on an unimaginable scale. I wonder whether, had the incompetent South Yorkshire Police and their senior officers accepted responsibility and apologised immediately, the families would have had closure and justice there and then. Instead, before the bodies were even cold, the establishment was peddling the line that drunken Liverpool fans were to blame.

The *Sun* newspaper, with its vile editor Kelvin MacKenzie, led the charge, presenting a ream of lies under the headline: "THE TRUTH." West Midlands Police (a force with an image of corruption) were drafted in to investigate and, surprise, surprise, declared their South Yorkshire colleagues blameless. All of this was given the nod of approval from the very top, right up to Margaret Thatcher and her government.

I'm sure that in their private clubs over brandy and cigars members of the establishment felt smug in the belief that their corrupt conspiracy had been successfully executed. But they hadn't reckoned on the tenacity, courage and outright obstinacy of Liverpool, a city that was used to standing up and fighting against injustice and adversity. It's in our DNA.

I don't wish to sound arrogant, but I don't believe any other city would have been able to take on the forces of the state and win. The fact that it took 30 years stands as testimony to the desperation of the establishment as they fought a rear-guard action, and to the unbelievable determination of the families demanding justice—not only for their loved ones, but for all Liverpool fans; indeed, for football fans everywhere.

The Hillsborough Family Support Group and the Hillsborough Justice Campaign unleashed a campaign the likes of which had never been seen. The whole city, Evertonians as well as reds, stood with them. Such solidarity in demanding 'Justice for the 96' made me proud of my city.

The support from Liverpool Football Club itself was outstanding. Manager Kenny Dalglish and the players conducted themselves with such grace in the immediate aftermath of the disaster, attending every single funeral. The club always stood by the families and campaigners. There was help, too, from Liverpool City Council and from other organisations all over the country, and indeed the world. The campaigners were blessed in having such a force to drive their efforts as Margaret Aspinall, the leading face of the Hillsborough Family Support Group. She displayed such dignity throughout, symbolising all that was good in the many people involved.

The initiatives people took to help were amazing. One such project, in the later stages of the campaign, was the Don't Buy the *Sun*/Justice Tour. Karie Murphy, who worked for Tom Watson and would later be Jeremy Corbyn's chief of staff, teamed up with Peter Hooton, one of Liverpool's favourite sons, to put together a number of gigs in Liverpool, Glasgow, London and Cardiff, highlighting not only the fight for justice over Hillsborough but also over the Shrewsbury 24 and the Orgreave Campaign of the miners. Pete's classic song with the Farm, 'All Together Now,' brilliantly captured the spirit of resistance to the establishment. I spoke at two of the events along with Tom Watson, my friend at the time.

Sadly, the wide support for the campaigners didn't extend to certain parts of the Labour Party. There were great hopes that an independent inquiry into the disaster would be possible after the election of a Labour government in 1997, but initially they were dashed. Jack Straw, home secretary from 1997-2001, didn't lift a finger. Neither did his successor, David Blunkett, from 2001-2004. Both were more concerned with not offending the police establishment than helping ordinary working people seek justice.

Every year a memorial service was held at Anfield in front of nearly 20,000 people in a capacity Kop. On the eve of the 20th anniversary service I attended a fundraiser for the campaign in Jamie Carragher's bar in Stanley Street. All the Liverpool players were very supportive of the campaigners but Jamie is one of us and has never forgotten where he comes from (his 23 Foundation does fantastic work for children in Merseyside and throughout the world). Andy Burnham was there—at the time he was secretary of state for culture, media and sport in Gordon Brown's government and was due to speak at the service the following day. I liked Andy, so I warned him he might get a rough ride given a Labour government had then been in office for 12 years and done nothing. Angela and Maria Eagle were with him. They assured him he'd be fine. Sure enough, the following day the boos rained down from the Kop when Andy was introduced. Though visibly shaken, to his great credit he committed himself there and then to doing more for the campaign. True to his word, he played a critical role in finally bringing about the independent inquiry.

A couple of years later, in 2011, in one of the most emotional experiences of my life, I watched from the visitors' gallery of the House of Commons as Liverpool MP and passionate red Steve Rotherham read the names and ages of every one of the 96. There was hardly a dry eye in the house. When he finished, spontaneous applause broke out in the chamber—the first time that had ever happened. Support from the Labour leadership finally became unequivocal under Jeremy Corbyn, who was solidly behind the campaigners. I felt proud when Dr Sheila Coleman, active in the Hillsborough Justice campaign, introduced Jeremy's 2016 Labour conference speech in Liverpool.

To see the police, politicians and scum media finally in retreat in the face of a successful campaign gladdened my heart. Particularly satisfying was the *Sun* being forced to apologise, and watching the pusillanimous McKenzie grovelling, not because he was genuinely sorry, but in an attempt to stem the boycott of the newspaper. Sales of the *Sun* in Liverpool plummeted by 90 per cent due to their disgusting lies and, to this day, they have never recovered. I caught a cab in 2020 and smiled when I saw a sticker that said: "Please do not read the *Sun* in this taxi."

As the real truth emerged, the police and the politicians fell over themselves in their backpedalling. When the court verdict finally came it was "unlawful killing." Justice had been achieved, although no one went to jail for their involvement. But the families, all of whom are heroes in my eyes, know that because of their courage and determination the men, women, boys and girls who died on that fateful day—15 April 1989—will never be forgotten and will never walk alone.

CHAPTER 7

BETRAYAL

It was like coming home to my family. Marching through the streets of Liverpool surrounded by dockers, their wives, kids, and the people of the city; trade union banners and makeshift placards held aloft; chants and jokes filling the air; a potent mix of belonging and determination swelling our hearts.

For two-and-a-half years in the mid-1990s, the Liverpool dockers held out on strike after 500 men were sacked for refusing to cross a picket line. They were tough times. But what I remember most about my trips back to Liverpool to support them is the palpable sense of togetherness and solidarity they forged in the face of adversity.

As an officer of a union that was shamefully engaged in selling out the strikers, I was ordered not to join the dockers' protest marches. There was no chance of me obeying that. Afterwards, I would go around the pubs where my old friends and comrades were drinking, whether in the appropriately named Slaughterhouse, the Queens, or Peppers. Despite the hardship, there was a lot of joy and humour there—people giving each other strength, in stark contrast to the lack of strength in the leadership of my union and the Labour Party at the time.

———

The trade union movement took a long time to gather itself after the defeats inflicted by the Thatcher government. Stripped of their confidence, unions became accomodationist—always looking to compromise rather than fight for the interests of their members—both in the industrial and the political arenas.

It was no coincidence that the period when this approach was most in vogue coincided with the rise of New Labour. But it was no coincidence, either, that the experience of workers being sold out while Labour refused to lift a finger triggered a backlash. The historic shift to the left in the trade union movement was a direct result and laid the foundations for the political developments that followed.

That momentous turnaround touched my life directly, from the low of the shameful betrayal of the Liverpool dockers in the mid-'90s to the high of getting my friend Tony Woodley elected as a left general secretary of the T&G in 2003. Those events thrust me into the heart of the action. Suddenly I found myself involved in shaping the course of history rather than reacting to it.

The journey began at the dawn of the 1990s with my appointment as a national officer for the T&G. I moved down to London to take up my position as national secretary for the General Workers' Trade Group. I would remain a national officer for the next 16 years. It was strange to leave Liverpool although my heart will forever be there.

I had not long landed in London when, to my shock and amazement, I was arrested. The previous December a ballot rigging scandal had gripped the T&G and an individual had maliciously told the police they had seen people, including me, "stuffing envelopes" in the union's Liverpool office. Through their investigation the police subsequently found this was totally unrelated to any ballot—the envelopes contained a humdrum mailing going out to branch members. But that didn't stop the media trying to traduce my name when my arrest was reported—with no subsequent mention of my innocence, of course. It was the first time I experienced how cynical and evil the media could be. Unfortunately, such treatment later became the norm as I was subjected to a constant stream of smears, innuendos and outright lies as general secretary of Unite. There's a horrible saying, "no smoke without fire," which ascribes guilt without any fair process. I can tell you that if you rub two lies together there will be lots of smoke, but no fire.

Once that unpleasant episode was behind me, I loved every minute of my new job, despite the dismal backdrop of the continued running down of our manufacturing industries. The experience I gained was invaluable as my involvement in the union widened throughout Britain and Ireland. I travelled from Penzance to Aberdeen, Belfast to Waterford, meeting shop stewards and regional officials and building up strong relationships. Without realising it at the time, this would stand me in good stead when I ran to be Unite's general secretary some years later.

One of the great benefits of working in the T&G's London HQ was its proximity to the National Pensioners' Convention's office in Holborn, where its president, the great Jack Jones, worked. It was such a pleasure to be able to periodically pop in to have a chat with the former T&G general secretary. They were nice half-hours. He would always greet me in the same way: "Hello son, how's the 'Pool? Have you been up there lately? How is everybody?" I had to pinch myself to believe I was chatting away with one of my heroes, a truly great man.

The new decade spelled the end of the line for Margaret Thatcher, brought down not by Labour leader Neil Kinnock but by a people's revolt against her hated poll tax ("events, dear boy, events" as Harold Macmillan might have said). The Conservative Party were spooked into getting rid of a prime minister who had looked invincible. It was a reminder of how misjudgements fuelled by arrogance can change fortunes overnight. The media gushed with sympathy as she left Downing Street in tears, but I thought of the tears of millions of working-class people whose lives her policies blighted. I felt the same when she died in 2013. A group of friends, including Tom Watson, went to a pub, not to celebrate her death, but to mourn the communities she destroyed. On both occasions I thought, "Good riddance."

1992 was a pivotal year, both for the country and my union. Against expectations, Neil Kinnock failed to defeat John Major in the general election. The debate started as to why, all over again. I believed then as I do now that you need to offer the electorate a clear alternative to inspire and enthuse them to support you.

The same year saw the retirement of T&G General Secretary Ron Todd, a good man whose gut instinct was always to lean left. Ron had a difficult time in the top job, having to cope with an executive council divided between left and right, while membership was plummeting due to the Thatcher government's assaults on manufacturing and trade unions. The right staged a walk out at one executive meeting, having first tipped off a delighted media. I learned then the importance of maintaining a united executive.

The left backed Bill Morris as its candidate to succeed Todd. There were reservations about Morris in some quarters—some political, and some born of a belief that not enough members would vote for a Black man. As I was still very much involved in the Broad Left group within the union, I was tasked with travelling to the more sceptical regions, in particular Ireland and Scotland, to persuade left comrades that Morris could win. It was an incredible achievement when he not only won, but won comfortably, and became the first Black general secretary of a trade union in Britain and Ireland.

Unfortunately, the hopes many of us on the left had for Bill's stewardship faded little by little. He drifted into a reliance on right-wing regional secretaries for support, whose influence grew to the consternation of the left. Sadly, he equated disagreement with disloyalty. That trait was on show when he decided that my old region of the union, the North West, needed to be taught a lesson. The region was known to be unorthodox and awkward, but the way it was treated revealed an intolerant attitude that I have always opposed. Officers were disciplined and sacked, creating tensions that led to a split in the Broad Left (never a good thing). Even Peter Haggar, the left's leader who was a brilliant political operator, was so disillusioned with Bill that in his most frustrated moments he talked of standing against him in any re-election. I don't believe he really would have done but it was a mark of how high feelings were running that he considered it. Sadly, Peter contracted cancer and we lost a fantastic comrade.

As the fighting spirit ebbed away from the T&G I also became disillusioned. My concerns about Morris' leadership were so deep that, along with the North West region, I found myself in a position I would never had expected: supporting his opponent Jack Dromey (whose politics I did not share) when Bill ran for re-election in 1995. Some friends on the left said I was wrong to oppose the first Black general secretary. I suppose they had a point. I was simply looking at the actions of a man who was slipping away from the vision we had hoped and fought for. I was angry at what I saw as a betrayal. I did feel uneasy in Dromey's campaign and quickly disappeared when Labour Party apparatchiks came to take it over. I disagreed with their methods—negative campaigning against Bill personally with the full help of the media. Ironically, some of the same people would subject me to the same treatment, only worse, when I ran for re-election as general secretary in 2017.

But I wasn't wrong about Morris. In fact, I was proved right in the most painful way possible. In September 1995, five young dock workers were sacked during a dispute about overtime pay. They had been hired by a subcontractor to do whatever they were told by the bosses, on worse terms than the majority of the dockers still working for the major employer, the Mersey Docks and Harbour Company. This subcontracting arrangement had one purpose: to undermine working conditions. After the abolition of the National Dock Labour Scheme and the defeat of the 1989 dockers strike, casualisation was returning to haunt the port.

The sacked workers formed a picket line. On the Liverpool docks solidarity wasn't just a word but a way of life. Five hundred brave dockers refused to cross the picket line—not only those employed by the subcontractor, but by Mersey Docks too. After all, they were from the same community, some even from the same families, doing the same work on the same docks. The employers responded by sacking them all. There followed one of the greatest fights by workers ever seen, lasting two-and-a-half years until 1998, making it one of the longest disputes in the history of the T&G.

Not that the union could claim much credit. While the shop stewards went above and beyond for their members, the T&G leadership refused to give them full and open support, citing as justification the Conservatives' anti-union legislation, which outlawed solidarity strikes. That didn't stop Morris trying to have it both ways. When John Bowers, the leader of the American east coast dockers' union the ILA, who unlike Morris had given great support and solidarity to Liverpool, came to the city to address a strikers' meeting in March 1996, Bill decided to speak alongside him, declaring: "When my grandchildren say to me in 15, 20, 25 years from now, 'Where were you when the Liverpool dockworkers were fighting for their jobs, their community, their dignity and their pride?' I want to be able to say: 'I was marching with them side by side.'"

If only that had happened. The dockers organised regular marches through Liverpool with huge support from the public and the emerging Women of the Waterfront group (the organised wives, partners and relatives of the dockers who became a powerful force). But the T&G wouldn't be seen near them. An edict came down from central office telling us officers that we shouldn't go on the marches for fear it would implicate the union and open it up to legal action. I ignored that, of course, and used to travel up to Liverpool whenever I could. These were my friends and comrades involved in a life and death struggle—five of them died from heart attacks during the dispute. I was proud to stand with them and full of anger at how they were being let down. I pledged to myself there and then that if I was ever in a position of power I would always stand with members in struggle, no matter what.

The determination and inventiveness of the dockers in those tough years was unbelievable, and has been brilliantly captured by my friend Mike Carden, one of the leaders of the strike, in his magnum opus 'Liverpool Dockers: A History of Rebellion.' They had high profile celebrity support, most famously from Liverpool footballer Robbie Fowler, who in March 1997 lifted his jersey after scoring in front of the Kop to reveal a T-shirt backing the dockers. His teammate and friend, Steve McManaman, wore the same top.

But aware they lacked industrial support from their union, the dockers looked abroad for solidarity. Internationalism is in the DNA of organised dockworkers. It comes from working with ships and crew from overseas, and from the historical experience of port employers and ship owners uniting across borders to break strikes and smash unions. It's why the International Transport Workers' Federation (ITF) exists. And it's probably why I have always had an international outlook to my politics.

The dockers made their own contacts with dock workers and transport unions in other countries, organised global dockers' conferences, and even sent a number of Liverpool dockers to America to set up picket lines outside ports in Baltimore and New York—literally flying pickets. Their campaign inspired international days of action. On one occasion, workers in 130 ports in 30 different countries took part. During the first phase of the dispute, this international solidarity put real pressure on the Mersey Docks and Harbour Company, which lost business as a result.

Morris' initial indifference to the dockers turned to negativity as the months passed by. He stopped the ITF from galvanising solidarity action. He started saying: "The leadership of the union has an obligation to preserve the fabric of the T&G." Whenever you hear a union leader talk about protecting the fabric of the union you know a sell-out is in the air.

Not once during the two-and-a-half-year dispute did Morris ask for my input. He dismissed all my attempts to be involved. I was a T&G national officer with 22 years' experience of the Mersey Docks and Harbour Company—11 as an employee and 11 as a union official. I knew all the company managers and all the shop stewards inside out. But I was not called upon. In a clear-the-air meeting with Morris after the strike, I asked him why. I suppose I already knew the answer—why would he want my opinion if he had decided to sell out the dockers? It's fair to say that what remained of our relationship evaporated, and in the years that followed I had to be on my guard against any mistakes he could use to secure my dismissal. It kept me on my toes.

The final hope for the dockers was the election of a Labour government in 1997. Surely, they thought, Labour ministers would instruct Mersey Docks to settle the dispute—the government owned a chunk of the company. It was heartbreaking to watch the realisation spread that Tony Blair and his acolytes had no intention of doing anything to help. Morris was not about to pressure the government to intervene, either. The dockers had no more avenues left.

I remember being called up to Liverpool to meet half-a-dozen of my friends who were shop stewards. "Lennie," they told me, "we are done. The men have no fight left in them. You need to get the leadership to get us a deal as quickly as possible." When I drove away from that bar in Mathew Street, my heart was heavy with sadness for these brave men who were accepting defeat.

The end of the dispute was bitter and miserable. All the jobs were lost. But if people expected the dockers to fade away they had forgotten this was Liverpool. Instead of being scattered to the winds, they created a focal point by moving into the CASA—a disused bar in Hope Street (how appropriate)—and making it into a vibrant social hub to service the community. My friends Mike Carden, Tony Nelson, Terry Teague and Andy Dwyer were the driving force in setting it up. The CASA became well known in Liverpool and 20 years on is still a centre of resistance against the powerful and a meeting place for those courageous dockers. As well as a bar, there are rooms for hosting meetings, theatre shows and events. Upstairs there's space for training, where many dockers reskilled by learning to work with computers. Mike named it the Initiative Factory (IF), taking great satisfaction from the fact no one realised 'if....' was a cult film that played to his anarchic sympathies.

The story of the Liverpool dockers was emblematic. A strong and productive workforce had the rug pulled from under it by the Thatcherite craze for subcontracting and casualisation. When the workers stood up for themselves they found their tradition of solidarity had been outlawed. Their union had become tame, unwilling to defend its members. And for those who saw this as a political attack that could ultimately only be beaten with a political response, New Labour offered no hope. These were lessons that trade unionists learned. The legitimacy of right wingers and accommodationists within the labour movement started to crumble.

―――――――

While the Liverpool dockers' dispute was at its height, a less heralded strike began at the Magnet Kitchens factory in Darlington. When, following a legal ballot, 321 union members went out on strike in August 1996 they were sacked and replaced by a scab workforce. The sacked workers were decent, hardworking people who were treated disgracefully by Magnet Kitchens back when the law gave no protection to strikers. Although they fought valiantly, as the weeks and months passed more and more strikers drifted away from the picket line to work elsewhere. The various workers on strike were represented by four unions— T&G; GMB; UCATT; AEU. The company refused to meet any of them. After about 18 months, with the strike petering out despite fantastic support from the local public and an incredible injection of activity from a women's support group, the dispute was handed over from the regional officials to national officers of the unions.

We decided to get creative. Working with two comrades from the GMB— my good friend Phil Davies and Steve Pryles, a great campaigner—we set out to embarrass the company. We organised occupations of Magnet Kitchens' stores on high streets and did banner drops from bridges. But our biggest coup was a chicken coop. We tracked down the CEO of Beresford, Magnet's parent company. He lived in the beautiful village of St Neots, Cambridgeshire, a different world from Darlington. Steve found and rented a plot of land opposite his luxury home. We stocked the land with chickens and put up a massive billboard proclaiming: "Chickens coming home to roost." Then we distributed leaflets around the village exposing the disgraceful treatment of the Darlington workers and the company's refusal to talk.

The stunt did the trick. For the first time, the CEO agreed to speak to the union, although only to me—he somehow had the impression I was the reasonable one while the GMB were troublemakers. I didn't disabuse him. We met in the luxury Rubens Hotel in Victoria, London. Here was the unacceptable face of capitalism made real—as far as he was concerned, the strikers were no more than units of production that had been discarded. He felt no responsibility for their plight. I pushed as hard as I could, but he was not going to reinstate the workers. The only move he would make was a payment of £850,000 to the union for us to distribute to the workers.

After discussions with Phil and the strike committee, I was tasked with producing a matrix to determine how the money should be shared between the workers based on how long they had stayed on strike. I spent many nights burning the midnight oil to come up with a fair system before presenting it to a mass meeting of the sacked workers. Situations like that are not always easy to handle. You need to be able to hold your own when the heckles come in. The amount of money we had to work with was derisory given the duration of the strike, and I also had to explain the fact that only the 56 workers still manning the picket line after 21 months were entitled to vote on the deal. Most of the strikers accepted it as the best we could get; it was agreed.

I often look back to disputes like the Magnet strike and the Liverpool dockers' ordeal and think we would have won if we'd had the sophisticated leverage techniques later developed by Unite. Those leverage techniques could be described as a kind of guerrilla warfare, working out where an employer is weak and applying pressure using unconventional methods. What we did in the Magnet strike was prototype version of a strategy that has been greatly advanced by Sharon Graham in Unite's organising department since. It's a shame that development came too late for those workers.

CHAPTER 8

COOL BRITANNIA

After 18 dark years under a vicious Tory government, a bright new dawn arrived at last. I remember the night of the general election on 1 May 1997 as one of my best. I watched the results come in at the Victoria Club across the road from parliament. It was a landslide for Labour, thanks to the combination of John Major's government looking tired and divided and Tony's Blair's ability to capture the imagination of the British public.

I left the club in the early hours and walked around the corner to Conservative Party HQ in Smith Square, where there was a gaggle of photographers and television crews waiting for Major's arrival. I can never resist an audience, so in the middle of the street at 3 a.m. I delivered a solo rendition of 'The Red Flag.' I was pleased to receive some applause from the journalists but, before I could launch into an encore, a policeman approached and said: "Sir, this is a residential area, I think you should go home."

"Officer," I replied, "that's good advice. Goodnight."

There's no doubt that working people made significant advances in the New Labour years. Behind the fleeting image of 'Cool Britannia' there were concrete gains, such as the introduction of the minimum wage, investment in public services, and big breakthroughs in social attitudes. Protection was given to workers who chose to withdraw their labour, meaning they couldn't be sacked in the first eight weeks of a strike, later extended to 12. I was overjoyed in 1998 when

the Good Friday Agreement was announced, an incredible achievement bringing to an end the violence in Northern Ireland.

But clouds began to slowly drift over the bright new dawn. New Labour's
vaunted 'third way' was based on the oxymoron of caring capitalism. In reality, it meant raising the white flag on the economic front and accepting the fun-
damental tenets of Thatcherism. Blair was brazen about his intention to "leave
British law the most restrictive on trade unions in the Western world." There
was no mistaking the message: Labour was not in the business of challenging
the establishment.

My growing disillusionment with New Labour was mirrored in my feelings
about the union of which I had always been so proud. It seemed to me we had
lost our fighting spirit and were becoming more accomodationist both industri-
ally and politically. As the millennium drew to a close, I began to think of other
options—perhaps a quieter life, catching up on reading, maybe trying my hand
at writing, certainly enjoying poetry in a relaxing way.

My love of poetry has since been discovered by journalists and often asked
about by interviewers, sometimes in an incredulous tone as though someone
from my background shouldn't enjoy such things. I'm a strong believer in poetry
being a statutory part of the school curriculum from an early age, having myself
missed out and only come to it, and to Shakespeare, in my twenties. While I don't
claim to be an expert, I have favourites. William Blake—an English revolutionary; the war poems of Wilfred Owen and Siegfried Sassoon—could there ever
be a more powerful anti-war poem than Owen's 'Dulce et Decorum Est'?; and
the beauty and passion of the Romantics—Percy Bysshe Shelley, Lord Byron and
John Keats. Shelley's 'The Masque of Anarchy' is a masterpiece that, of course,
gifted left wingers like me with the opportunity to recite many times the clarion
call, "Rise like lions."

Despite my disenchantment with the way things were going domestically,
I was amassing invaluable experience on the international front. I was engaged
with a number of global union federations, learning how comrades in other
countries operated. My involvement in the creation of 36 European works

councils gave me an inside perspective on the mechanics of the European Union. I also spent a lot of time connecting with individual trade unions from around the world and developed an especially close relationship with the leaders of North American unions the United Steelworkers, the SEIU and the Teamsters. Taking part in international solidarity actions confirmed what I had learned on the docks: workers are the same the world over, with the same problems and the same hopes.

Another opportunity to make friends from far afield came as an unwanted, but ultimately very enjoyable, surprise. In 1998, Bill Morris decided to send me away for two weeks to the Duke of Edinburgh's Commonwealth Study Conference in Canada, in a transparent attempt to get rid of me during an election for the deputy general secretary of the T&G (I was supporting an opponent of his favoured candidate). I tried all sorts to get out of the trip but Morris was insistent.

Every six years, the conference brought together 200 people from across the Commonwealth, supposedly comprising future leaders from business, the civil service and trade unions. Potential participants had to fill out an application form—which I thought was a formality—containing a section on "specialist subjects." I decided to get creative, rather than put football and chess, so I rang my friend Jim Mowatt for ideas. Off the top of his head, he rattled off architecture in sport; the Art Nouveau movement in Britain; and post-war provincial theatre. I thought they looked good on the form, until my secretary called to say the interview would be in a few days. Interview?

I called Jim in a panic and he told me not to worry. He had a book on sports stadia by Simon Inglis and one on British Art Nouveau from which I could snatch a couple of strap lines to get me through. When I asked about post-war provincial theatre he said: "You're a Scouser; the only people of any note are Alan Bleasdale, Willy Russell and Jimmy McGovern" (apologies to Alan Bennett).

The Commonwealth scheme was well supported by business organisations and, in the UK, it was British Airways that coordinated the 25 participants. I went for my interview in the company's palatial offices in Berkeley Square. After the pleasantries, a member of the interview panel said: "Len, we are fascinated by your specialist subjects, can you tell us about them?"

"Well yes," I said, "how long have you got?"

I talked about Cardiff Arms Park stadium and William Morris. I told them I knew Jimmy McGovern. They were transfixed. But soon I had used up my rehearsed lines. "Anyway, I'm taking up too much of your time," I said.

"No, no, Len, this is fascinating, go on," said a member of the panel called Deborah.

The cupboard was empty. Thinking quickly, I said: "No, honestly, I could be here all night. Deborah, will you be in Canada? Perhaps we could continue this there?" Deborah was in Canada, but fortunately she never picked up the conversation.

On the night before we flew out, the British contingent met in a hotel in Richmond to be briefed. During a drink afterwards, one of the party, a captain in the Royal Navy, started a conversation about "pay relativities." I was careful not to engage, conscious that Morris had warned me: "You are an ambassador of the T&G and I want you to behave yourself." I'm afraid that went out the window after the second glass of wine. The captain was dominating the conversation and being a little pompous, boasting of having briefly been in command of HMS Invincible.

I said: "I'm interested in this concept of pay relativities because here you are driving HMS Invisible around the Atlantic..."

"It's HMS Invincible," he said.

"Sorry, Invincible. I don't know what you're paid, but my bin men, who earn very little, are relatively more important to me because if they don't turn up my life is affected. Whereas, relatively speaking, you are not that important to me because I don't even know where HMS Invisible is."

"It's Invincible," he said in a raised voice. "Your argument is preposterous. Are you suggesting your bin men should get the same pay as me?"

"No, they should get more," I said.

Visibly agitated, he asked, "So you don't value the defence of the realm?" I replied that it depended who he was defending it against. He lost it completely and said: "You'd know how important it is if there was a Libyan missile headed your way." Everyone laughed. I had achieved my aim and it was time to leave.

Once we arrived at the beautiful Chateau Mont Tremblant in Quebec, the participants were split into groups (fortunately the captain was not in mine). As a teambuilding exercise we first had to choose five items from a list of 25 that we would want to have if our plane crashed in mountains inhabited by grizzly bears. I very quickly sat up while everyone else was still studying the list. The facilitator asked if I was OK. "Yes," I replied, "I only need two items." Everyone looked up, probably thinking "There's always one." I divulged my items: the bottle of vodka to get drunk and the gun to shoot myself when the bears arrived. The ice was broken and I began to get to know some great people.

One of them was a wonderful man about four feet six inches tall who would introduce himself in his lovely lilting accent with: "Hello, my name is Syral, I am a banker from Sri Lanka." On the final evening of the trip there was a grand ball with the Duke of Edinburgh in attendance. Syral had a cold so I bought him a couple of hot toddies. Unused to alcohol, he was soon tipsy, at which point it emerged that he knew the words to every Elvis Presley song and was determined to sing them. That was fine until the speeches started and we couldn't shut him up. I have to say, in Syral's defence, that the Duke of Edinburgh's speech sounded a lot better with the echoes of 'Blue Suede Shoes' reverberating around the ballroom.

There was another story from the trip which involved meeting the Duke himself. If the reader ever meets me, I might share it, but it would be wrong to put it in writing and, in any case, the libel laws mean my publisher wouldn't print it.

———————

As we entered the new millennium it's fair to say I was not brimming with enthusiasm. Perhaps my 50th birthday had brought on middle-age worries about where my life was going. Since the split in the Broad Left over Morris' treatment of the North West region I was more and more seen as the leader of a left opposition to the general secretary, which became a little debilitating. Morris was due to retire in 2003 and I knew I'd be pressured to run to succeed him. I also knew I'd have no chance of winning. It would be my last hurrah.

Despite Labour cruising to an easy victory in the 2001 general election, I was far from alone in my frustration at the state of politics and the trade union movement. The same feeling drove a collection of smaller unions to form themselves into a group dubbed 'the awkward squad.' They became a focus of opposition to New Labour. Mick Rix of ASLEF, Jeremy Dear of the NUJ, Andy Gilchrist of the FBU, Bob Crow of the RMT, and Mark Serwotka of PCS did a valiant job of keeping the flag of radicalism flying. But without the weight of the big unions, including my own, their impact was always limited.

This was the context for two watershed moments in British industrial and political history. The first was the defeat in 2002 of Sir Ken Jackson—Tony Blair's favourite trade unionist—as joint-general secretary of Amicus, a large new union formed the previous year from a merger that included the engineers' union, the powerhouse of the right. Sir Ken was a dominant figure and a key supporter of New Labour, so it sent shockwaves through the trade union movement when Derek Simpson, a relatively unknown challenger from the left, beat him.

Derek later told me a lovely story about his victory. Watching the count at the Electoral Reform Society, it appeared he had lost by a narrow margin. Rather than stay the night in London waiting for the declaration, he decided to drive back home to Sheffield. In the morning he went to tell his mum that he'd lost. She, like my mum, used to 'read the leaves'—remnants of tealeaves in the bottom of the cup that supposedly foretold the future. She said to Derek, "No, you haven't lost, there's a problem with the ballot." As he was trying to make her understand, he got a phone call from his team at the count telling him, "You'd better get back down here." They had discovered a batch of ballot papers in which the top one was for Jackson but those underneath were for Simpson. His narrow defeat was suddenly turned into a slender victory. I well remember the delight with which we greeted the news in the T&G head office.

The second watershed moment concerned my own union, and I was directly involved. It began in 2000 when BMW decided to pull out of the massive Rover car plant at Longbridge in the West Midlands, making 10,000 workers redundant. Cometh the hour, cometh the man. Tony Woodley, the T&G's national officer for the automotive sector, led the campaign to save the plant. He had to contend with pressure from the Labour Party, via Bill Morris, for a quick settlement to avoid a major issue in the 2001 general election. Yet, against expectations, the campaign was successful.

Tony had been a close friend for decades. I suddenly saw that he could be a credible candidate to run for the deputy general secretary position in 2001/2002, with a view to taking a shot at the top job in early 2003. In a typically modest way, Tony didn't think he had done anything special in the Longbridge dispute. "I was just doing my job," was his response when I told him he had given the finest media performance of any trade union leader in a generation—and he had won, something our movement wasn't used to. On a mission to persuade him, Jim Mowatt and I met Tony in a bar called The Thin Red Line (how apt) in Holborn. I said: "Let me build you a bandwagon and before it rolls you can have a look at it. If you think it's only got three wheels then we won't bother." He gave us the green light. I knew immediately that it would work because I could feel the mood in the union. Our activists were eager for change.

We also had a slice of luck. The two leading prospects for the deputy post, Barry Camfield and Jack Dromey, decided not to run in order to keep their power dry for the general secretary election. That was a fatal mistake. It allowed Tony to gather momentum and storm to victory, giving him a huge bounce going into the contest to lead the union nine months later. Everybody loves a winner.

This time we were up against the so-called big guns. Tony was far from the favourite, but Barry and Jack's dry powder proved to be more of a damp squib. Tony was an excellent candidate. I was his campaign manager and learned a lot from him—for example, when visiting workplaces, he wouldn't just meet workers in the daytime, he would go in on the previous night shift. No one else would do that. It would create a talking point among the workforce—"Do you know, that Tony Woodley was in here last night."

I was right about the mood in the union—it carried Tony to a comfortable victory in 2003, sending another shockwave rattling through the trade union movement. Suddenly, two of the biggest unions, the T&G and Amicus, had left general secretaries.

———————

Tony's victory brought a fighting spirit and an energy back to the T&G. He made me his assistant general secretary for strategy, in effect his aide-de-camp. I was delighted and excited by the prospect of making a difference. Those mid-life-crisis blues vanished. My thoughts of floating off to a cottage in the Welsh hills, reading and writing poetry, were shelved. We had got our union back.

The big idea at the centre of Tony's campaign had been the creation of an organising department. This involved establishing a team of professional organisers who would go into strategically chosen workplaces to build the fighting capacity of the workforce. I had persuaded Tony to embrace the concept and introduced him to my good friend Andy Stern, the leader of the American union the SEIU, which had pioneered this style of organising in the States. To be successful, the union had to devote significant resources to it. Tony was brave enough to invest on a scale that ensured the organising department became an integral part of the union. I believe the methods it developed in the T&G and subsequently in Unite will be vitally important for the future of the trade union movement.

Another priority for Tony was to reinstate two Irish officials, Mick O'Reilly and Eugene McGlone, who had been wrongly sacked by Bill Morris after a farcical and amateurish investigation by Deputy General Secretary Margaret Prosser. To reverse the decision, I suggested we seek a judicial review by an independent QC. John Hendy, a highly respected barrister very much of the left, was the man to do it. Although a friend, I knew his professional ethics meant he would do me no favours, but I was confident he would see the obvious miscarriage of justice.

So it proved, and Mick and Eugene were returned to work. The whole union, bar a few, were delighted.

With the T&G back under genuine left leadership 'the awkward squad' was tremendously boosted. More importantly, Tony became the driving force behind the establishment of the 'Big Four'—an unofficial association between the T&G, Amicus, Unison and the GMB. It was this alliance that decisively moved the TUC to the left and challenged New Labour in an effective way for the first time.

The new dawn that had accompanied Tony Blair's victory in 1997 was completely obscured by the illegal war in Iraq in 2003. With my family I joined the near two-million-strong anti-war march through London under the banner, 'Not in my name.' The French academic Dominique Reynié estimated that 36 million people protested in 600 cities around the world between January and April 2003. But the war went ahead, proving even more calamitous than its most outspoken opponents predicted. Hundreds of thousands of Iraqis were killed; more than 4,000 British personnel died; and the Middle East was set on fire, leaving a legacy that burns to this day. Blair's name will be linked with this disaster for eternity. I sometimes wonder if, in his private thoughts, contrary to his public statements, he wishes he could go back and take a different course. His three general election victories and peace in Northern Ireland would then have been a proud mark to leave behind.

Although Blair went on to win another general election in 2005, Iraq had sowed the seeds of New Labour's destruction. Blairism was shedding legitimacy just as the trade unions seemed finally to have recovered from the trauma of the 1980s. With the T&G back on track, the world felt very different from the despair of the Liverpool dockers' defeat a few years earlier. New Labour's betrayal of the unions had set in motion a historic shift to the left within the trade union movement that would later have dramatic consequences for British politics.

CHAPTER 9

COME TOGETHER

'Unite'—a word that would come to describe not only Britain's most powerful trade union but also a fighting, unflinching style of workers' representation—was adopted as a name in a moment of inspiration in a bar in Covent Garden. No brand consultants or advertising agencies were involved.

When two mighty trade unions—the T&G and Amicus—came together to form a new super-union in 2007, there was one question no one could satisfactorily answer—what would we call it? I suggested 'Beacon: shining the light for workers' or 'Infinity... and beyond,' with the condition that Tony Woodley and Derek Simpson, the general secretaries of the two organisations, would be compelled to change their names by deed poll to Buzz and Lightyear. They declined. A suggestion put forward by Andrew Murray, later to be my chief of staff, was ITSU, pronounced 'it's you,' standing for Industry, Transport and Services Union. I thought it was a great idea until I started noticing branches of the food chain ITSU on the high street.

The breakthrough came in 2006 when, with most of the other merger issues ironed out, the two unions' executive councils and senior officials gathered to celebrate the agreement. Tony and Derek each gave a speech. During Tony's contribution he suddenly pointed at someone wearing a 'Unite Against Fascism' T-shirt and shouted out: "There it is! That's what we should be called—Unite!" He turned to Derek who shrugged his shoulders and then nodded vigorously. And so Unite was born.

———

I often remind people that Unite only exists because, as individual unions, we struggled to stay afloat. The creation of Unite was the biggest example among a great series of trade union mergers, which were driven by cold, hard practicalities. Membership of TUC unions, which peaked at 13.2 million in 1979, had shrunk to just 7.9 million by 1996 as a result of the Tories' attack on traditional industries. Even with a Labour government after 1997 we continued to lose manufacturing jobs hand over fist.

By the mid-2000s the trade union movement was in some difficulty. Giants of the industrial era were a shadow of their former selves. Large unions feared they would no longer be viable. Membership of my union, the T&G, had fallen from 2.1 million when I became an official in 1979 to less than 1 million. Discussions across the movement were dominated by talk of mergers. I was right at the heart of the most ambitious plan of them all.

For the T&G, the natural merger was with the GMB. Both were general unions that already worked together in many industries. There had been merger talks in the early 1990s, but they came to nothing. After the GMB surprisingly elected a relative unknown in Kevin Curran to be its general secretary in 2003, suddenly the prospect was back under discussion. For reasons I still can't put my finger on, Kevin and Tony Woodley immediately struck up a rapport as if they were long-lost brothers—perhaps because Kevin, like Tony, was a man without an ego, a really decent and honest guy. However, his tenure was short-lived. In 2005, after some internal shenanigans, he was replaced by Paul Kenny, who proved much less enthusiastic about a tie-up.

One reason Tony and I were keen on merging with the GMB was a concern that our union might be marginalised if another large union, Amicus, continued to grow by absorbing smaller organisations. A potential solution was to merge with Amicus ourselves. I was not convinced. We'd just won back the T&G to make it a fighting, radical union; Amicus' culture was quite different (I later found there were many good people within Amicus who shared our outlook). Nevertheless, Tony raised the idea of a merger with Amicus' general secretary Derek Simpson who, it turned out, was himself fearful of us joining forces with the GMB. Soon we were talking about all three unions merging. But having just won power in the GMB, Paul Kenny had no intention of giving it up by going into another union as a smaller partner. The GMB fell by the wayside. The T&G and Amicus forged ahead.

The complexities involved in bringing together two organisations as large and diverse as the T&G and Amicus cannot be overstated. On Tony's behalf, I was involved in all the meetings as we hammered out the details. Any points that could not be agreed were placed to one side to be dealt with in a more informal way by a group of four of us: from Amicus, Les Bayliss and Steve Davidson; from the T&G, Jimmy Kelly and me. Had we not been allowed the flexibility to negotiate informally, Unite would not have happened. Frequently locked away in hotels and pubs, we got on well and found it surprisingly easy to thrash out outstanding issues, despite the different traditions of our unions. It was later suggested that Bayliss and Davidson were so compliant because they were confident of being able to take over the union and renege on anything they didn't like.

After many months of negotiations, by late 2006 we had a deal to promote to our members. I travelled around the T&G selling a positive message about what the new super-union could achieve. It worked: T&G members voted overwhelmingly in favour. Amicus came to the same decision. The biggest merger in British trade union history was sealed.

Sadly, the new union did not get off to an auspicious start. With the name settled as Unite, and the vesting day chosen to be 1 May 2007—International Workers Day—everything was prepared for Tony and Derek, the joint-general secretaries of the merged union, to host a triumphant launch in front of the media in Westminster. But as the journalists took their seats, only Tony had turned up. I was desperately rushing around trying to make contact with a member of Derek's crew. When I did, it emerged he was boycotting the event because Tony had done an early morning radio interview. Derek had taken umbrage at not being involved. At the historic moment of the official unveiling of Unite, he spat out his dummy. It was a sign of things to come.

The following three years, 2007-10, were a hard struggle as we got down to the real work of integrating the two unions. I was intent on driving Unite forward, but I found obstructions constantly being placed in my way by Derek's team. Part of it was down to very obvious cultural differences between the unions. The Amicus culture—to the extent that it had one—reflected a craft mentality that, historically, has always been there in the British trade union movement. It manifested itself as a superior attitude, as if Amicus represented craftsmen, while the T&G was a load of labourers, bus drivers and bin men.

I made a point of meeting Amicus' shop stewards and officers, listening to their hopes and concerns. There was so much to do, including bringing together the two left formations that stood candidates in internal elections—the National Broad Left in the T&G and Unity Gazette in Amicus—to create the United Left.

Contrary to media stories, Tony Woodley and Derek Simpson got on well personally but Tony became increasingly frustrated by the delaying tactics and dishonesty from Derek's team, epitomised by a lack of transparency on Amicus' finances. Relations soured. The effort of dealing with Amicus officials had a debilitating effect on Tony. He began to think he had made a mistake in agreeing the merger. He asked to meet at his home in Wallasey, Merseyside, where a barrister, John Benson QC, joined us. Unbeknown to me, Tony had charged John with producing an opinion on whether the T&G could demerge from Amicus. I was shocked. Tony was contemplating unravelling the biggest, most high-profile trade union merger.

The QC's opinion was that demerger, although difficult, was possible. When he left, Tony and I went into deep discussion. I argued that the creation of Unite was his great legacy. But Tony wasn't interested in that, only in the good of the union. Eventually I managed to convince him to give Unite one last go, in the hope that we could get the Amicus leadership to behave honourably.

At the time, Tony had come in for criticism within the T&G for bending over backwards to create a culture of trust—efforts that had not been reciprocated. So, in a final attempt to 'keep' Unite, Tony reversed his approach at the November 2008 joint-executive council meeting and launched a withering attack on the underhand practices and stalling by Derek's senior team. It was one of those moments where everyone in the room held their breath—including Derek, who didn't respond at all. The gambit worked. Although it was not all sweetness and light from there on, an uneasy peace was achieved.

Another crunch moment came with the merging of the two executive councils in May 2009 and the election of a chair. It was thought Steve Davidson, the chair of Amicus, should get the new role, but my closest friend and T&G comrade, Tony Woodhouse, had other ideas. He wasn't comfortable with Steve's style of chairmanship and was determined to stand himself. A confession: in the interests of unity, I tried to convince him not to. Fortunately, I failed. Tony went on to win and was immense in the new role, earning the respect of executive members from both unions. Looking back, I'm so relieved he didn't take my advice. Given the struggles that were to unfold, had Steve been chair, Unite wouldn't have developed the open, democratic, tolerant culture that it did. The role was crucial—it was Tony who often had to decide between the two general secretaries as differences emerged.

Meanwhile, in the outside world, Tony Blair had stepped down as prime minister (I was not unhappy to see him go) and been replaced by Gordon Brown. Tony Woodley and I met Brown on a number of occasions. He was far more at ease with trade unions than his predecessor. Unfortunately, he was still wedded to New Labour's 'third way' ideology. He failed to see the need for a more interventionist approach to bring investment into the manufacturing sector. It was a different story, of course, when the banks needed state intervention during the financial crisis of 2008. To be fair to Brown, he didn't get the credit he deserved for the role he played there, but he made a bad mistake by neglecting to lay down conditions on the banks in return for coming to their aid. Those at the top continued to rake it in, while the bank workers further down the ladder—as well as the public at large—paid the price for their recklessness. The bank workers' union UNIFI had previously been absorbed by Amicus and was now part of Unite. It was decimated as more and more frontline bank workers lost their jobs.

Across the board, the 2008 crash magnified the challenges faced by trade unions, making it even more important to coordinate our efforts. As the Big Four had been reduced to three by the merger of two of its members, the Communication Workers' Union, then led by Billy Hayes, a good friend of mine, was invited to join the leaders of the GMB, Unison and Unite to make us four again.

———————

The creation of Unite brought new opportunities on the international stage including the formation of Workers Uniting, a trans-Atlantic tie-up between Unite and the United Steelworkers in America. Workers Uniting was founded as a bona fide trade union in its own right, registered in the United States, Canada, Britain and Ireland. The idea, which came from Derek Simpson, was to go beyond the national, bilateral agreements that existed between unions to create a more binding relationship. It's fair to say Tony Woodley was not much interested in the concept at the outset, but I was very keen. I was present on behalf of the T&G section of Unite in Toronto when the new union was presented to the North American media and I signed the vesting document. It went on to be a great success, undertaking important solidarity action around the world. I couldn't have been more proud to be associated with it.

The leader of the United Steelworkers in America was Leo Gerard, a larger-than-life character who fought tirelessly for workers. I became great friends with Leo and his colleague Ken Neumann, who headed the union in Canada. The three of us were hewn from the same stone. It was through Leo that I met Napoleon Gomez Urrutia, the leader of the Mexican mineworkers' union Los Mineros, which joined Workers Uniting. Because of threats to his life, Napoleon lived in exile in Canada for 12 years. Despite this, he was re-elected several times by his members and continued to negotiate on their behalf with the mine owners, who were brought up to Canada to thrash out pay deals. I thought he and his wife, Oralia, were incredibly brave and courageous.

In 2018, having been asked by Andrés Manuel López Obrador to run on his slate, Napoleon stood for the Mexican Senate. As the left-wing López Obrador secured a historic landslide victory to become the president of Mexico, Napoleon was comfortably elected a Senator and could finally return to his homeland. He asked me to come to Mexico City to witness him taking the Oath of Office. I found I wasn't alone—5,000 Los Mineros miners travelled to the capital for the occasion. Dressed in red and green t-shirts, they marched from Revolution Square to the government building where the Oath ceremony took place. I was full of emotion as I marched beside them. What a privilege.

Ties of international solidarity proved invaluable to an important campaign to overturn a miscarriage of justice that had begun back in 1998 when five Cubans were unjustly gaoled in the US for espionage. The treatment of the Cuban Five, or the Miami Five as they were also known, which included solitary confinement and the denial of visitation rights, was condemned by human rights organisations and their 2001 trial was widely denounced as unsafe—in other words, they were innocent.

I had been a member of the Cuba Solidarity Campaign since its inception and was well aware of this cause. I persuaded Tony to take an interest in the campaign, introducing him to some of the wives of the Five, who travelled to the UK at conference time. Tony became hooked on righting an injustice and got deeply involved.

A big weakness of the campaign was that nobody in the US knew anything about the case, so we decided our objective was to break the silence there. Tony, Geoff Shears (the left-wing lawyer) and I flew out to Washington where I had arranged meetings with Leo Gerard, Mary Kay Henry and James Hoffa, the presidents of the powerful trade unions the United Steelworkers, the SEIU and the Teamsters respectively. They all committed to help and to try to influence the new president, Barack Obama. I also had the privilege of meeting the great civil rights lawyer, Leonard Weinglass, who was representing the Five.

The campaign stretched on for many years, with hundreds of people from around the world fighting for justice. Tony was right at the centre of it. I had long since succeeded him as general secretary when, on 17 December 2014, my secretary interrupted a meeting in my office to tell me Leo was on the phone with an urgent message. "Lennie," he said, "they are in the air. The Cubans are going home." I received the news with excitement and almost disbelief. I immediately rang Tony who was overjoyed. It was international solidarity at its finest.

———————

As Unite bedded in, the focus switched to the question of who would be the new union's next, sole general secretary. The issue of when the two joint-general secretaries would relinquish power had been negotiated during the merger. The retirement age of 65 was set in law at the time, requiring general secretaries to bow out at that milestone. Tony Woodley was three years younger than Derek Simpson, who was approaching 65, but we had agreed he would only serve one extra year as sole general secretary after the merger period (in the end Tony would forego that year and step aside at the same time as Derek to make way for me—an act of selflessness).

Because of technical, legal difficulties, Derek was required to run again for general secretary of the Amicus section in early 2009. He was expecting the usual contest from the ultra-left but was shocked when two of Amicus' national officers challenged him—Kevin Coyne and Paul Reuter. Derek won easily enough but wanted revenge by sacking Kevin Coyne and his brother Gerard, who had been involved in running a dirty campaign. Tony and I wouldn't let him, and by then we controlled the executive. I remember Derek and I standing in the garden patio of Esher College, where Unite ran training courses. Derek turned to me and said: "Len, Kevin Coyne is stupid and you'll have no problem dealing with him, but Gerard, as talentless as he is, is as treacherous as a snake and he'll come back to bite you." How right he was.

I liked Derek. He was good company, both socially and intellectually. But the trappings of office stoked his ego and changed him. He lost sight of what he originally fought for. He told his closest people his objective was to make Unite into an image of Amicus. Instead of looking for the best person to ensure Unite achieved its potential, he chose a narrow sectarian approach. He promoted, from nowhere, a man named Graham Goddard to the role of deputy general secretary and made it clear he would be Amicus' choice in a future election.

Tony and I took a different view. We were not interested in creating a T&G mark II. We wanted to find the right person to take the new union forward. Tony had a habit of coming up with leftfield ideas and suddenly suggested we ask Debbie Coulter, a capable deputy general secretary in the GMB then looking for a way out, if she would be interested in the top job at Unite. Tony's plan was to make her an assistant general secretary of the T&G section. Because Debbie would not be seen as having either a T&G or an Amicus identity, both unions could embrace her as an independent figure. She would need to win over the respective left groupings and develop a profile among the membership, but we would provide her with a platform to run for general secretary.

Tony and I met Debbie to explain our thoughts in my room in the Midland Hotel in Manchester during the Labour Party Conference in September 2008. She was rather overwhelmed by our suggestion and said she needed to think about it. In the meantime, I suggested another element of the plan to Tony: floating my name as a stalking horse candidate. The Amicus team would be horrified, making them more amenable to Debbie. A few days later, when I next saw Tony, he declared: "I must be stupid. The obvious is staring us in the face. Forget about Debbie, you're our candidate!"

I hadn't considered going for the top job. I regarded myself as a good second man, someone behind the scenes who could fix problems and come up with strategies. I said no, but Tony wanted to appoint me deputy general secretary to boost my status to match Amicus' Graham Goddard. I said, "No. No. No. Tony, I'm not being forced into something I don't want to do."

I continued to try to convince Debbie she should come on board. It was Christmas before she confirmed that she was moving on beyond the trade union movement. She thanked me and I wished her well. Meanwhile, Tony's efforts to persuade me were relentless. Despite my protests, his mind was set. At Tony's instigation, I was urged by lots of friends and colleagues to take up the gauntlet. It was very flattering, and I promised to think about it, but I was genuinely unsure if it was the right thing for me.

Throughout the winter and spring of 2009, Amicus floated the names of various national officers for the top job. The idea of any of them becoming general secretary was laughable but also alarming if, by some extraordinary aberration, one of them was successful. Tony used this to play on my conscience. "Are you going to risk losing everything you've fought for all your life?" he would ask. It was a good question. A number of people I respected were asking the same.

My mind was made up one summer evening when my wife Alicia said to me: "If you don't run and the union falls into the wrong hands, you'll never forgive yourself. If you do run and get beat then at least you'll have tried." I remembered how it felt when Bill Morris ran the T&G and I thought I'd lost the union I loved, and how Tony had picked us all up and put us on the path to being a decent, fighting organisation. I knew she was right. Other close comrades were telling me I had to be brave. The next morning, I told Tony and my supporters I would do it.

Just as Tony Woodley's handling of the Longbridge dispute burnished his credentials for the general secretary role, so a high-profile industrial action at a pivotal time was a vital part of my story. British Airways, led by CEO Willie Walsh—a man with a sure case of Napoleon Complex—launched a full-scale attack on its cabin crew workers, aiming to cut their number and erode their terms and conditions. It was, in essence, an attempt to break their union, BASSA (the British Airways Steward and Stewardess Association), which was part of Unite. But he hadn't counted on the incredible tenacity of our members.

Running from 2009-11, the dispute was the longest in aviation history and involved strike action that was planned to perfection. It was a watershed in modern day industrial relations. Twenty-two strike days cost British Airways £150 million in lost revenue. The leaders of the cabin crew were subjected to the full media onslaught. The press certainly put me front and centre as well—with the unintended consequence of boosting my name recognition and helping my chances of being elected general secretary. But that was not my motivation. For me, it was a privilege to represent such wonderful people.

These workers did not have a static workplace to meet and have a daily chat. At any time of day, 365 days a year, 6,000 of our then 12,000 members could be anywhere in the world, yet their solidarity was something to behold. They were a community. They kept in touch through a brilliant online communication system maintained by the BASSA branch. When we had to bring people together to physically relay information, BASSA would hold gatherings at Sandown Park or Kempton Park racecourse. These would be meetings of 4,000-5,000 men and women, most of them in their British Airways uniforms having just landed or about to fly off somewhere. On one occasion I stood on the sidelines with Brian Holmes, a member of Unite's executive who had come to give support. A big man, Brian is an ex-London docker who had carried on his shoulders Vic Turner, one of the Pentonville Five, when he was released from prison in 1972. Brian turned to me as we looked out on this strikingly attractive scene and said, "Lennie, I don't remember any of our dockers' meetings looking like this."

The workers were led by fantastic reps including BASSA's chair, Lizanne Malone, who was indefatigable, and its secretary, Duncan Holley, who displayed calm brilliance. The convenor, Nigel Stott, was one of the cleverest men I have ever met with an ability to explain things enticingly. He was supported by the superb Chris Harrison—the two of them were the class act of the aviation world. The meetings were brilliantly organised. Nigel had studied at RADA so there was more than a bit of theatre involved. The branch committee, thanks to Nigel, had adopted as their anthem Labi Siffre's 1987 song 'Something Inside So Strong,' after he saw a framed disc adorning my office wall. I told him the song inspired me because it speaks about every struggle against the rich and powerful, past, present and future, and how people power can always win. After that, at meetings the branch would play a video of the song on large screens, displaying the lyrics over pictures of past fighters and some of the leading reps. Everyone would jump to their feet to blast out the song with passion and pride. The sound of thousands of people singing these words was breathtaking:

Brothers and sisters
When they insist we're just not good enough

When we know better
Just look 'em in the eyes and say
We're gonna do it anyway
We're gonna do it anyway
We're gonna do it anyway
We're gonna do it anyway

It sent a shiver down my spine and brought tears to my eyes. I wanted to fight for these people.

For months we were engaged in complex negotiations with the company that stretched into the dark night hours. Such situations can be very stressful but there were moments of light relief. At a particularly awkward point in an adjournment—about 9 p.m.—my mobile rang. It was my mum's number. She was in her nineties at the time. I told the reps who it was and because of her age there was apprehension as I answered. "Lennie," said my mum, "I've run out of port, can you get me a bottle?" Everyone burst into laughter. From that night on, each time we gathered the reps would ask, "Is your mum OK, has she got enough port?"

In another long adjournment, I had to stand while talking to the reps because I was suffering from sciatica and was in a great deal of pain. "What are you taking for it?" I was asked. When I replied paracetamol there was laughter. Suddenly our adjournment room was transformed into a pharmacy as drugs from every corner of the world were produced. I don't know if they were 'Class A' drugs, but I certainly had a 'Class A' committee. I sampled a few, anything to relieve the pain. As a result, when we went back in to meet the management I was as high as a kite. The serious business was interrupted by my giggling and spontaneous bursts of laughter. I knew it was happening but couldn't control it. It was like an out-of-body experience. I was back in my youth on the beaches of North Wales.

There were times when it seemed the world was against BASSA. They were vilified by the media, denounced by the government, obstructed by the law, and traduced by their employer. Even within our own union there were senior people from Amicus who, it seemed, would have been happy to see them defeated.

The leaderships of the TUC and the conciliation service ACAS were less than helpful, constantly parroting the British Airways company line.

I, on the other hand, was proud to stand shoulder to shoulder with those workers. During the strikes the reps held regular family fun days at the ground of Bedfont and Feltham Football Club in Middlesex. There was music and song, kids' games and barbecues. I used to look around on those joyous days and see the strength of these determined people and feel sure that justice would prevail. Eventually, it would. But in the meantime, I had a general secretary election to fight.

CHAPTER 10

UNITING UNITE

What the hell had I got myself into? Here I was, a few thousand feet above the English Channel, stuck inside a tin can with propellers on it, bumping around in the turbulence like popcorn in a bag.

This wasn't what I had signed up for when I agreed to stand for general secretary. I didn't realise the campaign trail would include flying from Exeter to Guernsey to speak to some of the 1,600 Unite members on the island. The airline might as well have pulled back a giant rubber band and shot me across the sea; it would have felt safer.

I thanked whichever God happened to be on shift as we touched down on solid ground and disembarked the aeroplane to be met—to my great surprise—by flashbulbs and TV cameras. It may only have been the local Guernsey press, but for a moment I felt like a film star jetting in for a premiere.

I had been in front of the cameras before, speaking on behalf of the British Airways crew and many other groups of workers, but this was the first time I had experienced such attention simply for being me. It turned out that a visit from a candidate vying to lead the only general union in Guernsey was news on the island. Seeing such interest generated in a far-flung part of the country, it suddenly hit me how important this job would be.

———

Having decided to run for general secretary, I was in it to win it. All campaigning had to be conducted outside working hours. So while the British Airways dispute rumbled on, I devoted every ounce of extra energy I had to the task. First, I had to win the support of the left within the union. In September 2009, a hustings was arranged to decide the United Left's candidate. Manchester Free Trade Hall was packed to the rafters for the event. This is where my years as a key figure on the left of the union stood me in good stead. I knew them and they knew me. I was successful in winning the nomination.

I was determined to run as a unity candidate—not unity between left and right (I stood on a strong left-wing platform) but unity between the T&G and Amicus. I wanted to be a general secretary for all members of Unite, not just one section. We needed to bring the union together and allow it to develop its own culture and identity.

On that basis, I still held out a sliver of hope that I could gain the support of Amicus' leaders, none of whom had indicated a desire to run. Graham Goddard, Derek Simpson's handpicked candidate and a far more honourable man than the rest of the senior Amicus team, bowed out after he very sadly contracted cancer, from which he later died. I had a feeling Derek would happily have supported me until Amicus' assistant general secretary Les Bayliss announced he was standing. I suppose it was a strange way for Derek to round off his involvement in Unite. It had been a great moment for the left when he defeated Ken Jackson to become the general secretary of Amicus; now he was backing a candidate of the right to run Unite. It was sad the way it all ended for Derek, when he left the union under a cloud.

It was shaping up to be Amicus verses the T&G, precisely what I wanted to avoid. But there were other candidates in the race: Jerry Hicks, who mounted a conventional ultra-left bid, and Gail Cartmail, another Amicus assistant general secretary, whose campaign was clean and respectful. Gail produced the best moment of the contest when, in a *Guardian* article, she described her male rivals as acting as if we were in a scene from the film 'Reservoir Dogs'—brilliant!

Having run Tony Woodley's campaign for T&G general secretary, I knew how to do it and I had a great campaign manager of my own in Steve Turner, a very talented industrial officer. I worked hard—I always did in the three general secretary elections I contested. I loved every minute of it: travelling throughout the union, meeting old friends, making new ones, and sharing my vision. I would hold public meetings outside workplaces in the evening or on weekends. Sometimes the turnout would be 20-30 people, sometimes 200-300.

Where I could get permission from the companies, I'd go into the factories and workplaces. I'd usually speak in the canteen, so as not to disrupt the production line. At break time the workers would gather to eat. Shop stewards would get their attention: "Hang on everyone, just a quick five minutes to listen to Len McCluskey. We're supporting him." I'd stand up and say, "Hi everyone, look I don't want to spoil your meal," then do a quick spiel. I didn't have a set speech but I'm someone who can talk; it comes easily. What I had to say was always well received. Then I'd go around and chat to people. Sometimes I'd walk the production line with the shop stewards and greet the workers. I also used Tony's idea of speaking to the night shift, who were always impressed that I'd bothered. I loved engaging with people, debating issues and listening to our activists' ideas.

One line that always went down very well was that I would not be giving the Labour Party any blank cheques. There was real resentment among members at the amount of money we were handing over to the party without getting very much in return. I tapped into that resentment not only for electoral reasons; I felt it just as strongly.

Our powerful campaign was rewarded when I secured two-thirds of union branch nominations, with the rest split between my three rivals. Every campaign requires finances and we had a terrific response from those branches, enabling us to produce leaflets and reach the furthest flung parts of our organisation—even Guernsey.

Whenever I came back from a campaign event Tony Woodley would ask how it went. "Yeah, it was good Tony, good vibe," I'd say.

"What about Bayliss?" he would ask.

"No, there didn't seem to be any activity." And there wasn't. Bayliss wasn't a good speaker. He wasn't one for going out and connecting with members. Instead, his increasingly dirty and disgraceful campaign relied on the old

Amicus machine and the media. Tony used to say, "They know something we don't, they're talking about a silver bullet." There were constant rumours of this "silver bullet" that would "take McCluskey down" emanating from the group of spineless, mediocre Amicus national officials and communications officers running Bayliss' campaign. They spread a number of lies, but no silver bullet emerged. When their scurrilous tactics failed, they at least had the good grace to get Derek to give them a redundancy package. The calibre of these officers was such that one of them took the union's money on a Friday and started in a management role for a multinational company on the Monday, sitting opposite the same shop stewards he had previously purported to represent. Another re-emerged a little later as a 'consultant' to construction companies that were trying—and failing—to break a national agreement covering pay and conditions. These individuals were no loss to Unite.

Sensing that his only chance was to appeal to the old, right-wing traditions of Amicus, Bayliss came out against public sector strikes in response to austerity cuts and disgracefully attacked his own union's handling of the British Airways dispute while it was still underway, going so far as to tell the *Guardian* the fight was lost. Ironically, his positioning helped define the contest in terms that suited me, rather than as a battle between the two unions. "This election is now a clear left-right struggle for the future of Unite," I said in October 2010. "There are two visions on offer—of a union that puts its members first and stands up for them come what may in difficult times, or a union that puts managers and ministers first, that rolls over to have its tummy tickled by the employers every time the going gets tough."

By the end of the campaign I was exhausted. But it was all worthwhile when, on 21 November 2010, I was announced as the victor with 42 per cent of the vote. Bayliss, at one time thought to be a favourite, could only manage third with 19 per cent, beaten by the ultra-left Hicks. It gave me enormous satisfaction that activists and members had embraced my vision, and that we could now build Unite as a fighting, left trade union.

———————

New Year's Day 2011—my first day as Unite's general secretary. I sat down at the desk in my big new office on the top floor of Unite's HQ in Holborn and contemplated the multitude of problems facing the union. The previous day, Unite had posted a £50 million deficit in its accounts. There was a £150 million deficit in the pension fund. As the major manufacturing and finance union, we were still reeling from the effects of the 2008 crash as redundancies mounted. A new Conservative-Lib Dem coalition government was committed to unleashing vicious austerity on working people. A close friend had said to me, "Lennie, you must be mad."

I was up for the challenge. But there was a moment that morning, sitting at my desk, when I looked behind me and thought, "Oh, God, it's me that has to take these decisions. There's nobody else to take them." As Tony Woodley's aide-de-camp I could make all kinds of suggestions but he was the one who had to decide. There were times I was pleased it was him and not me. But now I had to make the calls.

I knew I needed a good team to support me. I once read that the greatness of a leader is determined by the calibre of the people they have around them. I am happy to be judged in that way. I was fortunate that most of my team had been comrades and friends for years and had worked together on my general secretary election campaign.

I was an obsessive fan of the American television programme 'The West Wing.' I had always seen myself as Leo, the chief of staff, sorting problems behind the scenes. Now that I was the frontman I was determined to create such a support for myself. The title Chief of Staff is used in the political and business arenas—not to mention in the military—but never in the trade union movement. I don't know why. But I wanted a chief of staff and I knew precisely who it should be: Andrew Murray, a brilliant intellect and a wonderful wordsmith. Our collaboration would go on to produce stimulating, sometimes controversial articles and inspiring speeches. I used to think my friend Jim Mowatt was the best-read person I'd ever met, but Andrew takes that accolade. He would become my closest confidante through 10 tumultuous years.

I also needed someone to do the heavy lifting. Steve Turner fit the bill perfectly. Steve had done a great job as my campaign manager and would later fulfil that role on two further occasions. I promoted Steve to assistant general secretary. I knew he would never let me down whenever any troubleshooting was needed. He proved me right. I asked Sharon Graham, a force of nature, to take charge of Unite's organising department. Her outstanding skills would contribute so much to Unite's industrial might.

My team was strengthened by the appointment of three more assistant general secretaries: Tony Burke, Gail Cartmail and Diana Holland. Gail, who had run against me, would go on to be totally loyal, always on top of her brief, and capable of doing any job asked of her. Diana had invaluable experience in the food and transport industrial sectors and had done more than most on equality issues. Tony, always a steady hand, was ever ready to assist.

My team would be completed later that year with the arrival of Howard Beckett, a committed socialist solicitor who had built a very successful practice primarily servicing working-class communities, including advising on welfare rights. He could have earned considerably more money continuing with his business but was so eager to come and work for me that he was prepared to sell it. When he rang his mum and dad to tell them, full of excitement, that he'd been appointed Unite's legal director, they were so proud that tears flowed. I made Howard an assistant general secretary as we integrated the legal department into our industrial work, instead of regarding it as an 'add on' service like in most unions.

One of my first and most satisfying acts as general secretary was to settle the British Airways dispute. It helped that CEO Willie Walsh moved to a new position in the airline's parent company, IAG. His successor, Keith Williams, was almost his opposite: decent, fair and interested in finding a solution. At our first meeting he said, "Len, I can have a war of attrition with you or seek an honourable settlement. I'd prefer the second option." I told him that was music to my ears. Along with our teams we locked ourselves away in a hotel for five days and successfully concluded one of the most bitter disputes of the day. At Williams' insistence, the settlement was facilitated by a clinical psychologist called Mark

Hamlin—in all my long years this was a first. His honesty and professionalism were critical to achieving a deal. The settlement gave dignity and respect to the cabin crew—the two things, in my experience, that workers everywhere want—and protected their earnings and terms and conditions.

It has always struck me how the whims of individual senior managers can have such an impact on the lives of so many workers. I have experienced many times new managers starting with a mentality of 'a new brush sweeps clean,' only for that brush to cause chaos in its application and leave devastation for workers in its wake. From the arrival of Walsh at British Airways, the company adopted a style of management that sought unneeded confrontation. For a period, Williams restored respect and harmony, but I am afraid this great British company has been detrimentally changed by Walsh's influence. He failed in his attempt to break the union, but some bosses bide their time for their moment of vengeance. Sadly, 10 years after the dispute, Walsh was at it again, taking advantage of the Covid-19 pandemic in 2020 to attack British Airways workers who faced another tough fight.

I have met many CEOs in my life and most have two common characteristics: they are charming and professional. I did not rate Walsh highly in either regard. The fact that workers find themselves at the mercy of such egos testifies to why trade unions are needed and are as relevant today as they have always been.

———————

Any general secretary of a major trade union is constantly buffeted by crashing waves. It's important to have a guiding philosophy to stay on course. I called mine 'principled pragmatism.' I doubt I coined the term, but from my earliest days as a shop steward, principled pragmatism is what I have practiced. It means ensuring the pragmatism required of any workers' leader to reach deals and solve problems never undermines the principles of solidarity and justice.

My position on Trident nuclear weapons is a case in point. I have been a unilateralist all my life. The T&G always opposed nuclear weapons, so it was a comfortable position to take. I had the luxury of not having to answer to anyone for my views. That changed when I was elected general secretary of Unite. Now I was a voice for all of our members. They had placed their trust in me to protect their jobs and communities. Unite represented many workers in the nuclear defence industry. Our members produced nuclear warheads at Aldermaston; our members built nuclear submarines in Barrow; our members transported the missiles to Faslane; our members installed and maintained the missiles on the submarines. If, as general secretary, I had said, "I'm opposed to nuclear weapons, they should be abolished overnight," I would have betrayed those members. And, in fact, there was a principled point to this: just as I found nuclear weapons immoral, I also found the destruction of communities and livelihoods immoral.

The shop stewards representing those workers were highly intelligent, good people. They were well aware that the world should be free from the threat of nuclear annihilation. They would participate in fabulous debates on this issue at our policy conferences. I remember at the 2016 conference the debate was of such high quality, and so balanced, that I felt overwhelming pride at being the general secretary of such a union. The statement that was passed that day emphasised how terrible nuclear weapons were, demanded progress on defence diversification to create skilled, alternative employment for workers, but said that until such a plan was pursued seriously by the government, we would defend our members' livelihoods and their communities. In subsequent years, our policy conferences rarely heard anti-Trident motions because workers' representatives had listened to each other, had the debate, and settled on a position.

Sadly, defence diversification has only ever been paid lip service by employers and governments (New Labour shamefully abolished the Defence Diversification Agency). The workers themselves remain the only people who have given it serious thought, producing an enormous amount of work on the concept and practicalities. Ironically, the politician who most strongly supported their efforts was the one they felt uneasy about—the most famous unilateralist of all, Jeremy Corbyn.

Principled pragmatism means being guided by unchanging principles while being sufficiently pragmatic to deal with the realities of life. I have taken the same approach to the issue of the climate crisis, including over increased capacity at Heathrow Airport to maintain its position as a transport hub. I fully recognise the urgency of the climate emergency, support reducing carbon emissions to zero as soon as possible, and believe wholeheartedly in the necessity of a real green industrial revolution. But it isn't Unite members working in polluting industries who should be made to bear the costs—there must be a just transition to greener jobs for those workers as we shift away from a fossil fuel economy. That takes significant government investment and oversight; in its absence, I am bound to support our members whose families and communities depend on the good, skilled jobs they have.

———————

I had been elected on a promise to bring the two unions together and that's the way, as general secretary, I was determined to lead. I wanted to create a union with its own culture—not a T&G culture or an Amicus culture, but a Unite culture. But in any merger, whether of trade unions or businesses, one of the two cultures emerges as the stronger. The T&G philosophy of being a proud, fighting-back union was always going to come through. To a large degree I had to restrict that. It was like having a horse that wanted to gallop away; I needed to ease it back a little or it would dominate Amicus. It didn't help that Amicus didn't have much of a culture of its own. Itself the product of mergers, it was not really one union, but five. It was only when I became general secretary that we found the Amicus leadership had done nothing to integrate them. They had all just carried on as they were, operating semi-autonomously.

Of course, my knowledge of the T&G was strong in every detail, but it was immediately clear this would be considerably more complex than just bringing two organisations together. Staff were on completely different terms and conditions, officials had different pay rates, and there were different expense regimes. Some of the things I had to deal with were unbelievable. I had to force people to come together as one group of officers.

Frankly, the union would have collapsed unless we had done something about the finances. Tony Woodley always struggled to get sight of Amicus' books, probably because they would have revealed some pretty sharp practices. Eventually, once the books were opened, my wonderful finance director Ed Sabisky and I could identify the measures needed—pulling resources together and setting out a proper financial strategy. Sadly, we lost Ed to a massive stroke in February 2020. Replacing him was very difficult.

It was important to mend the bitterly split Unite executive. It was divided primarily between the T&G and Amicus but also between left and right. Tony Woodhouse, the chair, tells me I am particularly good at bringing people together. While I can argue my case against political enemies, I also know that to win you need unity. I'm proud that, over time, the executive became more and more cohesive to the point where, although there were still factions, not a single member of the 70-strong council opposed me.

We were making good progress, but time was short to secure our gains. Running for the job in 2010, I had said I would only serve one term. That message was designed for Amicus activists, to tell them, "You're not electing me forever, just give the union an opportunity to settle down." It also happened to be true— it was written into Unite's rulebook that the general secretary had to resign at 65, reflecting the law of the land. I would be 65 when the next election was due. The issue of who from the left could succeed me was on our minds.

Steve Turner was the natural successor, but then a more surprising name began to be mentioned: Mark Serwotka. Mark was the general secretary of the PCS civil servants' union, solidly on the left, greatly admired, perhaps the finest orator in our movement. He indicated that PCS would be interested in a merger with Unite. We set up a number of meetings between senior lay members of our unions to get the ball rolling. Mark was attracted by the prospect of a merged union having more than half-a-million public sector workers, enabling it to challenge the more cautious attitude of the other public sector unions, in par- ticular, Unison. He would come in as deputy general secretary and head up this powerbase. He would then become an obvious left candidate for the top job. It was felt that Mark would quickly win over the left in Unite and, subsequently, the members. To Steve's great credit, despite this plan meaning he would no longer be in pole position to succeed me, he embraced it wholeheartedly, seeing its political importance.

Unfortunately, Mark contracted a rare disease that attacked his heart. He was critically ill for a long time. In his absence, those in PCS who opposed the merger were able to get the 2014 PCS conference to reject the proposal. I think it was a missed opportunity, but I am confident that in the not-too-distant future the merger with PCS will happen. Mark eventually had a successful heart transplant in 2016. I was so relieved, as was the whole movement. I had lost a good friend and comrade in Bob Crow in 2014, I didn't want to lose another.

Unite also held extensive merger talks with the TSSA rail workers' union. Their general secretary, my friend Manuel Cortes, entered into a number of discussions with the committees we set up. We came close but were ultimately unable to reach agreement.

While mergers were being discussed, the circumstances around the Unite general secretary election changed. The Cameron government twice amended the law, firstly so people of retirement age could ask their employer if they could continue, secondly so employees had the right to carry on working beyond 65. Our union rulebook was altered to reflect the change, meaning I could stand again if I wanted to. The left within the union began to say, "We need you to stay on, Len." But there was the further problem that an internal Unite election in 2015 would have clashed with the general election. So we had a debate about whether I should go again, and go early.

The massive task of uniting Unite was unfinished. Three years of hard slog, persuasion, and an element of ruthless determination had begun to establish a unity of purpose, a commonality of pay and conditions, and a Unite culture. People could see the prize, but it was still in the balance. The collective view— and it was a collective view, I would only have done it with the left's support— was that I should seek re-election two years early, in 2013. Some comrades were against it. I would be standing at the age of 63. Another term would take me to 68. At the time, Unite was campaigning under the slogan '68 is too late' for public sector workers. But the vast majority saw the logic of me continuing.

The 2013 general secretary campaign was a much cleaner and more comradely affair than 2010 had been. It was a head-to-head battle between me, backed by the United Left, and the ultra-leftist Jerry Hicks. The right wing didn't put anyone up but supported Hicks because they needed to get rid of me and thought the union might disintegrate under him. Realistically, there was never any chance that I would be beaten by Jerry—I secured more than 1,000 branch nominations to his 136. But I drummed it into people that we had to take the contest seriously. Interestingly, we found companies more willing to let me into the factories to speak to our members this time around. I must have been seen as the moderate!

The results were announced on 14 April 2013. I won comfortably with 64 per cent of the vote. Finally, the future of Unite as a cohesive, strong, fighting union was secure.

This had been a tough period. I felt a lot of responsibility. I was trying to bring the union together and all the while I had a horrible coalition government intent on attacking us and our people on the one hand, and a Labour Party that refused to recognise the task before it on the other.

I was sometimes accused by opponents on the right of being too political, of "using the union as a vehicle for [my] political views," as Les Bayliss put it in 2010. In fact, as general secretary, 90 per cent of my time was spent on industrial and union matters. Unite is an industrial union, but I strongly believe the industrial cannot be divorced from the political. Politics shapes the circumstances in which our members struggle and determines how hard they have to fight for the dignity and respect they are due.

For all the disappointments of New Labour, securing that bare minimum of respect had become a much harder task since Gordon Brown's defeat and the installation of a Conservative-Lib Dem coalition government. In 2010, Labour had gone through its own process of electing a new leader. Ed Miliband had beaten his brother David, despite the latter being much favoured by a media that saw him as Tony Blair mark II. As the general secretary of Labour's largest affiliated union, it was incumbent on me to build a relationship with Ed in the hope of securing the policies supported by my members.

It did not get off to a good start.

PART TWO

FROM FALKIRK TO FINSBURY PARK

CHAPTER 11

DEALING WITH MILIBAND

Ed Miliband was giving his first big conference speech as Labour leader in Manchester, and I had a front row seat.

I was still a candidate for the general secretary position at the time—my election would be announced two months later in November 2010. So there I was, a "senior union official," as all the journalists would soon be describing me, sat next to Tony Woodley and Derek Simpson, the joint-general secretaries of Unite, who had the cameras trained on them as they watched the speech.

The press had already branded Miliband a puppet of the 'union barons' after his win, despite the fact it was the votes of tens of thousands of individual trade union members—on top of nearly half the Labour Party membership—that got him over the line. But the jibe had stuck. I'm sure that's why Ed decided to have a pop at trade unions from the podium.

At the time Ed's speech was regarded as subversive for breaking several New Labour taboos—which was necessary. But read today it is pretty tame stuff. Yes, he rebuked the Blair and Brown governments for pandering to the financial sector, for their "naïve" faith in markets, and he was brave to bluntly assert that the Iraq War was wrong. But it seemed to me that every treat served up for the left had to be matched with a sop to the right. Iraq may have been a disaster, but the war in Afghanistan was beyond reproach. New Labour was wrong not to side with the "communities who want to save their local post office" from being sold off, but there wasn't "a public ownership solution to every problem." And then he turned to trade unions.

Miliband talked about having met exploited dinner ladies who "weren't interested in going on strike... but they wanted someone to help them get the basic standards of decency and fairness, and that is the role of trade unions in this country." To me, it sounded like Ed was living in a different world. A new coalition government had made absolutely clear its intention to attack working people through an austerity programme that would see wages frozen, conditions eroded, and good jobs cut. It was the duty of the labour movement to stand up for workers against this deliberate economic vandalism. Yet Miliband chose to turn his fire on those fighting back. "I have no truck, and you should have no truck, with overblown rhetoric about waves of irresponsible strikes," he said. "The public won't support them, I won't support them, and you shouldn't support them either."

Well, I've never heard of an "irresponsible strike." In all my experience I've never met a worker who liked going on strike. It's real grievances that drive industrial action, real fears about the future.

I couldn't keep it in. "Rubbish," I shouted.

It was a spontaneous outburst, over in a moment. But Tony Woodley's eyes and expression told me everything. Afterwards he was furious with me. I fronted it out and said: "For God's sake, Tony, so what? Nobody will notice." But I was thinking: "Oh God, what have I done? My mouth has gone into gear before my brain."

I couldn't put up with all the moaning so I got in my car and left Manchester early. As I was flying down the motorway the phone rang. It was Tony. "Hello," he said, "I've just watched Sky News. First item was you shouting 'Rubbish.' So much for nobody noticing." He put the phone down.

My front-row seat alongside the general secretaries meant I was in shot as the cameras filmed them. The footage was all over the media.

All I could do to fix it was write to Ed to apologise, admitting I had let my emotions get the better of me. But I did use the opportunity to explain why he had been wrong to talk about irresponsible strikes and to point out that he had given the media an open invitation to ask him, every time there was industrial action, whether it was responsible or irresponsible.

So began my frustrating and somewhat torturous relationship with Ed Miliband. Unfortunately, that episode foreshadowed much of what followed.

———————

Ed Miliband is a decent man who was correct in wanting to move his party away from the disappointment of the New Labour era and develop a more inclusive way of doing things. He captured the mood for change—that's why he won the leadership over his brother. But he was too lacking in the courage of his convictions to truly shake off the past. Sadly, that meant on the biggest issue of his time—austerity—he ended up on the wrong side of history. Ultimately, his timidity cost him at the ballot box.

I liked Ed personally and gave him as much political support as I could in the early years. He recognised New Labour's so-called Third Way had failed. City-first deregulation policies had ended in a historic financial collapse, and instead of showing contrition, those who were culpable, the spivs and the speculators, were demanding that working people pick up the tab. But what Miliband failed to understand—unlike his successor Jeremy Corbyn—was that to break with such thinking meant seriously challenging the status quo. Ed was neither strong enough nor committed enough to see that through. As he retreated from the radical positions he initially staked out, our relationship became increasingly strained.

A man many backed to lead the fight against austerity was soon promising austerity-lite. I don't think that was inevitable at the beginning of Miliband's leadership. In March 2011, he addressed a huge anti-austerity demonstration in Hyde Park called by the TUC. Neither Tony Blair nor Gordon Brown would have done that. But the lack of sure-footedness that would drag Miliband down was already apparent. In the run up to the event his team were plainly worried. They asked whether I thought he should do it and what reaction he was likely to receive. "Yeah he should speak," I told them, "he'll be fine." And so he was.

It was to be a short-lived stand against austerity, however. It's never a good sign when a leader makes a speech billed as a "relaunch." When they start talking about "difficult choices" you know they are really in trouble. That was the message Miliband delivered in January 2012. But it was the other Ed—Miliband's shadow chancellor, Ed Balls—who made the economic policy shift explicit. In a speech to the Fabian Society the same month he not only endorsed George Osborne's freeze on public sector pay but said it might continue under a Labour government. Interviewed by the *Guardian*, Balls destroyed any hope that Labour would oppose austerity, saying: "My starting point is, I am afraid, we are going to have to keep all these cuts... At this stage, we can make no commitments to reverse any of that, on spending or on tax." Labour's inspiring message, trotted out by Miliband on the Andrew Marr show that weekend, was: "If Labour was in power now... we wouldn't be cutting as far and as fast as the government." I hung my head thinking, "Ed, what kind of rallying cry is that?"

There's no doubt in my mind that this was the critical mistake of Miliband's leadership. Hindsight is a wonderful thing, of course—it is the only exact science. But in this case, I said the same at the time. "Balls' sudden embrace of austerity," I wrote in the *Guardian*, "challenges the whole course Ed Miliband has set for the party." By allowing himself to be "dragged back into the swamp of bond market orthodoxy" by the "four horsemen of the austerity apocalypse" (I named Balls, Liam Byrne, Jim Murphy and Stephen Twigg—shadow ministers who had endorsed savage spending cuts), Miliband was on the path to "certain general election defeat" unless he changed tack.

From early on I was conscious of serious tension between the two Eds. Miliband was the leader, but Balls was increasingly calling the economic shots. Balls was determined Labour must accept austerity as part of his obsessive quest for "credibility," while Miliband was more wary. I never understood how it was "credible" to endorse a brutal economic rampage aimed at your own supporters, especially when serious economists were saying it would be economically counterproductive. That kind of too-clever-by-half positioning may win you applause from a very narrow set of liberal journalists but not from the public.

I was told that Balls put his foot down before the Fabian speech, causing Miliband to say, "Well, you can tell the general secretaries then, because I'm not." So on the Friday night before the speech I learned what Balls was about to do from a voicemail message. I know he also rang Paul Kenny of the GMB and Dave Prentis of Unison. Needless to say, there was uproar. All the unions, especially those with members in the public sector, were furious. But Balls wanted to prove that he could be tough. Public sector workers would just have to swallow the cuts. That was his message and his belief and to be fair to him he never deviated from it. We know where it landed him—dancing on *Strictly*, Gangnam Style.

When I complained to Miliband about the austerity-lite position he told me to go and talk to Balls. So I did. I said: "Look, we're going through difficult times but you should consult with us trade unions, because even if we can't agree with you, we can help come up with language that satisfies your thoughts and doesn't make life impossible for us."

Chris Leslie was there with Balls—honestly, I wouldn't send him across the road with a message. He was in the shadow Treasury team; later, of course, he would defect from Corbyn's Labour to the much-hyped Change UK, only to lose his deposit in the 2019 election. Leslie said: "Exactly Len, I couldn't agree with you more. We have to be able to tell people that when Labour gets elected there will be at least another two years of austerity."

I looked at him in total disbelief and said: "Are you on the same planet as me? That's not what I'm saying at all."

On another occasion I asked Miliband and Balls the difference between austerity and austerity-lite, saying: "I can't quite make it out. Austerity is like sticking a knife in and killing someone. Austerity-lite is when you slit their wrists with a razor blade—they don't die immediately but eventually it has the same result."

At the time, all of us—Miliband included—thought the right of the party was much stronger than it really was. Pressure from the right bolstered Balls' position. I wanted to help Miliband by applying some pressure from the left.

So, in April 2013, in an interview with the *New Statesman*, I called out the "siren voices" of the austerity-enthusiasts. "If [Miliband] is brave enough to go for something radical, he'll be the next prime minister," I said. "If he gets seduced by the Jim Murphys and the Douglas Alexanders then the truth is that he'll be defeated and he'll be cast into the dustbin of history."

I'm afraid Ed didn't take my intervention the way I had hoped. His spokesman called me "reprehensible," "disloyal" and said I was trying to "divide the party." When you bat something at someone, sometimes they bat it back; I wasn't upset. And it didn't escape my notice when, later in 2013, Ed demoted Liam Byrne, Stephen Twigg and Jim Murphy, three of the most destructive Blairites. But sadly, there was no change in the direction of travel on economic policy, with the leadership making further commitments to eliminate the deficit by 2020 and bring in a welfare spending cap.

I wish Miliband had been strong enough to assert himself over Balls, although perhaps I am exaggerating the difference between the two. Miliband didn't seem to want to help himself. He aspired to be a unity leader and refused to build a support base, either in the party or in parliament. I said to him at one juncture: "Who are your close people? You need a group of supportive MPs. We've had Blairites and Brownites; you need Milibites." Being leader of the Labour Party is the most difficult job in politics—anyone in that role needs trusted people they can rely on. Jon Trickett, a rare working-class voice in his shadow cabinet, was one of the few people from the left that Miliband listened to. He tried to set up such a group of supportive MPs but Miliband wouldn't allow it.

Miliband was drifting, and I had no idea who was influencing him. I was desperately trying to find out because my job, as a general secretary dealing with a Labour leader, was to secure the maximum influence for my members. I met with all kinds of people: Arnie Graff, the American advisor brought over to develop the party's community organising; Jon Cruddas, whom Miliband made his policy coordinator; and Maurice Glasman, the thinker behind Blue Labour. I was saying to all of them, "Have you got his ear? Who's influencing him here?" No one seemed to know.

The meetings with Glasman were interesting because I wanted to understand Blue Labour, the trend within the party that paired support for economic intervention with socially conservative values of family and country. Many comrades on the left were very dismissive of it, but I hoped it might provide a route into Miliband's world, as he was said to be taken with Blue Labour's ideas. (Lisa Nandy, whom I admired, had been promoting similar views.) Unfortunately, I was wrong. Glasman had been very close to Miliband at one stage, but by the time I met him and other Blue Labour figures, I got the impression they were as frustrated as I was. Glasman told me: "I don't have any influence anymore. He's like a petulant prince, if you disagree with him that's it."

Miliband had retreated behind his small team in the Leader's Office. No one else could get near. Unfortunately, he had surrounded himself with entirely the wrong people. There were a few exceptions: I had time for Lucy Powell, his deputy chief of staff until she became an MP in 2012, and Simon Fletcher, his trade union liaison officer who later worked for both Jeremy Corbyn and Keir Starmer. But when you look at the others—the likes of Tom Baldwin, a former *Times* journalist who was his director of communications—you have to wonder how Miliband did as well as he did. There may have been some clever individuals among them but they mirrored Miliband's own weakness: they had no connection to real people. And they were by-and-large a bunch of right-wingers.

I was always struck by Miliband's advisors' lack of empathy for trade unions. Most of them—and unfortunately this applied to Miliband as well—didn't understand what unions were. The wider labour movement was an alien planet to them. They never got over the accusation that the unions had cheated David Miliband out of his rightful inheritance. I was angry that Ed never took that on. Among the party membership David beat Ed by 54 per cent to 46 in the final round of voting for the leadership—hardly the landslide that was portrayed.

A reluctance to challenge damaging untruths became characteristic. The Tories spent five years squeezing every last drop of political advantage from the note left in the Treasury in 2010 by the outgoing minister Liam Byrne, saying "I'm afraid there is no money." Miliband never condemned that for the childish act it was nor challenged the infantile understanding of economics it betrayed; instead, he put Byrne in his shadow cabinet. He wasn't strong enough to say, "Frankly, for the crime of pure stupidity, you can't be in my shadow cabinet—go and serve some time in the penal colony of the backbenches."

Most damaging of all, Miliband and Balls took a deliberate decision not to challenge the Tory mantra that Labour's public spending had somehow caused the 2008 recession. One of Miliband's advisors said, "there was no point in trying to contest their account of the past... we had to be future-oriented." In Unite we couldn't believe they were letting the Tories get away with it. It handed them a justification for austerity on a plate. When Miliband finally got around to taking on this nonsense—during a TV appearance in the 2015 election—it was far too late. Asked if Labour had spent too much in government, Miliband said "No." The audience laughed.

The result of the leadership's austerity-lite position was that Labour was cut off from the only source of political vibrancy in those years: the anti-austerity movement. This was a period of spontaneous outbursts of opposition—students protesting the tripling of tuition fees, the disabled highlighting cuts to their support, UK Uncut exposing tax injustice, the Occupy movement raising the issue of inequality, and a multitude of small local campaigns fighting cuts to libraries, childcare, hospitals, housing and much more.

The trade union movement was on the front line of the fight against austerity. We had to be—it was our members who were bearing the brunt of it. Two million workers took part in public sector strikes over changes to pensions in 2011. A million took strike action and joined protests over the public sector pay freeze in 2014. And then there were the demonstrations—400,000 in Hyde Park for the rally addressed by Ed Miliband in 2011; another large national demonstration in 2012. Up and down the country trade union branches and trades councils were the backbone of local anti-cuts campaigns.

As a new general secretary, I was determined that Unite should be at the forefront of this battle. I have what is perhaps an unusual outlook for a trade union leader. I don't believe that trade unionism should be confined to the workplace. The worker who feels the power of collective action in their job should take that experience back into their community. If you want to change things in the workplace, join a union, come together with your mates, and your voice will be that much louder. If you want to change society, the same rule applies—join with others and change society yourself. If you don't want to change society then fine, just accept the status quo and let people walk all over you.

I didn't want the anti-austerity movement to be segmented, with organised labour on one side and the groups carrying out spontaneous action on the other. It would be a far stronger movement if we worked together. So when the Occupy movement arrived in October 2011 with an encampment outside St Paul's Cathedral, I went down to associate organised labour with their challenge to the establishment. I believe I was the only general secretary of a major trade union to do so.

The camp was an incredible scene to behold, with its tents, its makeshift catering facility, its library and its Banksy art. It looked like a part of Glastonbury had been picked up and dropped amid the grey of the City of London. The occupiers were sat in a big circle on the paving stones holding their daily meeting—400 people, maybe more, listening to speakers. Someone said, "Who are you?"

"I'm Len McCluskey, can I speak?"

"Yeah, anyone can speak," he replied.

Very quickly it was my turn. With any public speaking you rely on feedback from your audience. When you hit a big line you expect the reassuring sound of applause. Well, I hit the first big line at the Occupy camp and there was silence, just a load of hands waving around in the air. I thought, "What the...?" I soldiered on and hit another good line. Again, no applause, but all the hands went up. And then I realised. This was the first time I'd encountered jazz hands, the silent gesture to indicate agreement used by these types of groups.

All my life I have believed in direct action. It's easy to pass a resolution in a smoke-filled room but physically going out and doing things takes real commitment. So when UK Uncut emerged, with sit-down protests in the shops of tax-avoiding companies, I was an instant supporter. I thought they were wonderful. They explained to me that it began with half-a-dozen of them sitting in a pub having a drink, moaning about the world, and deciding to do something about it by creating a network of activists that could carry out direct action with the element of surprise. And what an impact they had. Before UK Uncut came along, the issue of tax avoidance and evasion wasn't even on the radar. They soon changed that.

The idea of trying to bring all this activity together, from the traditions of direct action, community campaigning and organised labour, was the motivation behind the formation of the People's Assembly in 2013. It united local anti-cuts groups with big unions including the CWU and Unison. Unite was central to its creation and funding. Soon, People's Assemblies were springing up all around the country.

Of course, austerity was not only a UK phenomenon. Unite is a big trade union in Ireland, where austerity measures were even more severe, provoking a spirited fightback by the people. I was proud that Unite was at the heart of that, with our senior officer Brendan Ogle taking a leading role in the struggle against water charges in the Republic from 2014 as the coordinator of the Right2Water campaign. Out of that mobilisation came the Right2Change political campaign, based around a statement of principles that politicians were asked to commit to, which may have sown the seeds of a new political movement.

For a long time, I had an idea for a new form of trade union membership for people who were not in employment—those who had retired, been made redundant, or never been in work due to their health or circumstances. Whether they were 16 or 116, I wanted them to be able to join our family, to become Community members of Unite, so that we could organise them and strengthen their voice in society—the same way we strengthen the voice of workers at work.

If we really believed in solidarity and looking after one another, we had to take those values into the political arena and into the communities where we lived. Unite Community did just that. From the moment it was set up, it was at the forefront of the fight against austerity. It was our Unite Community activists who spearheaded the campaigns against the bedroom tax and universal credit. Unite Community flags could be seen flying at many fantastic demonstrations, small and large, throughout our nations.

What I witnessed in Britain in those years was an army of activists beginning to form up. They would later become the infantry of the Corbyn movement. But Miliband's Labour preferred to keep its distance, more concerned with winning that elusive "credibility" from the establishment than helping its own people. The leadership could hardly complain that they were seen as part of the problem by so many of those fighting back.

CHAPTER 12

FALKIRK

Ed Miliband was on the TV attacking my union. It was July 2013, about halfway through Ed's time in charge of the party. How sad that, like many Labour leaders before him, Miliband had decided that to look strong he needed to make a show of slapping down the unions. He had seized on a completely phoney scandal about a parliamentary selection in the Scottish seat of Falkirk as a pretext, and now he was making a speech about how he wanted to reform the link between the party and the trade unions. What he hadn't reckoned on was that I would agree with him.

I was in my office watching the speech with my team as Miliband accused us of operating "a politics of the machine, a politics that is rightly hated." It was an outrageous slur. But when he went on to say, "I do not want any individual to be paying money to the Labour Party in affiliation fees unless they have deliberately chosen to do so," I couldn't disagree. In fact, I was looking for a way to reduce Unite's massive affiliation payments. Now here was Miliband giving me the perfect excuse. I thought, "Thank you, Ed."

As soon as Miliband had finished, I said to my brilliant director of communications, Pauline Doyle, "Let's go down to College Green and speak to the media." The journalists and cameras were all there outside parliament expecting me to go to war with the Labour leader. But I had no intention of playing the big, bad, union dinosaur. Instead, in a host of interviews, I welcomed what he had said, to the journalists' obvious frustration. "Len, we're all surprised," I remember the BBC's Nick Robinson saying disappointedly as we were waiting to go on air.

That day was the most important of Miliband's leadership. It set in train a series of events that would lead to an outcome no one could have imagined at the time, least of all Miliband himself: Jeremy Corbyn becoming leader of the Labour Party. Dramatic reforms intended to weaken the unions and the left instead had the opposite effect. Unite was central to that being the case. While all the other major players miscalculated, I am proud of the role that we played. Had I gone down to College Green that day and blasted Miliband, history would have been very different.

———————

One of my defining characteristics, if I look back over my life, is that I have never been in favour of the status quo. I am always willing to say, "Well that might be OK, but it can be better." The usual instinct of trade union general secretaries is to keep everything the same in exchange for influence. I have never been satisfied with that. I don't mind throwing the pieces up in the air, because how they land will reveal new opportunities. And I have never been sentimental about the Labour Party.

The story of how Unite came to support reforms that would radically transform Labour begins with my campaign to become general secretary. In every workplace I visited, union members asked why we were giving so much money to a party they saw as working against them. There has always been a strain of anti-Labour sentiment within every trade union—some of it comes from the cadre of ultra-left rival parties, some from workers who don't vote or identify with Labour. But by 2010 that discontent had spread wider than ever—and was growing.

My answer to those who wanted to abandon Unite's association with Labour was always this: if you are a member of any organisation—it could be the local darts club or a political party—which doesn't have your values and doesn't speak with your voice, you have only two options. One is to leave and the other is to try to change it. My pitch was that we should try to change the Labour Party.

This was a party that millions of working-class people related to. That meant something. We should say: no more blank cheques, we want to be treated with respect, and we want Labour to be for *labour*.

That determination to try something different was an important plank of my mandate. As Labour's largest affiliate, it was no good whinging and moaning, it was up to us to organise. So as general secretary one of the first things I did was develop a new political strategy for the union, designed to put working-class values of collectivism, solidarity and community spirit—all of which had been marginalised by New Labour—back at the heart of the party and ensure they would be voiced in parliament.

The plan was simple: to seek out and support good people with working-class values to become the MPs of the future, and recruit members, activists and shop stewards to the party who would endorse union-supported candidates in selections. That way, through organising in democratic contests, we could rebalance the Parliamentary Labour Party away from the right. This same philosophy was also aimed at the Scottish Parliament, the Welsh Assembly, Stormont and the Dáil in Eire, as well as local councils.

The objective was sometimes misrepresented as standing more working-class candidates, rather than more candidates with working-class values. The difference is important: my great political hero, Tony Benn, could scarcely have been less working class, but his values, in my opinion, were working class—solidarity, community, looking after one another, and challenging the establishment. That was the essence of my experience growing up in working-class Liverpool, and the complete opposite of Margaret Thatcher's dictum, "There is no such thing as society." Compare Tony Benn with New Labour's Alan Johnson (whose autobiographical trilogy I enjoyed immensely) who is working class through and through but whose working-class values have, I believe, been lost. It's the values that matter to me. If there's a candidate with working-class values who is also a lorry driver or a docker or a supermarket worker, that is the cherry on the cake.

The political strategy was officially adopted by Unite in summer 2012 and produced as a booklet. It was inevitably attacked in the press and by the right of the party, who presented it as a malicious conspiracy. Of course, they knew that a union as big as Unite, with a clear-eyed plan and the resources to make it happen, was going to be a force to be reckoned with.

I wasn't the only one who wanted to shake up the Labour Party. The leadership itself aimed to breathe some life into the moribund party structures with the Refounding Labour review in 2011. I sympathised with Miliband's desire to stimulate some vibrancy at the grassroots. I was then attempting to bring some vibrancy in to Unite's branch structure, to prevent the union becoming too bureaucratic. At the time, Labour was a party with fewer than 200,000 members—a third of the size it became under Jeremy Corbyn. Local constituency parties up and down the country had been hollowed out during the New Labour years. Meetings were sparsely attended. There was no energy, no life in the organisation. It was dying. Sadly, Refounding Labour was a missed opportunity to turn things around. Its proposals failed to excite support.

As a new general secretary who had won on a left platform of radical change, I was continually being challenged from the left by activists who were, understandably, exasperated by Labour. Impetus built behind the idea of disaffiliating from the party. Imagine the political earthquake that would have caused. We were Labour's biggest donor and biggest affiliate. The party would have struggled to run an effective election campaign without Unite's money. Politics would have changed forever, in unpredictable ways.

Naturally there was scepticism about how real the threat of disaffiliation was. I can reveal that we came closer than most people realised. The pressure within the union for disaffiliation reached a high water mark around our 2012 and 2014 policy conferences. Had I favoured disaffiliation, I am quite sure I could have persuaded Unite's executive and conference. I can recall many tense moments at policy conferences where I have turned the hall, and turned the union, with a speech. That ability doesn't just come out of thin air, and it's not only about rhetorical delivery. It's the result of the trust and respect earned over many years as a national officer and a leading figure on the left of the T&G that means delegates who may disagree with me on a particular issue will still support me because they know I'm on their side.

I understood the arguments for disaffiliation and it was not inconceivable to me. We had just been through 13 years of a Labour government that refused to loosen the shackles on trade unions; millions of our people were living below the poverty line; the gap between rich and poor was wider; we had lost a million manufacturing jobs because the government was not willing to intervene; and yet here we were still handing over huge sums of money to the Labour Party, which under Miliband constantly seemed to be taking one step forward, two steps back.

Had Unite chosen to disaffiliate, the logical next step would have been to establish an alternative political vehicle to represent the interests of our members and our class: a new Workers' Party. The idea was under discussion. We knew that any serious new party would need to have a base or it would be blown away like dust, as Change UK found in 2019. For a new Workers' Party, the base would obviously be organised labour. I am not 100 per cent sure we would have been able to persuade enough other trade unions to join us to make it work, but I believe it might have been possible. The RMT, led by my close comrade and friend Bob Crow until his death in 2014, would have been involved. We would have tried to convince the CWU and other affiliated unions to join us. As a first step, we would have organised a conference to assess the power that could be assembled and whether a new party would be viable.

We didn't reach that stage. Instead, we continued to try to move Labour to the left by winning selections, in accordance with our political strategy. It was against this backdrop that the Falkirk 'scandal' blew up.

————————

It began with a punch. Eric Joyce, the Blairite MP for Falkirk—once dubbed New Labour's 'Minister for Newsnight' for his eagerness to go on the airwaves to defend the Iraq War, and subsequently a convicted child sex offender—got drunk in a House of Commons bar one evening in 2012, lost his temper and thumped and head-butted several MPs. His exit from the party in disgrace left Falkirk Labour needing a new candidate.

This was exactly the situation Unite's political strategy had been designed for. Falkirk was seen as a safe Labour seat (ironically, given everything that followed, the Scottish National Party would take it with a massive swing at the 2015 election), and the constituency was home to the Grangemouth oil refinery, a huge industrial facility with a unionised workforce represented by Unite. The union's Scottish region set about finding a candidate who embodied our working-class values.

At first, they settled on Stevie Deans, chair of Unite in Scotland and of the local Labour party and a lovely, decent man. But when he decided not to run, the team approached Karie Murphy, a member of Unite's political committee in Scotland and a former chair of Scottish Labour, who had been running Stevie's campaign. Karie, later to become a central figure in the Corbyn project, said she would run if she had the support of the industrial workers. She met the shop stewards and got the thumbs up.

In line with our political strategy, Stevie—who was now running Karie's campaign—set about recruiting new members to the party ahead of the selection contest. He signed up his colleagues at Grangemouth, where he worked, and his friends in the local pubs. Pretty soon he had recruited around 100 new members.

At the time, the Labour Party ran a scheme called Union Join by which trade unions could subsidise the first year's membership fees of workers recruited to the party from within their own ranks. That made it very easy to sign up Unite members at Grangemouth, because for them it was free. The Union Join scheme was an invention of Tony Blair, used heavily by the shop workers' union USDAW, which is on the right of the trade union movement. I remember USDAW promoting a video of Blair encouraging its use. Personally, I have never liked it. I disagree with the whole idea of unions subsidising membership fees. I am one of those people who believes that paying money to join something generates a sense of commitment and connection.

My one regret over Falkirk is that Unite used the Union Join scheme. It was perfectly within the rules, but it was not a good look to have 100 new members suddenly drafted into a local party which, because it had been hollowed out during the New Labour years, had only around 100 members to start with. Stevie and Karie's recruitment drive was too effective. It became very evident to the local right wingers that something was happening that threatened their control. They cried foul.

Soon the Labour right, led by Peter Mandelson, was up in arms, claiming we were trying to manipulate the selection. They saw an opportunity to kick up a controversy to push Unite back. As far as the Blairites were concerned, Labour belonged to them. Here was Unite threatening their cosy little club—first getting Ed elected and forcing poor David to go off and make millions elsewhere, now targeting selection contests throughout the party. It was all too much for them. They sensed that the power of the Blairite sect Progress was on the wane, but their network still extended into Labour HQ, where Iain McNicol was general secretary, and they could rely on their friends in the press. They had the clout to turn Falkirk into a 'scandal,' have the selection contest suspended, and get an internal investigation launched.

The Labour Party has a long track record of using sham investigations to do people in. Nine times out of ten, they get away with it. But the target isn't usually their largest affiliate and biggest funder. So it was doubly insulting that what transpired was the most amateur stitch-up you will ever see. McNicol's people didn't even have the decency to do it professionally. Whether that was due to arrogance or incompetence I don't know—probably a mixture of both.

There is a trick to these kinds of investigations. Look closely enough into any political process and you will usually find discrepancies that can be cast in the worst possible light. That's what Labour HQ was hoping for. Unfortunately for them, they found nothing. Their investigation concluded with an internal report in June 2013 that was a disgrace. The executive summary on the cover page claimed Unite had attempted to manipulate party processes, recruit members without their knowledge, and frustrate the investigation. But the rest of the report might as well have been blank—it contained no evidence to back up its incendiary claims. It was such a one-sided and half-hearted effort that, incredibly, the investigators hadn't even bothered to interview Karie or Stevie. Remarkably, buried in an appendix was the revelation that the Blairite candidate in Falkirk, Gregor Poynton, husband of the then Labour MP Gemma Doyle, had recruited new members to the party and paid their membership fees himself, which was completely against the rules. But the investigators hadn't followed that up—it wasn't the discrepancy they were looking for.

I was all in favour of the report being published. Unsurprisingly, Labour refused. There was no mystery as to why: when the *Guardian* finally obtained the report the following year, the newspaper's analysis began: "The Falkirk report arrives at eight conclusions in its executive summary, leaked to the press and widely interpreted as damning proof of forgery, bullying and 'machine politics' by Unite... But there is only limited evidence in the report which supports these conclusions."

Of course, at the height of the 'scandal' no one knew how thin the evidence was. All anyone had to go on was the innuendo and briefings coming from Labour slamming my union.

I knew then that I was in a real fight; that the people around Miliband—and possibly the leader himself—had decided that this was his moment to take on the unions, and that big, bad Len McCluskey had been cast as the villain. But I couldn't have predicted what happened next: Miliband reported my union to the police. The magnitude of the insult is difficult to convey. To say I was incandescent would be putting it mildly. I will never forgive him for it. He didn't even have the decency to tell me personally; I found out about it in the media. None of the other general secretaries could believe it either; the whole trade union movement was shocked. It was quite extraordinary.

It took the police only a short time to conclude there were no grounds for an investigation, but by then the damage was done. The press had a field day. Unite's name was dragged through the mud. Karie and Stevie were suspended from the party. Tom Watson—my flatmate and friend at the time—resigned his shadow front bench role in disgust at Miliband's decision to make this into a macho moment.

The statements issued by Miliband and the Leader's Office were, let's say, less than comradely. Trade unions were described as a "vested interest" equivalent to Rupert Murdoch. What had happened in Falkirk was, apparently, "corrupt." This came on top of constant attacks from a vicious media that already had its sights set on me as one of the most powerful voices on the left.

It was all manna from heaven for the Tory prime minister, David Cameron, who portrayed Miliband as a puppet whose strings were being pulled by yours truly. Taunting Miliband at prime minister's questions on 3 July 2013, Cameron said: "The right honourable gentleman goes up and down the country speaking for Len McCluskey." Well, if only. Cameron took to name-checking me every week from the dispatch box. I'm still a little annoyed I never got invited to his Christmas party, I thought we had become rather well acquainted.

It's difficult to describe how it feels to be under attack from the entire media and political class. It hurts, especially when family and friends read the rubbish that's written about you. You can never be completely anaesthetised to it. What I suffered was just a fraction of what they later threw at Jeremy Corbyn, but it was more than enough. The best way to cope is to treat it as a badge of honour. I was being attacked because I was doing a good job for my class. I've always believed that trade unions should be prominent in public life, not hidden away in a corner; having my name and that of my union at the centre of the news did have value in that sense. As Oscar Wilde wrote, "There is only one thing in the world worse than being talked about, and that is not being talked about." Part of me was secretly proud to hear Cameron say my name at every prime minister's questions, but another part was saying, "I hope to God Ed isn't falling for this."

Unfortunately, I think he was. Why did Miliband walk into the trap and turn on his own side? I believe it all goes back to his election as leader, and the accusation that the trade unions installed him. His advisors wanted to exorcise that demon, and were egging him on to have a set-piece confrontation with the unions. I think Miliband went along with it because he feared the 'Red Ed' tag, he disliked being taunted by Cameron, and he was looking for an opportunity to "show his mettle as leader," as his team briefed the press.

Miliband saw trade unions through a liberal prism that made legitimate collectivist structures appear crooked. I remember an extraordinary conversation I had with him in his office when I had to explain the basics of collectivism. I said if I negotiate a pay deal with a company on behalf of 100 workers, and 60 vote in favour and 40 against, then 100 of them have accepted it. I don't go back to the employer and say, "Well these 60 have accepted it but I'm sorry, you'll have to wait for the other 40." Miliband said that taught him a lot.

What still makes me angry is that an opportunistic political stunt had severe consequences for the lives of many people, and yet it was all built on sand—neither Karie, nor Stevie, nor Unite had done anything wrong. The only fraud that took place was the Labour Party's investigation. After Police Scotland said there was nothing to answer for, the party made an abrupt U-turn in September 2013 and cleared Karie and Stevie of any wrongdoing. Yet neither they nor Unite ever received an apology.

The Falkirk 'scandal' triggered one of the major industrial disputes of my time as general secretary. Grangemouth, the oil refinery within the constituency of Falkirk, is one of the largest manufacturing sites in the UK. Stevie was a Unite convenor at the facility and INEOS, the company that runs Grangemouth, had been itching to take us on for some time. INEOS is owned by the billionaire Jim Ratcliffe, by some reports the richest man in Britain. A couple of years earlier he lost a battle with the workforce over pensions. He's the type of individual who was always going to seek retribution.

When the political storm hit in July 2013, with Stevie at its centre, INEOS seized their chance and suspended him for, they said, using company computers for Labour Party business. His workmates resisted and the union threatened strike action. The company chose to escalate. The facility is split between a chemical processing plant and a petrol refinery jetty. The company effectively told the workers it would close the chemical plant unless they accepted a 'rescue

With mum, dad, and our Kath at 9 Iris Street, Liverpool.

Mum and dad ballroom
dancing at St Richard's
Club.

The day of my Holy
Communion. How
did this angelic
boy become public
enemy no. 1?

Me and dad at the beach in North Wales.

With my mum and big sister Kath at Christmas.

Cycling between picket lines on the docks while
on strike for six weeks in 1972.

We're not English, we are Scouse.

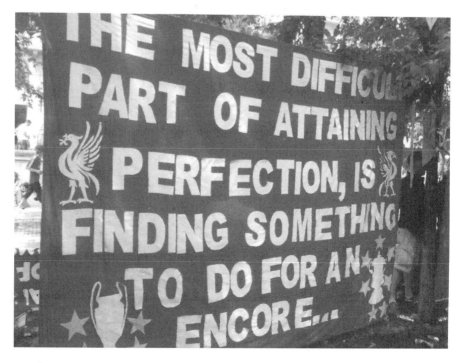

The banners made by Liverpool fans are works of art for me. This one was
made by my great-nephew Adam when he was 15.

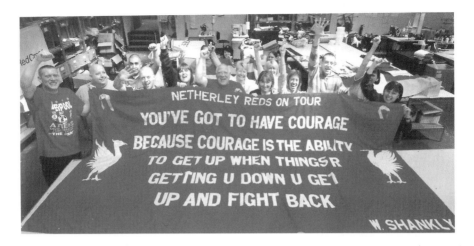

The messages reflect the indomitable character of Liverpool and its people.

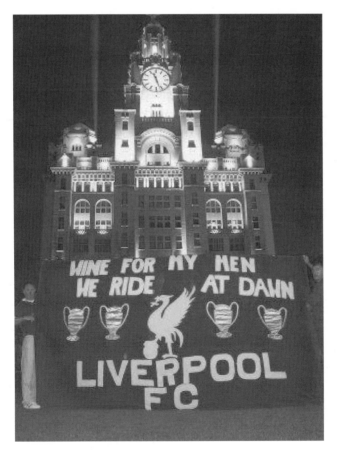

One of the most iconic Liverpool banner slogans and
nobody knows where the quote comes from.

The banners travel with the fans—this one is in Istanbul for a Champions League final that was the most beautiful dream.

The 96 who died in the Hillsborough disaster will never be forgotten.

Marching with the dockers.

Laughter at a BASSA gathering during the British Airways dispute.

package.' Of course, the rescue they had in mind was the kind that cuts pay, pensions and conditions.

I got directly involved in the dispute as I realised our officers and the workers were in some difficulty. The Scottish Labour Party leadership didn't contact me once, in stark contrast to the SNP first minister, Alex Salmond, who bent over backwards to help and with whom I had a series of meetings. He saw that a vital strategic interest for the Scottish economy was dependent on the whim of one billionaire. He was trying to persuade the Chinese, who owned 50 per cent of the jetty, to find another company to buy out INEOS' half and run the facility under a tripartite system with Unite having a golden ticket. Unfortunately, that didn't come to pass but I couldn't have asked for more support from Salmond.

General secretaries are very good at taking credit for victories; they're less visible when things go bad. But I went up to Grangemouth to take the defeat. Given INEOS' threat to close the chemical plant, we had to step back, accept the package that slashed our members' conditions, and commit to abide by it for three years, which we did. We have been able to claw back some of those losses in the time since, but it was a very bad period. Stevie had to resign from his job at Grangemouth and from his position as chair of Falkirk Constituency Labour Party, and in February 2014 INEOS sacked another of our excellent conveners at the refinery, Mark Lyon.

I am in no doubt that by blowing up a phoney controversy Miliband weakened the industrial strength of the workers at Grangemouth and cost them both financially and in their working conditions. I suspect Unite would have had a confrontation with INEOS at some juncture in any case, but the national political situation provided the catalyst Ratcliffe needed, throwing us into battle at an explosive time when we were at a severe disadvantage—all thanks to the political leadership of organised labour.

―――――――――

At the height of the Falkirk controversy, on 9 July 2013, Miliband tried to seize the initiative with a speech on the relationship between the party and the unions. His big proposal was that trade union members should have to 'opt in' to become affiliated Labour members and contribute a portion of their subs to the party. As it was, trade unions usually affiliated all their members through a collective decision, with individuals able to opt out if they wished. Miliband's idea had nothing to do with Falkirk. He had, in fact, already scrapped the Union Join scheme—which was fine by me. This new proposal was intended as an attack on the power of trade unions within the party. Making trade unionists 'opt in' might sound like a dull, technical change, but it meant there would be far fewer affiliated members, potentially leaving us with less clout.

The Labour right was delighted with Miliband's proposal. Tony Blair made one of his regular rare interventions to call it "bold and strong." Understandably, then, almost the entire left was against the idea—except me. I knew when I went down to talk to the media on College Green that day to welcome Miliband's proposal that I would be standing apart from my comrades. But I thought Miliband had a point. Unite was affiliating a million members to the Labour Party, very many of whom didn't even vote Labour. It used to be the case that union branches would send tens of delegates to CLP meetings, but by 2013 there were very few. If trade unionists had to agree to become affiliated members, I believed they would feel more connection to the party and be more likely to get involved. And if that meant unions had to put in a bit of effort to engage with them, instead of taking them for granted from the safety of a bureaucratic bubble, then so much the better.

I also saw a chance to save a lot of money. Affiliating a million members was expensive. With the Falkirk controversy raging, it wasn't easy to see what we were getting for it. I had become frustrated with Miliband and, if I'm honest, I had started to lose faith in Labour. I wanted to slash the amount we paid to subsidise the wages of Labour Party staff who, as far as I could tell, were being directed to spend much of their time attacking my union. But I was worried that if I cut our affiliation payments I would be accused of weakening the party. Miliband's speech gave me an opening to cut our affiliation fee in half, saving £1.5 million a year which we used for other political objectives—on campaigns, activism and funding particular MPs and candidates—which vastly increased Unite's influence.

I knew I would face a backlash from the left and from other trade unions for the stance I took. It's fair to say the other general secretaries of the Big Four unions were not happy with me. They wanted to slice my head off. Paul Kenny (GMB), Dave Prentis (Unison), and Billy Hayes (CWU) got me in a room and demanded, "What the fuck are you playing at? You know this is ridiculous."

"First of all, it's me and my union that are under attack in the media, not you lot," I responded. "If you think for one minute I'm going on telly to have a go at Miliband and be seen as a dinosaur, you're living in a different world and you're dealing with a different person. But secondly, I agree with him. I genuinely believe we should win over our members to commit to the Labour Party."

I came at this from a different angle from them because they were generally happy with the status quo, I wasn't. Why not shake things up and see what happens? And anyway, Miliband didn't have the power to impose anything; he needed our agreement to vote through changes to the party's rules, and that gave us the ability to shape the final settlement.

Miliband gave the job of negotiating the reforms to Ray Collins, a former general secretary of the Labour Party and assistant general secretary of the T&G. He was an old political opponent of mine, but a friend. Ray knew that Unite was his way in. If he could keep me onside, he would succeed. I had already expressed support for the 'opt in' proposal but we knew there was a hidden agenda behind it. The system put forward by Collins was basically the same as one devised during earlier cross-party talks on state funding of political parties, with the aim of banning large affiliation fees but allowing trade union members to make what were effectively small, individual donations from their subs, collected and passed on by their trade union. The Blairites were big fans of the idea because state funding would mean they didn't have to answer to organised labour. As for Miliband and his team, they may have had one eye on an alliance with the Liberal Democrats after the election, with reforms to party funding providing the foundation of any coalition deal. But Miliband may also have simply believed in the principle of opting in, as I did.

The other general secretaries said I was being naïve, but I wasn't suggesting we walk into this blindly. We would set conditions: one was that we would have five years to transition to the new system. That gave us time to talk to our members. (In Unite we subsequently made contact with up to half-a-million members. More than 200,000 said they were happy to be collectively part of the Labour Party and more than 100,000 wanted to become affiliated supporters. It was a great exercise, one we have continued since.)

I wasn't oblivious to a scenario in which the trade unions didn't put the work in and ended up with as few as 50,000 affiliated members between us. That would then fuel a demand from the Blairites to reduce or scrap the 50 per cent of the vote that we held at Labour Conference—the key to severing Labour's ties with the unions. But it was up to us to make sure that didn't happen, and as I kept pointing out to people, Collins wasn't even mentioning the 50 per cent share at Conference.

But Collins did propose changes to the way Labour elects its leader. The electoral college system that Labour used had three sections: MPs, party members and affiliated members. Because there were different numbers of each, the weight of a single vote varied according to who cast it—in 2010 one MP's vote was worth the same as the votes of 477 party members or 794 affiliated members. Collins didn't want a situation where, with far fewer affiliated members, a trade unionist's vote carried *more* weight than a party member's. Plus, Miliband's embarrassment at winning more support from trade unionists than members or MPs in his own election meant there was a desire to do something about the electoral college.

Collins came to me with an extraordinary proposal. At a meeting in my office he showed me a document. I was so amazed by what I read that I asked him to talk me through it again. He was offering to scrap the electoral college altogether and move to a one-member-one-vote system. No longer would a third of the vote for the leader be reserved for just a few hundred MPs. A Labour

MP would have the same say over who leads the party as an affiliated member. I managed to restrain myself from saying, "Well, that's unbelievable, the PLP are giving up their power?" But when he had gone I kept saying, "I cannot believe this."

When the Big Four met, I said: "Do you understand what's happening with the electoral college? I'm not sure the MPs will accept this, but what's being offered to us is, in my eyes, extraordinary." We had the most right-wing PLP of my lifetime forfeiting their position of privilege. One of my colleagues said, "But they're taking away our 33 per cent, too." But we didn't have 33 per cent. The voting in the affiliates section of the electoral college had been conducted on a one-member-one-vote basis since John Smith's time. We could hope to influence our members in who to vote for, but they had minds of their own—in 1994 T&G members voted for Tony Blair to be leader against our recommendation of Margaret Beckett. I said, "It means nothing to us to move to one-member-one-vote, other than we have to go out and engage with our members. But this opportunity to cut out the PLP, who are a drag anchor on everything we're doing, is irresistible." Eventually Paul Kenny said to me, "You're right about this electoral college."

The quid pro quo for MPs was a hike in the number of nominations a leadership contender would need to secure from their colleagues in the Commons in order to stand. Instead of having a disproportionate influence on the vote itself, MPs would be the gatekeepers, limiting the choice put before members. The point was to ensure no left candidate could get into the race and do embarrassingly well.

As it stood, a contender had to secure nominations from 12.5 per cent of the PLP to get on the ballot. Collins proposed raising that to 25 per cent. That was never going to fly with the trade unions, so he came back with 20 per cent. There was still no chance of Unite accepting it. I said, "Ray, you need to go and speak to Dave Prentis," because at the time Dave was saying he would have nothing to do with the whole process. "Go and offer him something. Draw him in." Ray and Dave agreed a 15 per cent threshold. Funnily enough, Blairite true believers were also pushing for a lower threshold, aware their numbers in the PLP were not as great as was commonly assumed. As the 2015 leadership race would show, the 15 per cent bar was just low enough for both Jeremy Corbyn and the Blairite Liz Kendall to clear. Had it been 20 per cent, there would have been no chance, at least for the left.

The final element in the new system for electing the leader was the extension of the vote to non-members—registered supporters. The Blairites were convinced this would help the right, as non-members were bound to be to the right of the party faithful. I thought the scheme could be used to appeal to the thousands of socialists who had left Labour in the Blair-Brown years. That came to pass in 2015, but looking at it today I don't support giving non-members a say over who leads the party. There is no need for them—Corbyn proved that you can still have a mass political party in the 21st century if you give people something to believe in.

So, after months of to and fro, there was a deal. Affiliated members would need to opt in, the electoral college would be scrapped, the nomination threshold would be raised only slightly, and registered supporters would be given a vote. The Collins Review, as it was known, was put to the vote at a special conference in March 2014. It passed comfortably.

In taking such a pro-Collins position I could have ended up with a black eye, but I felt instinctively it was the right thing to do. Fortunately, history has vindicated the stance I took. Jon Lansman, a veteran of Labour politics and co-founder of the left-wing, Corbyn-supporting organisation Momentum, summed it up nicely when he said: "If Len had spoken against it then we would have defeated the Collins Review and Jeremy Corbyn would not have been leader of the Labour Party, which is obviously an irony."

I wish I could say I foresaw the second coming of JC. I can't. But I did see an opportunity to break what was there, and I thought it would mean a left leadership candidate could do better in a future contest. Lansman is right: Corbyn would not have been possible without Collins, or without Unite.

At the time, it was the Labour right that was celebrating. Tony Blair praised Miliband's "courage and leadership" and pundits rejoiced that the next Labour leader would now definitely be a Blairite. A year-and-a-half later their worst nightmares would come true. Talk about the law of unintended consequences.

CHAPTER 13

THE ROAD TO DEFEAT

I'd been summoned to Ed Miliband's office for a telling off. In his own unique fashion Ed was reprimanding me for writing an article warning that if Scottish Labour elected Jim Murphy, an ultra-Blairite, as its leader, it would be a "sentence of political death for many Scottish Labour MPs," and for Labour's chances in the next general election.

It was November 2014, a few months since the Scottish people had rejected independence in a referendum, but only after giving the British establishment the fright of its life by taking it right to the wire. Jon Trickett was there in Ed's office with us. Miliband was telling me how unhelpful it was for me to attack colleagues using "vicious language."

"What vicious language, Ed," I asked, "can you be more specific?"

Miliband looked a little uncertain and said he hadn't actually read the article, Jon had told him about it.

"Well, Ed, let me give you one piece of advice," I said. "If you're going to attack me for something I've written, it would be a good idea for you to read it first."

We talked about Jim Murphy. I asked how the Scottish working class could be expected to get behind a man who was an unashamed champion of the very ideology that had lost us so much support north of the border and pushed workers in their droves to the SNP. We spoke of the implications if that happened. Eventually, I said, "Ed, you should call Jim in and say you're about to announce that the next leader of Scottish Labour has to be a member of the Scottish parliament"—ruling out Murphy, who held a Westminster seat.

Ed's response left me stunned: "I'm keeping out of it."

"Well, that's fucking unbelievable," I said. "What happens in Scotland could be the difference between you being prime minister or not, and you're keeping out of it?" It was to be a prophetic statement.

I've never felt as politically depressed as I did after that conversation. Four years into Miliband's leadership, after all the frustration of austerity-lite and Falkirk, I still couldn't find a way to get through to him. I desperately wanted him to win the general election but I thought Labour was heading for disaster in Scotland. "Labour faces the loss of perhaps dozens of Scottish seats," I had predicted in the article Miliband took exception to. "Without those MPs, the struggle to evict the Tory-Lib Dem coalition and elect a majority Labour government starts to look hideously difficult."

As I was walking through parliament after leaving Miliband's office, I bumped into Tom Watson. "I'm banging my head against a brick wall with Ed," I said. Tom told me I needed to get to know him better and suggested I try socialising with him. My response can be imagined.

———————

Labour's fate in the 2015 general election wasn't entirely sealed in Scotland, but the road to defeat started north of the border. We in Unite had been telling Scottish Labour for many years that it had to wake up and smell the coffee. It could get away with taking the Scottish working class for granted when there was no real alternative, but an agile and alert party had arrived to fill the vacuum.

I watched the rise of the SNP with both horror and fascination. Here was a case study in what can happen if the Labour Party abandons its radical traditions. The SNP used to be mocked as 'Tartan Tories,' but they recast themselves as a social democratic party and stole Labour's clothes. With a charismatic leader in Alex Salmond, followed by another charismatic leader in Nicola Sturgeon, they were a formidable threat. It beggared belief that Scottish Labour couldn't see it.

The rot went back well before the independence referendum of 2014. The SNP won Govan in Glasgow from Labour in the 2007 Scottish parliamentary election—Sturgeon was the victorious candidate. In 2011 they took control of Holyrood under a system designed to prevent a majority government. By the time the referendum came around in 2014, there had already been a shift under the surface with more progressive voters identifying with independence.

Labour was losing the Scottish working class—that was being communicated to us loud and clear by Unite members. To the fury of our regional secretary in Scotland, Pat Rafferty, our concerns were dismissed out of hand by the Scottish Labour Party, which was more Blairite than its English or Welsh equivalents. When Pat and I met the Scottish Labour leader, Johann Lamont, and the shadow Scottish secretary, Margaret Curran, in Pat's office in Glasgow, we warned that the coming referendum could have serious consequences for Labour's base and urged them to push for 'devo max'—a real extension of powers for the Scottish parliament—to be an option on the ballot paper. We thought it had the best chance of uniting those on both sides of the argument. Lamont and Curran were utterly dismissive. Lamont declared: "We will put independence to the sword once and for all." Fat chance of that. Both Pat and I were astonished and dismayed at their arrogance.

It was no use pretending the Scottish working class wasn't divided on the issue. I was advised that half Unite's membership in Scotland favoured independence, the other half was against. To back either Yes or No in the referendum would have split the union down the middle, so we adopted a neutral position.

As the referendum campaign unfolded, a stark contrast emerged. There was huge vibrancy on the Yes to independence side—not just embodied by the SNP but expressed by the younger left in the Radical Independence Campaign— while those urging No were headed up by Better Together, with staid Labour politicians sharing platforms with staid Tories and Liberals. I remember the appalling imagery of a train packed full of English Labour MPs travelling up to Glasgow to tell Scots how to vote. Associating Labour with Better Together and sharing platforms with Tories was a disastrous mistake. Our members were telling us traditional Labour voters were furious.

There were calls for me to go up and join the campaign. I remember the Blairite commentator John McTernan writing in the *Scotsman* that he wanted one man to come to Scotland to support the No campaign and that was me, describing me as the authentic voice of the working class. Ed Miliband rang and said, "Len, I desperately need you up here, we've got to fight for this."

I said, "Well, Ed, look, unfortunately my hands are tied, my union has adopted a neutral position."

What I didn't tell Ed was that if I'd had the luxury of speaking as an individual, I would have argued for independence. Had I been a socialist in Scotland I would have seen Westminster as a drag anchor holding us back from building a fairer society. I would have backed independence on the basis that it would give Scots a better chance of implementing socialist policies. As for the argument that such a path meant abandoning workers in the rest of the UK, I would have hoped it would encourage English workers to get up off their knees. Later, my position on this changed when the political context was transformed by Jeremy Corbyn, who rekindled the hope that socialism could make gains across the UK.

On the day of the referendum vote I was in George Square in Glasgow where the Yes campaigners were massing. It was incredible—full of young people and energy. It felt strange, because I expected No to win, and thought that come midnight those people would be disappointed. As I walked back to my hotel three lads and a girl shouted, "It's Len McCluskey" (Glasgow is a city where I get recognised a lot). They asked how I would have voted if I'd been able to. I said I would have voted Yes. The four of them cheered and ran back to the square.

My thoughts went back to the meeting with Lamont and Curran. Had Labour embraced 'devo max,' those four Scots, along with thousands of other young people, wouldn't have felt so betrayed and let down by the party. I believe the option would have won the day and the looming SNP tsunami could have been averted.

Lessons must be learned. Labour's continued opposition to another independence referendum is, I believe, an error. It should instead embrace a new vote, without initially committing to one side or the other, but say it will openly debate and engage with the public to decide its position. Old-style unionism gives the Conservatives a foothold, much of it wrapped up in Protestant identity. Labour's only path back to relevance lies in reclaiming from the SNP the mantle of radicalism and hope. Of course, I understand the socialist argument that class shapes the daily lives of Scots and that we shouldn't get diverted into a constitutional issue. I've made that case many times myself. But if Scottish workers keep responding by saying, "Fuck you," that's real politics that Labour needs to come to terms with.

If supporting another referendum is outside the bounds of possibility for Scottish Labour, then it will need to be imaginative in proposing an alternative or be condemned to the political wilderness. A way forward might be to engage seriously in a debate about federalism. As I write, a number of mayors, most notably Andy Burnham in Greater Manchester, are challenging the UK government for a fairer distribution of wealth. Such brave and defiant leadership may provide a model for uniting people behind demands for power to be brought closer to the people. I've long been attracted to the idea of having a constitutional convention to hammer out these matters.

In the aftermath of the referendum, Lamont resigned. Unite and most of the trade unions backed Neil Findlay, the left candidate, to succeed her, but Jim Murphy emerged as the favourite, promising to "do a Tony Blair" and end Labour's losing streak. He was precisely the opposite of what Scottish Labour needed if it was to have any hope of countering the SNP's positive appeal, as I told Miliband in his office on the day he called me in for a dressing down.

I would have been delighted to have been proved wrong. Unfortunately, what befell Labour in Scotland in May 2015 was much worse than even my darkest warnings. We lost 40 of our 41 Scottish seats as the SNP virtually swept the board, taking 56 of 59 constituencies, including Murphy's seat of East

Renfrewshire and also Falkirk, the supposedly safe Labour seat that had been at the centre of so much grief.

According to the psephologist Professor John Curtice, Labour was out-flanked on its left. "Those who voted Labour in 2010 but subsequently switched their support to the SNP after the referendum," he concluded, "were both dis-proportionately in favour of a more equal society and more likely to regard the SNP as the party that shared that view." I believe there was also a desire to give the establishment a slap in the face, and, especially after the spectacle of the Better Together campaign, Labour was perceived to be the establishment.

The wipeout in Scotland held many lessons for Labour. It showed the dan-ger of losing touch with our working-class base and being seen to side with the status quo. It was a prelude to what happened in the party's English heartlands in the 2019 election, when working-class communities that had been Labour for generations abandoned us. The comparison isn't exact, but it was a warning of what could happen.

There is a postscript to the story of Scottish Labour's demise. In 2017, when I was campaigning in my third general secretary election, I came out of Glasgow Airport late at night and waited at the taxi rank. Suddenly, I heard a voice say, "I hope you lose, Len." I turned around to see Jim Murphy, but he was already walking away. The snide way in which he did it said everything about the man. He didn't even give me the opportunity to say, "Well, you know all about losing, Jim."

I had serious doubts about Ed Miliband's chances of winning the 2015 general election, but I hoped against hope that he would. Despite my anger with him over Falkirk, I acknowledged that he had broken from New Labour. His most popular policies were those that sounded left wing: raising income tax for high earners, increasing the minimum wage, restricting zero-hours contracts, freez-ing energy prices—all good announcements that gave activists a boost. I also thought he was brave to oppose the bombing of Syria in summer 2013.

One area where the unions were heavily involved was on the workers' rights agenda—but this was kept secret from the public. Miliband appointed John Monks, a former general secretary of the TUC who I liked, to develop a workers' charter and a programme of action to put British workers on a more level playing field with our sisters and brothers in Europe. The central thrust and most radical element was the reintroduction of sectoral collective bargaining, allowing trade unions across a whole sector of the economy to negotiate a collective agreement with employers to cover every worker in that field, preventing companies competing by undercutting on pay and conditions and setting workers against each other. Monks' agenda would have undone the Tory trade union laws that shackle British workers and swapped the race to the bottom culture for a rate for the job society.

Miliband and his policy advisor Torsten Bell were on board with the plan but wanted it to fly under the radar going into the 2015 election. It certainly wouldn't be in the manifesto. It was typical of the attitude that regards trade unions as an embarrassment and a vote loser—a case of, "We'll give workers rights, but let's not tell the workers." Still, it would have been a major advance.

That uneasiness about who we were and the values we held was echoed in other areas of policy, most famously with the "Controls on immigration" mugs. They were a terrible response to the threat of UKIP—who were making headway in many working-class areas—by playing to the most base fears people held. The mugs reflected an entirely wrong way to approach immigration—talking up "legitimate concerns" without dealing with the issues that contributed to those concerns. I didn't agree either with those who wanted to shut down the conversation on the grounds that talking about immigration panders to a right-wing agenda. I took the view that you have to both talk about immigration *and* deal with the issues that arise from it, otherwise you leave a vacuum to be filled by the most despicable, racist opportunists.

What was too often ignored in the debate was the brutal exploitation of the migrant workers themselves. For example, of the 3,500 workers in the massive Sports Direct warehouse in Shirebrook, Derbyshire, 3,000 were migrant and agency workers—and some of the agencies would only take on migrant workers. Why? Because they were easier to exploit. Unite exposed the conditions faced by those staff, including the case of a Polish woman who gave birth in the warehouse toilets because she was scared that if she missed her shift she would lose her job and her accommodation. Any abuse of working people, wherever they come from, should be fought against. It was telling that Labour had a plan to do just that—the Monks plan—but kept it under wraps, while promoting the immigration mugs.

Another area where Labour played into the agenda of our opponents was on the deficit. It was self-defeating for the leadership to go along with the idea that the deficit was the most important issue facing the country; doubly harmful to allow the falsehood to persist that it was high because of Labour; and, given that's where we put ourselves, triply damaging for Miliband to then forget to mention it at all in his final conference speech before the election. That speech was delivered without notes, a trick that looks impressive but is inherently superficial because it draws people's attention to the technique rather than the content. Miliband fell into a trap of his own making. The mistake allowed the media to portray him as hapless.

Miliband's performance in the 2015 election campaign itself was good, but he was already fixed in the public's imagination as a weak leader. The Tories were merciless in driving that home with a poster of Miliband in the pocket of Alex Salmond, scaremongering that in the event of a hung parliament the SNP would call the shots. I began to receive feedback in the union that workers were buying into the idea of "these fucking Scots running the show." It was very powerful.

On the night of the election, I was in a pub in South London waiting for the exit poll. I still thought Labour might win, but as soon as the figures were revealed I knew it was over. The Tories had cannibalised the Lib Dems in the South West and the SNP had obliterated Labour in Scotland. Some desperately wanted to believe the prediction was wrong, but I just went home.

Some good did come of that election. Unite's political strategy helped excellent candidates get selected to contest winnable seats. The poor result meant much of that effort was in vain, but there were several Unite-supported candidates who did get elected in 2015, some of whom almost immediately played a crucial role in the rise of Jeremy Corbyn.

One thought nags me to this day: what would have happened if Labour had gone to the country on an unashamedly anti-austerity programme that addressed the real problems people faced, in an era before Brexit hung like a cloud over British politics? Just two years later Jeremy Corbyn would do just that and, despite facing opposition from the media and his own party that was far more ferocious than anything Miliband had to contend with, he showed there was an appetite in the country for bold, radical change. It is immensely difficult to break with the economic orthodoxy, but had Miliband been willing to do it, history could have been very different.

CHAPTER 14

THE RISE OF JEREMY CORBYN

The race to succeed Ed Miliband as Labour leader had been running for a month when I bumped into the favourite, Andy Burnham, at a trade union drinks reception in parliament.

From the moment Miliband had announced his resignation on election night, hopefuls had been jostling to replace him—Burnham, Yvette Cooper and just about every Blairite in the parliamentary party. The debate was depressing. The Blairites were straight out of the blocks with their explanation for Labour's defeat: Miliband had been too left wing, alienating "aspirational" voters—or those who "aspire to shop in Waitrose," as Tristram Hunt put it (I kid you not). The Blairites had been waiting for their moment to take back the party, and their confidence seemed to convince everyone else it had arrived.

The contest was pulled to the right as candidates competed to win the support of fellow MPs, whose nominations they needed to get a place on the ballot paper. The contenders fell over themselves to attack the last Labour government's public spending; Cooper came out in support of the Tories' cut to corporation tax; and Burnham attacked the mansion tax.

Andy was to the left of the other candidates, but he lurched rightwards, abandoning the soft-left ground he could have made his own. He was so desperate to avoid being seen as another Miliband that he announced his campaign would accept no funding from trade unions.

Andy was a friend, so when he came over to greet me at the crowded reception in parliament I asked him frankly, "What game are you playing?" He thought he needed to woo the right, believing that the left wouldn't vote for any of the other candidates. "There is such a thing as being too clever for your own good," I said. "You do know that today Jeremy has thrown his hat into the ring?" He looked at his friend and mine, Steve Rotherham, who confirmed it was true.

It was 3 June 2015. In another room in the Houses of Parliament, the Socialist Campaign Group, a tiny collection of honourable but largely ignored left-wing Labour MPs, had met to decide whether to stand a candidate. They had no expectation of winning, but felt they needed to do something to change the awful leadership debate. After Diane Abbott and John McDonnell ruled themselves out, McDonnell turned to Jeremy Corbyn and said: "Your turn." Corbyn agreed to do it. The course of Labour Party history was about to alter.

No one thought so at the time, of course. When I told Andy that Jeremy was standing, he didn't even know. I had previously reassured him he was likely to secure Unite's endorsement for leader. But now I told him that if Jeremy got on the ballot paper that would no longer be the case. "You understand that changes the dynamics dramatically?" I said. Neither of us knew quite how dramatically.

––––––––––––

I've been involved in politics all my life, but I've never felt anything like the excitement that gripped me in the summer of 2015. Jeremy Corbyn's rise to the Labour leadership was unbelievable. Conventional wisdom said it couldn't happen. All summer I thought, "Something's bound to stop us, it can't go on like this." The prospect of the left leading the Labour Party was unlikely enough; the idea of doing it with a candidate like Jeremy—unambitious, unpolished and unknown beyond the left—was so far-fetched it would be rejected by film studios if written as a script. A man who was no Tony Benn when it came to oratory somehow touched the pulse of everyone on the left who was desperate for change. It was electric.

It was a long shot that Jeremy would even secure a place in the contest. He had to win enough nominations from MPs to clear the threshold of 15 per cent of the Parliamentary Labour Party. The trade unions had managed to lower that threshold to what we thought was an achievable level during the Collins Review negotiations, but even so, it was a tall order for Jeremy and his allies to persuade 35 MPs to back him in the space of just 12 days. The other candidates had been ticking off nominations for weeks. John McDonnell wasn't sure it could be done, having twice failed to clear a lower threshold himself. But Jeremy had a big advantage: his colleagues liked him. He was seen as friendly and unthreatening. And many MPs were quietly alarmed at how far to the right the leadership debate had gone.

As soon as Jeremy announced he was standing, I was in no doubt where my sympathies lay. My frustration with Ed Miliband was that he hadn't been determined enough to challenge the economic status quo. Andy Burnham's early pronouncements showed he had no intention of doing so either. I had no such fears about Jeremy. But, as the general secretary of Unite, my job was to influence the next leader on behalf of my members. No one—least of all the man himself—predicted that would be Jeremy. Within Unite we had a debate about what to do. If Jeremy failed to get on the ballot paper Unite would be backing Andy, so we couldn't burn our bridges. We decided not to publicly call for MPs to nominate Jeremy but worked behind the scenes, keeping a check on the nominations and quietly doing what we could to help.

Corbyn's small team did an incredible job of calling and cajoling potential nominators, but there was another force at play that was quite new to me: social media. Thousands of party members and trade unionists emerged out of nowhere to bombard MPs with messages saying, "Give us a debate." I hadn't realised how powerful that could be. Corbyn's people were convinced that several nominators who would never have helped a left candidate in previous contests were persuaded by online pressure.

By the final morning of the nomination phase, 15 June 2015, Jeremy had picked up 18 of the 35 endorsements he needed, with several more MPs promising to hand in their signed forms to the PLP office in parliament before the midday deadline. During the morning some surprising names arrived to nominate him—most famously Margaret Beckett, at the time a good friend of mine with a long history of working with the T&G and Unite. I don't know if that's what swayed her. I was sad later on to see her call herself a moron for nominating Jeremy and then become part of a group that undermined him.

As the deadline of noon drew near, Jeremy's team believed they had scraped their way to 33 nominations. John McDonnell, new MP Cat Smith and veteran left-wing organiser Jon Lansman were in the PLP office making desperate, last ditch efforts to persuade four wavering MPs to give their endorsement. All four said they would only do so if Jeremy needed just one more name to clear the bar.

Meanwhile, Tom Watson, who was then a candidate for the deputy leadership, was hanging around just outside the office, busy on his phone. Earlier that day Lansman had called me to ask if I could persuade Watson to help the Corbyn campaign get over the line. As it happened, I had already spoken to him. He had explained to me that he wasn't going to nominate anyone for leader because he was hoping to become deputy and would need to work with whoever won. Well, it's funny how that worked out. But I agreed with the logic. Instead of nominating Corbyn himself, Watson promised to use his influence to persuade some of his allies to do so. But as the deadline approached I spoke to him again and said, "If Corbyn fails by one and you haven't nominated him when you were being asked to, then the left, which is much of your support, won't forgive you." He said if one vote was needed he would do it.

So when Watson was standing outside the PLP office absorbed by his phone with just minutes to go, he was texting the MPs inside the office urging them to nominate so that he didn't have to. Lansman came out in a panic, telling Watson his nomination was needed because the others weren't doing it. Watson said, "I think you've got it, don't worry, they'll do it."

Inside the office McDonnell literally got on his knees to beg for two more nominations as the seconds ticked down. Farcically, it later turned out that Corbyn only needed one—his team had missed one in their calculations. But in the end it didn't matter—two MPs, Gordon Marsden and Andrew Smith, stepped forward to hand in their forms.

The PLP's veto over a left winger leading the party—which had been weakened by the trade unions in the Collins negotiations and challenged by the campaigning efforts of thousands—had been overcome.

———————

I was ecstatic when the news came through that Jeremy Corbyn was on the ballot paper. Suddenly, it was going to be an interesting contest. It didn't occur to me that he could win, but I thought he would build support for ideas and policies that had been totally ignored up to that point.

The immediate issue was that Jeremy had no campaign infrastructure and no money. His team was just a few dedicated people giving their time for free. These were crucial days at the outset of the contest. Jeremy could quickly have become a laughing stock if his operation was revealed to be shambolic and amateurish. For Unite to fund a candidate, our executive council would usually have to vote to endorse them. But the urgency was too great, so I authorised a £50,000 loan to the Corbyn campaign, enabling them to hire staff and buy materials. Other unions pitched in too, including the TSSA which provided an office.

My attention then turned to Unite's official endorsement. As far I was concerned, Corbyn was our candidate. Very early on I said to my chief of staff, Andrew Murray, "I'll be supporting Corbyn. My task is how do we make certain that we carry the executive with us?" There was no chance of Unite backing the Blairite candidate, Liz Kendall. A number of executive members who weren't even particularly on the left said they would resign from the Labour Party if she became leader. There was little support for Yvette Cooper, and she wasn't in the ballpark for me. That meant it was between Corbyn and Andy Burnham.

In truth, the executive was always going to favour Corbyn because 43 of its 63 members were part of the United Left group and most would follow my line. But I had to make certain we took people with us. I wanted to allow the executive to arrive at its decision in a way that minimised the friction within the union. My style of managing these things was to listen to all sides, argue with them if need be, but ensure everyone understood where others were coming from. That's how I had successfully unified the union since 2011. I saw it as my responsibility to maintain that unity. Plus, at that point in the contest I thought Burnham was likely to win. In that eventuality I would need to have influence with him, so I was careful not to create the impression that I had railroaded the union into supporting Corbyn against its wishes.

Some in the press misinterpreted this as me clinging on to the hope of backing Burnham and reported that the executive overruled me. Nothing could be further from the truth. When the executive met in Brighton on 5 July 2015 to decide which candidate to endorse, I was delighted that Corbyn won the vote with ease, 34 votes to 14, with Burnham's supporters comfortable with the decision. Had I not wanted it to be Corbyn, the numbers would have looked very different.

I've no doubt that was a critical moment in Jeremy's rise. Until then, he was the outsider, the also-ran, the novelty candidate standing simply to widen the debate. What Unite's endorsement gave him above all else was legitimacy—the kudos of being backed by Labour's biggest and most powerful affiliate. It made people want to jump on his bandwagon, not least activists in other trade unions.

Unite nominated Corbyn early in the contest, although we were still beaten to it by two smaller unions—the train drivers' ASLEF and the bakers' BWAFU, as well as the RMT and the FBU which were not affiliated to Labour. But crucially, Unite's endorsement came well before the decision of the other giant, the public sector union Unison. Dave Prentis and the Unison leadership would have preferred Cooper, but they were facing a grassroots revolt within their union and Unite's nomination put them in a difficult position. Eventually, they had to give way. Once Unison came out for Corbyn the momentum was unstoppable. I'm sure Unite's endorsement also influenced the choice of the CWU postal workers' union. Corbyn ended up winning the backing of six Labour affiliates, including the railway workers' TSSA, representing the overwhelming majority of workers in affiliated trade unions.

Unite's endorsement meant Corbyn had money to spend. As soon as our executive council officially nominated him we poured resources into the campaign. We donated £100,000 on top of the earlier loan, provided office space in our headquarters for volunteer campaigners, and seconded staff, including Anneliese Midgley from our political department, who became deputy to Corbyn's campaign manager Simon Fletcher, a good man with whom we had worked closely over the years.

Unlike the other unions, Unite threw everything at getting our members signed up to vote. The complicated Collins Review system meant trade unionists not only had to opt in to paying a share of the affiliation fee to Labour, but had to opt in again if they wanted a vote on the leader. The five-year implementation period for this arrangement—negotiated in the expectation of Ed Miliband remaining leader—now had to be condensed into a few months. Whereas under the old system 2.7 million trade unionists were eligible to vote, we feared that unless the unions made an effort, a derisory number would opt in, putting wind in the sails of those who wanted to cut Labour's ties with organised labour. And that's exactly what would have happened, had it not been for Unite. We signed up over 100,000 of our members in a few weeks, making up the majority of the 150,000 affiliated supporters who received a ballot paper. Of course, every one of them was free to vote as they wished, but I believe Unite's endorsement did persuade most of our eligible members to back Jeremy.

Alongside our pick for leader, we also had to back someone for deputy. I hoped we would support Tom Watson, but there was a push on the executive for Angela Eagle, who would give gender balance to the leadership team and was then seen as more to the left than her opponents. Again, I wanted to maintain as much unity as I possibly could, so we actually nominated both of them and gave each a donation of £50,000. Tom then came back asking for a further £20,000, which we provided. Years later, when relations between Tom and I had soured and he was trying to engineer my replacement as general secretary by Gerard Coyne, he made a public dig about Unite members wanting to know where all their money went. I thought, "What a short memory, Tom, you should know."

––––––––––

It was when I arrived at Unite headquarters late one evening to find 400 volunteers squashed into every available inch of the office making phone calls for Jeremy Corbyn that I truly felt the buzz his movement had generated. Young people were everywhere; the best of a generation that I never thought I'd see getting involved in party politics. There were volunteers from all class backgrounds and every ethnicity. Lifelong trade union activists sat next to students getting their first taste of politics. All of them were single-minded in making the impossible possible. It felt exhilarating.

I got the same feeling at Jeremy's mass rallies. We became used to him drawing in the crowds in the years that followed, but in the summer of 2015 it was startling. Here were thousands of people queuing around the block to pack out venues to listen to a veteran backbencher just say what he believed. It was extraordinary and inspirational.

Jeremy's campaign was the nucleus around which a genuine movement came together. Contrary to the media myth, it wasn't a case of outsiders or entryists overrunning the Labour Party. In the first few weeks of the campaign, before most of the press had even noticed he was standing, Jeremy had the bulk of existing Labour Party members backing him—those loyal Labour men and women who believed in socialism but had always been told they had to bite their tongue. Here was a candidate saying they didn't have to. Then, as the endorsements racked up, the trade union movement swung behind him. Those fighters for dignity and workers' rights knew Jeremy well. Unlike most of his colleagues in parliament, he was never scared to be seen on a picket line with them. His years of dedication to every worthwhile cause meant he was also trusted by the social movements: the peace campaigners, the international solidarity advocates, the disability rights activists, the anti-racist fighters, the Occupiers, the environmentalists and, of course, the now massive anti-austerity movement. Many of them weren't even in the Labour Party but here was a reason to join—or at least pay £3 to get a vote as a registered supporter. Tens of thousands took the opportunity.

When all those people came together with one aim, it set off a chain reaction—the movement exploded. People suddenly rediscovered something that had been missing from our movement for many years: hope, the most powerful of the emotions; hope that there could be a better future for all. Like so many others, I wanted to be part of it. It was like jumping into a fast-flowing river—just diving in and seeing where it took us.

I remember watching three young people on the news. They were asked why they were so excited about Corbyn. They replied they had never heard anyone say the things he was saying. Journalists and commentators may have scoffed at his ideas and said they were from the past (unfairly, as it so happened), but anyone under the age of 30 had only ever been told that there was no alternative. Now, for the first time in decades, an alternative to austerity and neoliberalism was being placed before them.

That's what the British establishment was afraid of. They were shaken to the core as the popularity of Corbyn's ideas became obvious. And that was the reason the media—including the supposedly left-liberal media—launched vicious attacks day in, day out, from the moment a Corbyn victory looked possible.

It soon became clear to everyone that the establishment extended into the heart of the Labour Party itself. The party machine was mobilised against Jeremy. We now know that in Labour HQ the idea of stopping the contest was actively discussed. His supporters were purged and denied membership. Meanwhile, twisted figures from the New Labour past were wheeled out to denounce the outsider threatening to disrupt their cosy club. Tony Blair tried it three times; it only boosted Jeremy's appeal.

The hostility of the PLP became unmistakable as MPs collaborated with the hostile media to brand Corbyn a dangerous extremist. But he embarrassed them all in parliament by breaking the whip to become the only leadership candidate to vote against the Tories' cruel Welfare Bill on 20 July 2015. The decision of the Labour front bench to abstain on the Bill exposed how far the PLP had spun off from the wider party and lost its moral bearings. For most members and trade unionists, there was no question that Labour should vote against legislation that would plunge hundreds of thousands of children into poverty. If members wanted a leader who felt the same, Corbyn was the only choice. His campaign went stratospheric. I kept asking my people, "Is he really in with a chance?" The answer came back, "Yes." All the polls, all the campaign data, showed things were just getting better and better.

The Welfare Bill spelled the end of any real challenge from Andy Burnham who, against his better judgement, followed the whip and abstained. He would later admit his regret. He would have won if Jeremy hadn't entered the contest. Although he was not a right-winger, those around him were. He was being advised on strategy by Michael Dugher, then an MP, later a lobbyist for the gambling industry. People like Tom Watson used to tell me Dugher was a great campaigner. The campaign he ran for Andy was amateurish and diabolical and must go down as the worst in Labour Party history.

Yvette Cooper was an experienced performer, but everything she put forward was hollow and vacuous. The Blairite candidate Liz Kendall was particularly poor. Her eventual result, winning 4.5 per cent, was astonishingly bad. It exposed that the right of the Labour Party had nothing to offer. There was a dearth of visionary policies because Blairism had run its course. The right was probably at its weakest point in history. They still had their organisations Progress and Labour First; they still had money, profile and access to the media; but it was all a mirage.

Jeremy's campaign showed that those who appeared mighty in the Labour Party could be brushed aside if the conditions allowed. He was simply brilliant: so relaxed, so comfortable, so at ease with himself. His off-the-cuff speeches were hardly rhetorical tours de force, but it didn't matter. Here was a man who wasn't like the other politicians, who wasn't trained and rehearsed to within an inch of his life. Here was a man who wasn't afraid, a man you felt couldn't be bought. All those years of New Labour's message discipline had produced bland politicians who never said what they really thought, if they had any thoughts. Jeremy excited people because he was the opposite of that. The Jeremy of summer 2015 was a breath of fresh air. I only saw that Jeremy again once, in the 2017 general election. I wish he'd always been there.

By the eve of the result being announced, victory was already in the bag. I spoke at Jeremy's final campaign rally in Islington on 10 September 2015. It was a wonderful atmosphere; a celebration. That didn't stop me getting into trouble though. I told the audience: "Seventeen weeks ago I was listening to the debate,

I was listening to Liz, Yvette and Andy, and I reached for the nearest, sharpest object so that I could slit my wrists because the blandness and the sameness of that was depressing." Well, the next morning I had all these angry emails telling me how offensive I had been. At first I thought it was some kind of joke but as I read on I realised, Christ almighty, people wanted me to put on a hair shirt and walk across hot coals. It turned out 10 September was World Suicide Prevention Day. What are the chances? I had to write back to all of them apologising and promising to make a donation to charity.

I didn't go to the conference for the announcement of the result on 12 September 2015. I was very conscious that the media could turn Jeremy's victory into a Unite or a Len McCluskey thing, as they had done to Ed Miliband. The last thing I wanted to do was contaminate Jeremy—he was going to have enough problems of his own. So I watched the result being announced on TV—and what a result it was.

Jim Kennedy, Unite national officer and the chair of Labour's National Executive Committee, read out the figures. Burnham won 80,000 votes; Cooper 72,000. Then came Corbyn: 251,000 votes. I was bowled over. I hadn't expected it to be that emphatic. Kennedy had to wait for the pandemonium in the hall to subside before delivering another shock: Kendall's paltry haul of 19,000 votes. Corbyn won 59.5 per cent in a four-horse race, giving him a landslide victory in the first round with no second preference votes needed. He won in every section: members (49.6 per cent); trade unionists (57.5 per cent); and £3 registered supporters (83.9 per cent). My one worry had been that Jeremy would do significantly worse among members than the other two sections, undermining the legitimacy of his leadership. The result banished that notion, and I later read that he won handsomely even among longstanding party members from the New Labour era.

I joined Jeremy's celebrations later that afternoon in the Sanctuary pub in Westminster, and also went across the road to The Old Star pub where Tom Watson was enjoying his victory in the deputy contest. It was a great day. Jeremy's thumping mandate should have commanded respect right across the party—and from humbled Labour MPs in particular. Instead, the wreckers got to work immediately.

CHAPTER 15

OUT OF THE FRYING PAN INTO THE FIRE

"Look, which one of you is going to fucking step up to the plate?" I said.

Paul Mason, Owen Jones, Kevin Maguire and Seumas Milne looked back at me. None volunteered.

"Are you all two-bit revolutionaries? Which one of you is going to get out the ammunition and go to the front line?"

The five of us, together with my chief of staff, Andrew Murray, were in the Pink Room in the Stafford Hotel in London. I had invited the journalists to come for a meal shortly before Jeremy Corbyn's stunning victory in the 2015 leadership contest. I was paying.

"We're going to get our person in there but he's got no one around him. Which one of you is going to be his director of communications?" I persisted.

There was silence. I felt like hitting them all with a frying pan. Then, one by one, they made their excuses. Paul Mason said he needed to stick with his job at Channel 4 News. In a way, given Paul's later political journey, that was a blessing in disguise. Owen Jones argued he'd be more use as a supportive columnist at the *Guardian*. I liked Owen a lot and he was certainly quite brilliant at projecting the left's cause in the media—especially on TV, the camera loved him—so that seemed reasonable. Kevin Maguire, for whom I have great affection, was never a Corbyn-supporter to start with, I don't know why.

"Well, Seumas, that leaves you," I said.

Now, I love the bones of Seumas. He has a brilliant mind. But sometimes he prevaricates. He wasn't sure. To be honest, nobody was sure.

Meanwhile, the media were lying in wait, incandescent that someone from outside their bubble was about to occupy the top job. They would take any opportunity to make our new left-wing leader look amateur and shambolic. Facing them were just a handful of good comrades hopelessly out of their depth. It would be a rocky beginning.

———————

When Jeremy Corbyn was elected with a landslide, the left thought it was time to pop the champagne corks and party in the streets. It was only when dawn broke that the weaknesses of his campaign, of the movement, and of individuals were cast in an unforgiving light. Only then did the enormity of the task before us hit home. The truth was, we were nowhere near power, neither in the country nor even in the Labour Party.

Had Andy Burnham or Yvette Cooper won the leadership, their network of allies would have slotted smoothly into the Leader's Office. What suddenly became clear after Jeremy's victory was that nobody around him knew what they were doing. I don't criticise them for that. None of them had done anything like it before. Mistakes were being made left, right and centre and there was no guru figure to say, "Woah, no, no, no, you're doing this wrong"—including me. I'd never led the Labour Party; I didn't know what it entailed and, in any case, I had my own job to do—which was as complicated and full-on as ever.

But I was conscious of my responsibility. Without taking anything away from the hundreds of thousands of people who helped put Jeremy where he was, it couldn't have happened without Unite. That put an onus on us to make it work, and I desperately wanted it to work. I was five years into my time as general secretary, I was still overhauling my union, and now here was an even more daunting task. With any other Labour leader my job would have been—as it was with Ed Miliband—working out how to exert influence. With Jeremy, I was part of the Corbyn project, essential to it. It was a much bigger role for me.

None of that meant I was calling the shots—far from it. That much was evident even before Jeremy won. In the final weeks of the leadership contest, as victory became more certain, a broad cross-section of people privately expressed their doubts about Jeremy's plan to make John McDonnell his shadow chancellor. Neither Dave Prentis nor Paul Kenny could stand McDonnell due to past run-ins, but the concerns went well beyond them to other left comrades. All kinds of people were saying, "It can't be John McDonnell, it can't be." He was too abrasive, too provocative, too controversial. That message was communicated to Jeremy and John by Unite's Steve Turner at a meeting of Corbyn's closest allies in early September 2015. It didn't change their minds. So people started to say, "Well somebody's going to have to tell Jeremy directly." And it landed on me.

Jeremy came to my office on the Wednesday before the weekend of his victory. We sat down together. "First of all, you're going to win and that's an unbelievable achievement," I said. "You're then going to need to choose a shadow cabinet. You can't pick John as your shadow chancellor. I know he's your mate but it's a mistake. I'm speaking on behalf of a whole host of your comrades here, we think John is too divisive and you're going to have to think of someone else, maybe Angela Eagle" (this last idea was not my best). For 10 minutes I pressed the point, even discussing the possibility of splitting the job of chancellor in two—as Harold Wilson had done in the 1960s when he created the role of Secretary of State for Economic Affairs to reduce the power of the Treasury—giving John control of long-term economic strategy while someone else managed the day-to-day finances. (Ironically John later proposed a version of this idea himself in the run-up to the 2019 election, except with him as chancellor.)

When I finished my spiel I half expected Jeremy to say, "That's a load of bollocks, Len." But that wouldn't be Jeremy. Instead, he asked: "Have you spoken to John about this?"

"No," I said, surprised.

"Why don't you speak to John?" Jeremy asked.

"Well... OK," I replied, somewhat confused.

The very next day John was sat in the same chair that Jeremy had occupied 24 hours earlier. I said: "Look, John, you're Jeremy's best mate, you're putting him in an awkward position, you really should say, 'Don't put me in there.'"

John replied: "Len, fine. That's not going to happen. I'm going to be shadow chancellor." He explained it was essential that the leader and chancellor were tight because they were going to present a genuine alternative to the economic orthodoxy. They couldn't afford for the top two to be pulling in different directions—Labour had suffered badly because of the disagreements between Tony Blair and Gordon Brown and Ed Miliband and Ed Balls.

"Fair enough," I said, "that's a strong argument. I'm not going to convince you, but I've discharged my duty."

A fortnight later, at the Labour Party Conference in Brighton, John delivered the best speech I've ever heard from a shadow chancellor (or a chancellor, for that matter). His "bank manager" tone was exactly what was called for, playing against type. The framing of the speech was brilliant and the content ambitious. I thought this was a guy who knew what he was doing. I sent word that I'd like to meet him.

When John arrived at the small Queensbury Arms pub round the back of the Metropole Hotel at 9.30 that night, I greeted him by saying: "John, I owe you an apology."

"No, you don't," he said.

"I absolutely do," I insisted. "I've just witnessed one of the finest speeches I've ever heard and I now realise that I was wrong. So were others, but I was wrong. You are absolutely the right man for this job."

To this day I stand by that. While John and I later disagreed on Brexit strategy, I thought he was a brilliant shadow chancellor who would have made a great chancellor. Transforming the debate about the economy, against all the odds, was an extraordinary achievement. In a few years, austerity economics went from being the accepted orthodoxy of the mainstream and a selling point for the Tories, to something no one wanted to admit they had ever believed in.

That was largely down to John's success in articulating an alternative and fleshing out the economic policies needed to achieve it.

Jeremy's determination to make John his shadow chancellor dominated the process of assembling a shadow cabinet. The resistance from the Parliamentary Labour Party was fierce, with some MPs refusing to serve if John was given the job. But it was Jeremy's priority, and he was willing to compromise elsewhere in order to get it.

If, from the start, I had really had the influence I was sometimes credited with, the majority of Jeremy's first shadow cabinet wouldn't have been appointed. In Unite we wrote down our suggestions for each ministerial position and submitted the names. I'm afraid few of them made it.

Jeremy's first move was to reappoint Ed Miliband's chief whip, Rosie Winterton. She was a wily old operator who was never onside. On the day after Jeremy won the leadership, a Sunday, Winterton would only permit the leader and his chief of staff Simon Fletcher into her office to put together a shadow cabinet. John was apparently told to stay outside because of some archaic rule. At this point, someone should have said "No," but both Jeremy and Simon were conflict averse. I've no doubt that had Karie Murphy—who later took over as Jeremy's chief of staff—been involved from the beginning she would have told Rosie where to go, got John in the room, and insisted the two of them take their time to get it right.

As it was, the shadow cabinet appointed by Jeremy, Rosie and Simon was a disaster. I don't criticise Jeremy for that. He was under enormous pressure, with no experience to draw on, a shortage of MPs willing to work with him, and a chief whip he didn't trust. Assembling a shadow cabinet is difficult and complex. But when the names were announced to the press that Sunday night I thought, "How has this happened?" We had a shadow cabinet the bulk of which not only came from a different faction from the leader, but actively hated everything he represented—some of the most venomous, treacherous snakes in the party. Most of them would only manage a few months before resigning in a coup. Michael Dugher, of all people, was shadow secretary of state for culture, media and sport. I don't know if he just misunderstood his role, but he seemed to think the media part of his brief meant he had to tell journalists what was happening in every shadow cabinet meeting and drip-feed them poison. It was like putting Dracula in charge of the blood bank.

It wasn't like the media needed any encouragement to attack Jeremy in those early days, yet he was left with no protection—there was no infrastructure around him. Even on the night he appointed his shadow cabinet, there was no car to take him home and he ended up walking through the streets of Westminster after midnight followed by a Sky News journalist barking questions he wouldn't answer. Then there was the controversy over him not singing the national anthem at a Battle of Britain memorial service. The attacks were coming in by the minute but he had no communications team to rebut them.

That's why I had organised the meeting with Paul Mason, Owen Jones, Kevin Maguire and Seumas Milne, in the hope of having someone in place. Seumas was persuaded to leave his job as a columnist for the *Guardian* and become Jeremy's executive director of strategy and communications. McDonnell wasn't keen when I suggested it—he always had an issue with Seumas, perhaps because of their different political backgrounds. But Jeremy had enormous respect for him.

Yet it was six weeks into Corbyn's leadership before Seumas could unravel himself from his contract and take up his new role in late October 2015. Despite his efforts to help behind the scenes, those six weeks of damaging media coverage left their mark. When rumour spread about Seumas' likely appointment, the attacks were immediate. He was briefed against by MPs and knifed in the back by old colleagues. The picture painted of him as an ice cold, ruthless operative was a million miles away from the warm, kind, humorous man I knew—although they were right about his political steeliness. I thought, "Wow, if this is what it's like when a member of staff is appointed, we're in for a rough ride."

I think it was difficult for Seumas to begin with. He was stepping into a role he had never done before. He was used to writing to a deadline, job done. In the Leader's Office it was all go, 24 hours a day, with, at that time, few resources to call upon. But had it not been for his unwavering confidence and calmness under pressure, the Corbyn leadership would have been lost. Those that have sought to blame him for every misstep, and especially for the 2019 election defeat—including those from the left—are shockingly wrong.

———————

The moment the dysfunction at the heart of the Labour Party burst into public consciousness was the parliamentary debate on bombing ISIS in Syria at the start of December 2015. The spectacle of Jeremy Corbyn opening proceedings with a speech against military action, only for his shadow foreign secretary Hilary Benn to wind up the debate from the same dispatch box, for the same party, arguing the opposite case was just ridiculous. Benn's speech was praised to the heavens by the Tories, lobby journalists and warmongers everywhere, including Tony Blair. I thought it was a disgrace. His attempt to cast the RAF's bombing campaign as following in the footsteps of the trade unionists and socialists of the International Brigades who volunteered to fight fascism in Spain in the 1930s was disgusting. My political hero, his father Tony Benn, must have been turning in his grave.

On the day of the vote, I received a call from Tom Watson as I was sitting in a plane at Heathrow waiting to fly off to New York. He was agonising over voting in favour of the bombing. I urged him not to. "But, Len," he said, "I've been briefed by MI6 on all of the issues involved."

I replied: "For fuck's sake, Tom, there's a surprise—the British security services have come up with good reasons to bomb. Please remember Iraq. Don't do it."

He did anyway.

The following day I had the privilege of meeting UN Deputy Secretary General Jan Eliasson. It was supposed to be a five-minute 'meet and greet' set up by my friend Mark Seddon who worked in the UN at the time. It lasted one-and-a-half hours. What an incredibly impressive man I found him to be. He made it clear with the force of reason that the decision to bomb taken by the British parliament the night before was wrong. I thought to myself, "I wish he was the one briefing Tom instead of the British security services."

By this point, a few months into Jeremy's tenure, I had become exasperated by the failure of Corbyn and the Leader's Office to stamp their authority on the party. I said publicly that Jeremy was on a "learning curve." What I meant was I wanted to see him lead with greater firmness. I believe he should have sacked Benn before giving him the chance to make that speech from the front bench and faced down a shadow cabinet revolt rather than concede a free vote on the issue to Labour MPs.

To be fair, the leadership did try to impose its will. Knowing that many, perhaps a majority, of Labour MPs were fond of bombing things, Jeremy had emailed Labour members asking for their views on the matter. Seventy-five per cent of responses opposed military action. That strength of feeling from below helped limit the number of Labour parliamentarians who voted with the government to 66, about a quarter of the PLP. I had also done my bit to pile on the pressure, writing in an article that, "If those Westminster bubble-dwellers who hanker back to the politics of the past cannot show the elected leader—and those who voted for him—more respect, then they are writing their own political obituaries. So be it—but the price should not be paid in Syrian lives." It was reported that those words provoked anger at a meeting of the PLP. I was conscious that I was becoming a hate figure for the right wing of the party and the media. They were starting to believe that to get rid of Jeremy, they would need to get rid of me as well.

Some thought their chance to depose Jeremy might come sooner than that, immediately after the Syria vote, in the Oldham West and Royton by-election called following the death of Michael Meacher. There was talk that UKIP was going to take the seat. In fact, to the bafflement of the media, Labour won comfortably, increasing its share of the vote by seven points. That bought Jeremy some time and space and meant he was able to conduct a limited reshuffle in January 2016, finally sacking the despicable Dugher but still allowing Benn to continue in post.

———————

In those early months, Jeremy Corbyn's operation was a mess. The Leader of the Opposition's office (LOTO) was a complex institution. So many things needed attention that few people on the left had ever had to think about—short money, staffing, parliamentary procedures, managing the PLP, dealing with the party machine. Getting to grips with all of that while under laser-sharp scrutiny from journalists desperate to exploit every minor stumble was a nightmare for an inexperienced team—and that's before factoring in the relentless wrecking and briefing by MPs and the incessant campaign by party bureaucrats to leak and block everything the Leader's Office wanted to do.

Jeremy had appointed Simon Fletcher as his chief of staff. That seemed sensible—Simon had run Ken Livingstone's mayoral operation and worked for Ed Miliband. He was known to have a very sharp brain and to be good at campaigns. He had taken on the running of Corbyn's leadership bid when there was no real likelihood of winning and little prospect of getting a job out of it. So it was quite right that Jeremy hired him. The problem was, just like Jeremy, he didn't like confrontation. That was not a good combination in the circumstances.

Simon's deputy was Anneliese Midgley, previously of Unite. The two of them were close friends, from the same stable. Like Simon, Anneliese had worked for Livingstone and was also good at campaigns. She had done well for Unite. But neither were equipped for dealing with the myriad of problems that confronted them.

At best, the operation could be described as slipshod, made up largely of people who had jumped on the Corbyn campaign as it was rising, had done a fantastic job, but were now drowning. I was soon getting reports that the office was chaotic, staff felt desperate, morale was through the floor, and discipline had broken down.

I went to see John McDonnell around Christmas in 2015 and he confirmed to me that it was a "fucking disaster." I suspect John would have cut through these staffing problems very quickly if he had been in charge, but Jeremy was loath to sack anyone. I said, "Well look John, the only thing I can think of is I can take Anneliese back to Unite to make the necessary change for Karie Murphy to take over as deputy chief of staff and start to pull things together." John welcomed the idea.

My confidence in Karie's abilities was not blind faith. She was an unbelievably strong working-class woman, Glaswegian through-and-through, precisely the kind of fighter Jeremy needed in his corner—with the added bonus that she brought industrial experience which was missing in the operation. Much later, as Karie became more high profile, rumours abounded about our personal connection. The media, desperate for a way to undermine Corbyn, constantly threatened to expose that we were involved. We had no intention of providing them with that ammunition, so we engaged the press in a game of cat and mouse, getting Howard Beckett to use his legal genius to knock out gossipy stories. We wanted our relationship to be kept private, away from the public gaze.

Andrew Murray had first raised the idea of Karie going into LOTO. He asked me if I thought she could be chief of staff. I wasn't sure. Nobody was sure. At the time Karie didn't know what it entailed and didn't have a close connection with Jeremy. So we suggested the idea of her going in as deputy.

I arranged to meet Anneliese and Simon at the Blue Boar Bar near St James' Park. I offered Anneliese the job of political director of Unite—a prestigious role. She was flattered and after some discussion agreed to take it. She did a good job.

Karie started in LOTO as office manager in February 2016. As soon as she got there she called me and said, "Oh my God, it's fucking unbelievable." Staff would come and go whenever they pleased. People would roll in at 11.30 a.m., Karie would say "Where have you been?" and it would turn out they had been "working late" the night before—in the pub. There was no discipline at all.

Karie got on well with Simon but it was clear he wasn't suited to the role of chief of staff—nice guy, good comrade, but not right for that job. Fairly quickly, through sheer force of personality, Karie took effective control and began to knock the place together. Eventually, in June 2016, Simon decided to formally move aside and become Corbyn's campaigns director, before leaving LOTO in February of the following year. It took a while before Karie was officially given the title Chief of Staff. Jeremy didn't like the phrase, thinking it too militaristic, and Karie wasn't a bit interested in the formalities. I insisted it was important. It was only in October 2017, when Andrew Murray, my chief of staff, began assisting in Jeremy's office as a consultant, that I persuaded Karie to speak to Jeremy and get him to agree the title. People needed to know there was only one chief of staff and that was Karie.

I dread to think what would have happened if Karie hadn't gone into LOTO. It would probably have collapsed completely. Even her critics (and she did gain a few) conceded that she professionalised what had been a shambolic operation. She hardened it up. From then on, the attacks on the Corbyn project were no longer for stupid, avoidable mistakes, they were political attacks that could be anticipated and countered. Suddenly, Seumas had an ally in Karie, and together with Andrew Fisher, who was appointed executive director of policy around the same time, the trio formed a very strong bond that powered the project forward.

Jeremy even began to smarten himself up. He was certainly looking more the part and coming across well in media interviews. The May 2016 local elections came amid forecasts of doom, but just as in the Oldham by-election, Labour outperformed expectations, beating the Tories in projected national vote share. Things seemed to be getting on track. But then we were straight into the European referendum campaign, and British politics was about to be turned on its head.

———

It was clear to me from quite early on that the Remain campaign was in some difficulty in 2016. The trade union movement, with the exception of the RMT, was solidly in favour of staying in the European Union. But many of our members were not.

The evolution of my own position on the EU mirrored that of the left in general. I was opposed to the UK being in the Common Market in the 1975 referendum, part of the Bennite 'No' vote. We saw it as a bosses' club that would undermine the organised working class. But by 1988, when European Commission President Jacques Delors came to speak to the TUC at the instigation of T&G General Secretary Ron Todd, attitudes were changing, primarily because Margaret Thatcher was kicking the living daylights out of us. Here was Delors laying out a vision of a social Europe, with protections for workers' rights and collective bargaining enshrined at the European level. Along with most of the trade union movement, I cautiously bought into it.

In subsequent decades it became evident that the promised social dimension was not living up to its billing. The European Union remained, basically, a business club in the way it operated. I saw that first hand through my involvement in many European works councils as a T&G officer. By the time of the 2016 referendum I couldn't argue that the status quo was brilliant, but I didn't think leaving was a sensible option, especially for our manufacturing sector. I said the same thing about the EU as I had said about the Labour Party: if you're part of an organisation you aren't happy with there are two options: try to change it, or leave. We hadn't had the chance to try to change the EU in a leftwards direction. Obviously, we weren't going to get that chance under a Conservative government, but there was now the prospect of a radical Labour government coming to power and working with socialist parties and trade unions across Europe. So my position, and that of Unite, was: remain and reform. That was an easy slogan to say; it would be rather more difficult to bring it to fruition. But the alternative—a disorderly exit under Tory stewardship—would be costly for Unite's members.

That was also the conclusion reached by Jeremy Corbyn. He didn't have much option. Had the Labour leadership advocated Leave the party would have split asunder, but he knew very well the shortcomings of the EU, especially on issues of democracy. Remain and reform was the correct position: we wanted to stay in Europe, but there were all kinds of things that needed to be put right. That was a more genuine stance than the one taken by the Europhiles—including many who should have known better—who presented the EU as some kind of utopia. It just wasn't believable either in the referendum campaign or in the years after it, which is one reason why they eventually went down to total defeat. The vitriol thrown at Jeremy when he rated his passion for the EU as "seven, seven-and-a-half" out of 10 was so misguided. His view was far closer to the feelings of millions of people than that of his ultra-Remain critics. Repeated polls during the referendum campaign showed him to be the first or second most trusted politician on the issue, and easily the most trusted Labour figure.

Jeremy was also attacked for not joining the official establishment Remain campaign and for refusing to share platforms with Tories. Again, he was absolutely right to insist on a separate campaign and to make different arguments, as anyone who paid attention to the calamitous Scottish referendum experience knew. Neither did I have any sympathy with those who claimed a lack of effort on his part was to blame for Remain losing. He did vastly more than every other member of the shadow cabinet, including all those who would later use the result as a pretext to resign. Alan Johnson, in charge Labour's referendum campaign, didn't get an ounce of criticism for his own performance—and nor should he. But he was invisible in comparison. What actually happened was that the media became obsessed with divisions in the Tory party, dumbing down the issues at stake into a personality contest between Boris Johnson and David Cameron, and barely gave any coverage to the Labour message.

Beneath the superficial picture painted by the media, things were changing on the ground. Remain might have been the only respectable position in liberal, middle-class circles but there was a spirit of revolt brewing among the working class. I could feel it as I went around the country campaigning. In workplaces I visited our shop stewards and activists would say, "Len, we get what you're saying to us, but we've got to tell you that on the shop floor our members are absolutely hostile to the EU." I thought, "My God, this is going to be really interesting and it may even be close."

Midway through the campaign I bumped into Boris Johnson just inside the entrance to Portcullis House in Westminster. "Hello Len," he said. I didn't know him well but we had attended some of the same events over the years.

"How do you think it's going—the campaign?" he asked.

"Oh, I don't think it's going too well. I think a lot of our members will be voting Leave."

"Yes, yes," he said, "that's what I'm picking up."

I couldn't resist having a pop at him. "You'll be trying to take over here next," I said. "That'll be no good to us because you hate trade unions."

"That's not true," he claimed. "I don't hate trade unions. I think trade unions are a good thing."

"OK then," I said. "As soon as you get into Number 10 I'll be expecting you to give me a call."

He promised he would. He never did.

David Cameron did though, in a roundabout way. I was in Belfast during the latter half of the campaign when Frances O'Grady, the general secretary of the TUC, rang and told me the prime minister had asked the chancellor George Osborne to meet the general secretaries of Unison and the GMB, Dave Prentis and Tim Roache, and me. Behind the scenes, the government had indicated to Tom Watson and Labour's chief whip Rosie Winterton that it wanted trade unions to do more for the Remain cause. They replied that perhaps trade unions were too busy trying to defend themselves from the Tories' vindictive Trade Union Bill then going through parliament. The government responded that it could modify the Bill, and so Tom and Rosie set up a meeting. It wasn't unusual for a Conservative government to meet the TUC, but since Margaret Thatcher's time it had not been the done thing for the most senior Tory ministers to meet individual trade union general secretaries.

The government offered two time slots for the meeting, one of which Dave couldn't make and the other I couldn't. Since I was in Belfast I told them to go ahead without me, but Frances said they were particularly interested in me being at the meeting, they wanted to see the whites of my eyes. So I flew back and Frances, Tim, Rosie, Tom and I met the chancellor and a few of his team. They asked if we could do more. My view was yes, we would do anything, provided the government addressed certain problems with its Bill. They were very receptive. For example, we were concerned about a provision allowing anyone to ask the Certification Officer to investigate a trade union. They assured us a minister would speak from the dispatch box to clarify that wasn't the intention of the Bill and the facility would be withdrawn if it was used in such a way. Sure enough, that clarification was given.

It was a good deal as far as I was concerned because, in fact, Unite had already done all we could for the Remain side. When Alan Johnson had called me at the outset of the campaign I cut to the chase and asked how much he wanted. The maximum allowable was £250,000, he said. "You've got it," I told him.

The government was right to be worried about what was happening in working-class communities beyond its reach. People who had experienced nothing but decline in their local area saw voting Leave as a way to shake things up, to slap the metropolitan elite in the face for decades of neglect. So when the result became clear in the early hours of 24 June 2016 I was not shocked. I thought about the bumpy road ahead—including for the labour movement, which would have to deal with the fact a large number of our people had rejected the position of their representatives at work and in politics. It would require some humility and understanding on the part of trade union leaders and the PLP to regain their trust. The PLP, however, had other priorities.

CHAPTER 16

THE CHICKEN COUP

It was the weekend after Britain voted to leave the European Union. The government was in turmoil. The prime minister had announced his resignation. The Tories looked on the brink of a split. The country's future was uncertain—no one had a clue what would happen next. Millions of people were anxious. Racist hate crimes were surging. But as I flicked between news programmes, all they were talking about was a coup against the leader of the Labour Party.

All day it went on as one shadow minister after another resigned live on TV. Late the previous night, on learning that his shadow foreign secretary Hilary Benn was plotting a coup against him, Jeremy Corbyn had called his great friend's son and sacked him. That fired the starting gun on the coordinated resignations: first Heidi Alexander before 9 a.m., then Gloria De Piero at 11, Ian Murray at noon, Lilian Greenwood at 1, and so on. Twelve resigned throughout the day and eight more the next—most, not all, scurrilous individuals who should never have been in the shadow cabinet to begin with. The crescendo came when Angela Eagle brought herself to tears over her own resignation on air. What a pitiful display.

The sheer arrogance of these MPs—who owed their stature to being in the shadow cabinet, not the other way around—attempting to cancel the democratic choice of hundreds of thousands of Labour members by inflicting as much damage as possible on their own party left me aghast. It was a betrayal that should never be forgiven. With each one that went, part of me thought, "Fuck them. Good job they've gone. Replace them immediately." And that's exactly what happened. Corbyn refused to be bullied out, while some of the worst people in the Labour Party purged themselves from his shadow cabinet, leaving it a considerably better team.

Watching those resignations, I didn't have a moment's doubt that I would be doing everything possible to defend Corbyn's leadership.

———————

The 'chicken coup' of summer 2016 was one of the most extraordinary and shameful episodes in the history of the Labour Party. It confirmed the worst accusation levelled at the Parliamentary Labour Party and the bureaucracy in HQ: that they would rather destroy their party than allow the left to succeed. But it also brought out the best in the movement that had formed around Jeremy Corbyn, mobilising hundreds of thousands of people to take politics into their own hands and cut the MPs down to size. The role played by the trade unions was critical. This was the moment when, without Unite, Corbyn would have gone under.

The result of the EU referendum was the pretext used by MPs for the putsch they had been threatening to launch since day one of Corbyn's leadership. Of course, it made no sense. Labour had delivered two-thirds of its voters for Remain. As for the other third, anyone who thought the result would have been different had Jeremy told the Labour heartlands all was well with the EU was living in a dream world. It was easy to do that from an oligarch's yacht or a bank boardroom but it wasn't so convincing in our deindustrialised cities and towns.

Labour politicians had urgent work to do protecting employment rights and jobs from Conservatives who saw Brexit as a mandate to introduce a free-market dystopia at the expense of working people. Instead, they decided this was the moment to turn inwards, let the Tories off the hook and busy themselves with overturning a landslide leadership election held just nine months earlier.

Margaret Hodge led the charge on the day after the referendum, proposing a vote of no confidence in the leader. What a hypocrite—here was an MP blaming Corbyn for the result and yet her own constituency ignored her advice and voted overwhelmingly to Leave, one of the few to do so in the Remain strong-hold of London. When the PLP's confidence vote was taken a few days later—in a secret ballot, because the MPs didn't have the guts to answer for their actions to their local members—172 voted no confidence, 75 per cent of the parliamentary party. These were people you would never want alongside you on the battlefield.

From the outset, supporters of Corbyn, including me, were saying if MPs wanted to get rid of the leader they should put up a challenger and take him on democratically—the rules allowed it. But they wouldn't do that because they knew he would win. That's why they came up with novel, unconstitutional ways to force him to resign, like the vote of no confidence, the staged shadow cabinet resignations, and the old tactic of simply abusing him to his face at a disgraceful meeting of the PLP on 27 June when they attempted, in Diane Abbott's words, to "break him as a man." What despicable, spineless people they were.

However, they hadn't reckoned on Corbyn's inner strength, or on the strength of those who rallied around him. At the same time as that infamous PLP meeting was taking place, a spontaneous demonstration gathered in Parliament Square. Thousands turned out to give a message of defiance to the PLP. Corbyn went directly from being pilloried by MPs in Westminster's Committee Room 14—told by no-marks he wasn't "fit to be prime minister" and that resign-ing would be "the most important contribution you can make to the Labour Party"—to being cheered to the heavens by a large and emotional crowd out-side. It can't have done his morale any harm.

The party experienced the most spectacular membership surge ever seen in those days and weeks, with 130,000 new members joining in a fortnight. Online, more people signed a motion of confidence in Corbyn than had voted for him in the original leadership election.

That's not to say these weren't precarious times for LOTO. The pressure was enormous. Some of Corbyn's allies among MPs buckled. People who should have known better advised him to go. Karie Murphy played a critical role by shielding Jeremy from personal lobbying by MPs. At one point Andy Burnham—who to his credit had initially refused to join the public resignations—coordinated a group of supportive MPs who intended to tell Jeremy privately they were going to stand down. Karie thwarted them by calling Jeremy, who was on his way into parliament, and telling him to turn around while she locked the door to the Leader's Office and picked off the waverers one by one.

I was resolved to do whatever I could to shore up Corbyn's position, including intervening on broadcast media and in print to warn the plotters that if their betrayal succeeded in ousting the leader without a democratic contest, they would split the party. But the most important thing I could do was to bring the other unions with me.

I pulled together a coalition of trade unions that went well beyond those that had supported Corbyn in the first leadership contest. Importantly, it included the GMB, which had sat it out in 2015, and Unison, which despite having endorsed Corbyn had a leadership who, I think it's fair to say, were not his biggest fans. As it happened, it wasn't difficult to persuade them—my pitch was that what was being done was a fucking outrage. No one could argue with that. There was a feeling that Jeremy and John deserved a chance. My task was to catch that common ground to get a unified position.

A statement signed by the general secretaries of 12 trade unions—Unite, Unison, GMB, CWU, UCATT, TSSA, ASLEF, FBU, Musicians' Union, BECTU, the Bakers and the NUM—was issued on 24 June, before the shadow cabinet resignations began. It said: "The last thing Labour needs is a manufactured leadership row of its own in the midst of this crisis and we call upon all Labour MPs not to engage in any such indulgence."

The PLP ignored our advice so on 29 June we put out another statement saying, "our members and millions of others will be looking with dismay at the events in parliament," and telling MPs to "respect the authority of the Party's leader." At the time, with the Labour establishment attempting to force Jeremy's resignation or prevent him from standing in another contest, merely getting into a leadership election looked like it would be a victory, so the statement said Corbyn "should not be challenged except through the proper democratic procedures provided for in the Party's constitution."

Crucially, having a unified position meant I was able to speak for the trade unions in negotiations behind the scenes. I cleared that with all the other unions, including even the traditionally right-wing USDAW. I knew who I would be negotiating with—the man who had positioned himself as the PLP's *de facto* leader in the crisis: Tom Watson.

———————

I first met Tom Watson in 2010. I was living in my friend Jim Mowatt's house in Bermondsey, London. Tom needed a place to stay and, the following year, he moved in with Jim and me. In the course of the two years we lived together Tom and I struck up a strong friendship. He was good fun, intelligent, not obviously ambitious. He liked music and we enjoyed many nights out in Soho's nightclubs and bars. He was a nice fella, a decent, good friend.

Politically, he came from the right wing of the party. He had worked for the right-wing engineers' union the AEU. They had catapulted him into parliament. He said he was "dazzled" by Tony Blair but became much closer to Gordon Brown and ended up organising the 'curry house plot' that forced Blair from office. By the time I knew him, Tom was certainly moving left. In our debates and discussions he progressively became more radical. He would take a lot of advice from me. I think Karie Murphy also influenced him—she worked for him in parliament and was his confidante, carrying him through some dark times in his personal life.

Tom was brave in taking on the Murdoch press from 2011, which earned him support from the left. When the News of the World was closed due to the phone hacking scandal Jim Mowatt and I gave Tom a framed copy of its final edition, which he kept on display in his office. After Tom published his book, 'Dial M for Murdoch,' I remember saying over a drink: "Tom, you've become a working-class hero." He denied it, but I told him, "You have, but take a piece of advice from me: don't ever betray the left because, if you do, they will never, ever forgive you."

Why I said that I don't know. I really didn't expect him to betray the left, but, of course, I knew he was a complex MP who liked the Machiavellian side of politics. There were doubters among my friends and within my union. Our chair, Tony Woodhouse, always thought Tom was a phoney, something he has reminded me of many times.

By 2015, when he ran for deputy leader, Tom had discovered he could have great success by positioning himself as essentially soft left. So what happened to turn him into the nemesis of the left that he became? Only Tom knows. I've been asked many times and I genuinely don't have an answer. My best guess is that the radicalism of Jeremy Corbyn, his willingness to rock the boat, spooked Tom and caused him to retreat back to his old networks on the right of the PLP and in party HQ, where he had strong relationships with General Secretary Iain McNicol and his cronies. Those people looked to Tom, as deputy leader, to be their figurehead, which probably both appealed to him and put him under a degree of pressure.

What I know for sure is that by the time of the coup he was lost to us. He had become duplicitous, which leads to disloyalty. He would say he was loyal to the party but, as I repeatedly pointed out, the job of the deputy was to support the leader—debate and disagree in private, of course, but support the leader in public. That support was never forthcoming from Tom, which is why a vicious, disreputable, right-wing PLP trusted him to be their unofficial shop steward when the crisis arrived.

The key meeting took place in Tom's office on Thursday, 7 July 2016. By then the coup had stalled. Corbyn had simply refused to resign and the plotters didn't know what to do. They were still desperate to avoid having to take him on in a democratic contest. Activists were mocking their prevarication and cowardice, branding their insurrection a 'chicken coup.'

In the room with Tom and me were the chief whip, Rosie Winterton, and the chair of the PLP, John Cryer (who was pretty irrelevant). My remit was to say: "Back off, there should be no challenge to Corbyn, he deserves an opportunity." They raised the usual objections—the opinion polls were a disaster (in fact, Labour had polled level with the Tories on the very day the staged resignations began), he was a weak leader who didn't perform well in the referendum.

I said these accusations were outrageous—he had only just been elected. They responded by asking how long they should wait—until it was too late? That sparked a discussion about the possibility of a two-year breathing space with an agreement to look again at Jeremy's performance and polling in specific parts of the country in 2018 (believing the next general election would be in 2020). What I was desperate to do was buy time for Jeremy and John, to give them a real shot at it. They were under a level of pressure that, frankly, I thought they might not survive.

I went from Tom's room to the Leader's Office to report back to Jeremy, John, Karie and Seumas Milne. I told them I was trying to hold off the PLP and we were discussing having another look in 2018. They didn't agree to that idea—I don't remember if they even reacted to it because I floated it very tentatively—but they were aware of the priority to buy time.

When I returned to Tom's office, he was now unambiguously pushing for Jeremy to step down. "Let me make something crystal clear," I said, "that isn't on the table. I haven't come here with any option at all for Jeremy Corbyn to step down. That will not happen—I'm speaking on behalf of every single trade union—that will not happen so you can forget that. I'm prepared to talk about seeing where we are two years out from the next election, but that's all."

Rosie said we would all need to think and meet again and suggested Monday. I said I would be down in Brighton from the weekend for Unite's policy conference. Tom asked if it was possible to meet on Sunday in Brighton, because his dad lived on the South Coast and Sunday was his birthday. The date was set. I would facilitate the meeting and invite other leading general secretaries.

I made arrangements for Dave Prentis of Unison, Dave Ward of the CWU and John Hannett of USDAW to come down to Brighton; Tim Roache of the GMB couldn't make it. As John would be coming from Manchester, Unite booked him a room in the Grand Hotel.

The following day, 8 July, Jeremy Corbyn had an article about Brexit in the *Guardian*. Towards the end of the piece he addressed the situation in the party, writing:

I have made clear I am ready to reach out to Labour MPs who oppose my leadership—and work with the whole party to provide the alternative the country needs. That's why I am pleased that trade union leaders are exploring ways to bridge the gap and work together more effectively. But MPs also need to respect the democracy of our party and the views of Labour's membership... Those who want to challenge my leadership are free to do so in a democratic contest, in which I will be a candidate.

I received a text from Tom:

Hello Len, this article by Jeremy in today's *Guardian* will probably end my ability to hold the PLP back today. It's not been widely read yet but suspect when it does we'll just have to expect the rest is inevitable.

I replied:

I'm not sure why you feel so pessimistic, Tom, the article just about gets it right... As I said yesterday, you haven't got a magic wand and if you can't hold people together so be it. I've got the other GSs to now engage in what will be difficult negotiations but ones where, if we had the time, I believe could produce a solution. Your belief that the courts might rule Jeremy out [from being on the ballot in a leadership contest] will undoubtedly split the party and there's no doubt in my mind that some of the right of the party want that. The idea of Unite disaffiliating would suit them and they are not interested in Labour losing elections so, as I said yesterday, we should just stay focused on trying to do the principled thing and if it falters we can walk away with our heads held high.

Tom responded:

It's that he says there is no other prospect than a challenge to his leadership. Let's see what happens when MPs have read it.

I wrote back:

He also said that he wants to reach out and he is in talks with the unions. A statement about a challenge is the only way to unseat him now, is a statement of fact. Tom, if you are getting cold feet just let me know, please.

I received no reply. A bit later on I text again:

Tom, Brighton looks good, Dave Ward, Dave Prentis, John Hannett and me, Tim can't make it but that's OK, maybe Paul Kenny will deputise. Tell Rosie and John, the Grand Hotel, lunch provided, I'll ring you later.

Again, no reply. I persisted:

Tom, can you confirm that you are all coming to Brighton, 2pm?

The following morning I drove down to Brighton with Jim Mowatt. I turned on the radio in the car and the breaking news was that Tom Watson had pulled out of negotiations with the trade unions. I was furious.

That moment marked the death of a friendship. I haven't spoken to Tom since, save for a few barbed texts two years later when his attempt to unseat me as Unite's general secretary failed.

Livid, I put out what journalists described as an "incredibly strong statement." I said I was "dismayed" by Tom's actions, which I labelled "an act of sabotage." I pointed out the arrangements for the meeting had been "requested by Tom Watson and his colleagues, specifically for Mr Watson's convenience." I also accused him of a "deeply disingenuous manoeuvre" by suggesting that Jeremy's *Guardian* article marked a change of position, since "Jeremy Corbyn's resignation as the leader was not on the agenda."

I don't know why Tom couldn't manage the courtesy of letting me know he was pulling out of the talks. I read somewhere that he said he was scared to. Had he picked up the phone and said, "Lennie, this is a waste of time, I can't move the PLP and, to be honest, your refusal to persuade Jeremy to step down means it's just pointless," I would have said, "Fine, come down to Brighton and we'll put together a joint statement and end our discussions in a comradely fashion." For him to not even contact me—his friend—beggared belief.

Tom had entered discussions as Mr Fixer for the PLP with a view to doing Corbyn in. I can only assume he realised he wasn't going to be able to deliver that. Perhaps his real motivation was to become interim leader without having to get his hands dirty. Maybe he thought he could then cobble together enough support to stay on without a contest. Neither a leadership challenge nor a two-year breathing space would lead to that outcome, so perhaps he decided there was nothing in the talks for him. Whatever the truth, it was a squalid, ignoble way to end a valued friendship.

―――――――

While the negotiations were taking place, others were preparing for a leadership challenge that increasingly seemed the only way out. During her tearful performance on TV on 27 June, Angela Eagle had insisted her decision to resign was a spontaneous response to the sacking of Hilary Benn. But John McDonnell had suspected her of planning a challenge for some time. So, a while before the coup, I went to ask Angela—who had been my friend since she and her twin sister Maria joined my Constituency Labour Party in Crosby, Liverpool, aged 16—if it was true. Typical of her, she started complaining about not being properly respected by the leadership. I said, "Angela, that's a load of rubbish. You're the shadow first secretary of state and the top woman in the shadow cabinet. Anyway, I'm asking you a simple question: have you been approached to run?" She said she wasn't going to run.

Once the coup broke it immediately became clear that Angela was, in fact, going to run. She had a website registered, a campaign seemingly ready to go, and was reportedly being advised by some of the worst elements from the New Labour era. But she didn't want to run against Jeremy Corbyn, so she prevaricated for two weeks hoping he would resign, incurring ridicule every time she made a statement announcing she would imminently be making a statement. That was slightly unfair, because one reason she kept delaying was that I was asking her to wait for the negotiations with Tom Watson to reach a conclusion.

When Tom scuppered the talks, Angela finally declared herself a challenger. I called her. "I'm not saying this as a general secretary of a union but as a friend who has known you for a long time," I told her. "You are being used and you will suffer." The rest is history. Her woeful media performances and a disastrous press conference, during which most of the media walked out to cover a more exciting story, meant her candidacy was as short-lived and humiliating as it was dishonourable. Her own CLP in Wallasey turned against her, leading to its suspension by the party machine on charges that were questionable at best. Had the 2017 snap election not intervened, denying her local party the chance to have a say over its candidate for the seat, she would have been deselected.

With their customary sense of loyalty, the PLP dropped the faltering Angela like a stone and instead summoned up their brightest and best talent: Owen Smith. Owen had been Jeremy's shadow work and pensions secretary before resigning on TV as part of a contingent of departing soft-left MPs that included Lisa Nandy. He came to my office to tell me he was thinking of throwing his hat into the ring and promised he wouldn't attack Jeremy. He agreed with all Jeremy's policies, he said, but thought he was the better person to deliver them. I told him, first of all, he would inevitably be pressured to attack Jeremy, and second, he was going to lose.

The fact we were, by this point, into a formal leadership contest represented something of a triumph for Jeremy. He had not been forced out, and a battle that had hitherto been fought in the TV studios and the corridors of Westminster would now be undertaken in the open, among the party membership, where Jeremy thrived. But there was one more obstacle to clear first.

It had been feared all along that where the PLP had failed, the party machine might succeed. We knew, and our enemies knew, that if Corbyn was on the ballot paper in a fair leadership election he would win. So for hostile party officials, ensuring he couldn't even join the contest was their number one priority. The party rulebook seemed to suggest an incumbent leader would automatically be in the race if a challenger triggered a leadership challenge. But an alternative reading held that the leader would have to go through the process of securing MPs' nominations in order to stand. In 2015, Corbyn had just scraped 35 endorsements. But the threshold was higher when there was no vacancy for the top job, meaning, in this scenario, Jeremy would need to secure 51 nominations. There was very little chance of that.

The question of whether Corbyn had an automatic place on the ballot was to be decided at a meeting of the National Executive Committee, Labour's governing body. At the time, the left didn't control the NEC. Many of those in and around the leadership had little understanding of how it worked. At Unite we realised that we, too, had to get more involved in the intricacies of the committee than had ever been necessary in the Miliband era. We stepped into the role of coordinating and rallying the left elements on the NEC, especially the trade union representatives.

On the other side, Labour's general secretary Iain McNicol and his senior staff were seen to be working hand in glove with right-wing representatives on the NEC and were prepared to use every trick in the book to fix the result they wanted. The long-anticipated meeting was called at 24 hours' notice for 12 July when two left representatives, one of them Unite's Martin Meyer, were away on holiday. Both managed to get back. It was decided that votes would be taken in secret to prevent the "intimidation" of NEC members, although the real reason was to encourage trade union delegates to vote against the position of their unions.

McNicol himself was reportedly prepared to put his job on the line to keep Corbyn off the ballot. His big play was to circulate legal advice to the meeting that said the leader had to secure fresh nominations. Had that been accepted, the matter might not even have been put to a vote—McNicol could have insisted the law was the law. But at Unite we'd been expecting such a move. We didn't trust McNicol as far as we could throw him, so I had asked our legal director, Howard Beckett, to commission our own advice. He was absolutely brilliant at covering off the legal angles with our barristers. At the NEC meeting, McNicol only allowed the author of his suspect opinion to make a presentation, but Unite and other left representatives challenged his interpretation using our advice.

I was getting updates in my office as the meeting progressed. It was nail-biting stuff; touch and go. Eventually, after many hours, the news came through that we had won the day. The NEC had voted 18 to 14 that Jeremy did not need to seek nominations. In saying so, the NEC was legally correct—the matter later went to the High Court, which agreed with Unite's interpretation of the rulebook. McNicol's legal opinion had been wrong.

It's no exaggeration to say that on 12 July 2016, Unite put Jeremy Corbyn on the ballot paper. The role played by Howard Beckett was critical to the outcome of the meeting. Without us, Jeremy might well have gone under there and then.

Having lost the main battle, McNicol and his allies nevertheless managed to win later votes to restrict the franchise and reduce Corbyn's advantage in the leadership election. A retrospective freeze date was imposed, meaning only those who had been members for at least six months could vote, disenfranchising at a stroke a quarter of the party membership—which had swelled to more than half a million under Corbyn, an incredible phenomenon. The fee to become a registered supporter was hiked from £3 to £25. In the days following the meeting, party officials launched a new purge of members, debarring some left wingers on the flimsiest of pretexts.

But no matter how the party machine tried to skew the contest, the sheer numbers massing to defend Corbyn overwhelmed it. The members excluded by the freeze date signed up as registered supporters instead—despite the £25 fee. In a deliberately short 48-hour window, 180,000 people applied for registered supporter status (doing wonders for the party's finances). Once the campaigns got out on the road, Corbyn was met by thousands of supporters everywhere he went. The rallies were far larger than in 2015. I saw Jeremy speak on St George's Plateau in Liverpool on 1 August. The rain did its best to dampen proceedings, but 10,000 people came out to support him regardless. Lime Street had to be closed. Two days earlier, Owen Smith had held his own outdoor rally in Liverpool. It attracted fewer than 100 people, even though he was giving away free ice cream. I was told that once the attendees got their ice cream, half of them disappeared before Smith spoke. Once again, I was so, so proud of my city.

The race was a foregone conclusion. Smith's imitation act on policy meant the only serious dividing line between the two candidates was his pledge to support a second Brexit referendum, but in 2016 that failed to excite the membership. Desperate, Smith reneged on his promise not to attack Jeremy and instead adopted a scorched earth strategy, launching vicious attacks on sections of his own party. It was an unedifying spectacle. It was also disappointing to see the unified position of the trade unions during the coup fragment slightly for the leadership contest, with the GMB and USDAW backing Smith, although Corbyn was supported by more affiliated unions than in 2015.

When the result was announced at the Labour Party Conference in Liverpool on 24 September, Corbyn won by a bigger margin than he had the previous year, taking 62 per cent of the vote. Given the tirade of abuse and lies unleashed against him in the interim, that was quite remarkable. The right's attempt to depose him had greatly strengthened the left. On austerity, the economy and domestic issues Corbyn's agenda was totally dominant—the right hadn't even dared challenge it.

But, although the right was beaten on ideas, they had no intention of calling off their campaign of sabotage. They were well dug-in—the left could easily win a one-member-one-vote leadership election, but its strength wasn't represented in the structures of the party. Corbyn's opponents even had control of the 2016 conference. So, when it was my turn to speak, I thought it was important to have a pop at the merchants of doom, but I wasn't certain how it would go down. I said:

> I've heard people lecture us about the futility of principles without power, but comrades, we've also seen where power without principles leads to. It leads to disillusionment, disappointment and ultimate defeat. Of course, we must win power, but we must also use power for our people, for working people. So I ask all of you not to be debilitated by the media and those within our own ranks who seek to undermine your confidence in the fight that lies ahead. And I say to the merchants of doom, in the words of Shakespeare's Henry V, if you have no stomach for this fight, depart the battlefield.

As I said "depart the battlefield" the whole place erupted. I was taken aback. I looked out at a blur of people rising to their feet, but directly in my eyeline one individual with flowing white hair stood out, even though he was right at the back: it was Tosh MacDonald, a great comrade, then president of the ASLEF train drivers' union, jumping up and cheering. I've been fortunate to deliver some electrifying speeches over the years but that was perhaps my best moment. It was an extraordinary response.

In summer 2016 the PLP and the Labour bureaucracy openly and shamelessly sought to reverse the democratic choice of the party and impose their will. But uniquely in Labour Party history, they failed. Party members and trade unions simply said no. The outcome revealed the power that lay at the grassroots. For me, it further vindicated the stance Unite took over the Collins Review in 2014. When an empowered membership and resolute trade unions were in alliance, they made a mighty force.

CHAPTER 17

A CLOSE CALL

"It's too close to call, Len," said Steve Turner down the line.

My heart sank. "Really?" I asked. "My God, Steve."

For each general secretary election I contested, Steve Turner, my campaign manager, would monitor the count. The process was in the hands of an external company, Electoral Reform Services. The count took two days—on the first, the envelopes would be opened and the ballot papers laid on tables; on the second, the votes would be sorted into separate piles. Candidates could nominate someone to be in the room to observe. Steve was there for me.

The previous two times I had stood for general secretary, Steve had called me from the count on the first day to tell me I had won. He didn't need to wait for the ballots to be separated out; he could get a feel for the result by watching as the envelopes were opened, so comfortable was my margin of victory. This time was different.

My third general secretary campaign, ending in April 2017, was quite unlike the other two. It was a dirty, filthy affair. My main opponent, Gerard Coyne, ran an entirely negative campaign based on smears, innuendo and personal attacks. It was unpleasant, uncomradely and unforgivable. I was sure our members would see through it.

That's why Steve's words came as a body blow. I was shocked. I didn't sleep that night.

I asked Steve to keep me up to date the following day—"I want the truth, no false hope." As the votes were counted it remained "too close to call." One time he said, "We're ahead, but only just." But Coyne's people started tweeting that their man had won. Was it true? "Well, you know, it is close, Len," Steve told me.

The clock ticked on into the afternoon and I began to contemplate the unthinkable. It was difficult to understand how this had happened.

I became philosophical. If it was defeat, so be it. I would clear out my office immediately. I wouldn't hang around. I didn't trust myself if I came face-to-face with Coyne after the way he had behaved.

Then the phone rang again. I picked up: "Hello?"

Steve simply said: "Congratulations, General Secretary."

———————

After the coup against Jeremy Corbyn failed in the Labour Party, its plotters didn't just retreat to their lair. Instead, they looked for new terrain on which to wage the same battle. They turned their attention to Unite.

There is no doubt that the 2017 Unite general secretary election was a proxy war. The Labour right and the establishment saw it as an opportunity to kill two birds with one stone. If they could take me down, they could take Jeremy down. Of course, they saw getting rid of me as a scalp in its own right, but the story of the campaign—the vast resources lavished on my opponent, the underhand methods he used, the media onslaught—would make no sense outside that context.

The campaign ran from December 2016 until April 2017—after Jeremy's second emphatic victory, but before his fantastic performance in the 2017 general election. His position then was far from impregnable. We now know from a leaked Labour Party report that preparations for another leadership contest, dubbed Operation Cupcake, were being discussed by the most senior Labour officials. Suddenly there was an opportunity in Unite to remove one of the main pillars of Corbyn's support.

The man the forces of the right were relying on to do it was Gerard Coyne, Unite's regional secretary in the West Midlands. In my opinion, he was one of my worst regional secretaries, a man of no real ability. There was nothing in his character or accomplishments to warrant his large ego. Were it not for the group of right-wing MPs and officials sometimes dubbed the 'West Midlands mafia'—the likes of John Speller, Jess Phillips and Tom Watson—I'm sure Coyne would have remained a man of no consequence. But their networks and access to money turbo-boosted his campaign.

Ironically, the opportunity was presented to them in part because I was anxious to shore up Corbyn's support ahead of a general election expected in 2020. My term ran to 2018, but if I had stood for re-election then I would have been asking to lead the union until the age of 73, which I thought was too late. Privately, I thought 2020 would be the right time for me to go. I didn't want to bow out before then—my God, I'd been a member of the Labour Party for half a century and there had never before been a chance like this. Better to have my election a year early and, if successful, give Corbyn and his team a solid and durable foundation. That was the view of many on the left. Of course, we didn't know Theresa May would call a snap election in 2017. Had I waited until 2018, by which time Jeremy had become unassailable, I'm sure the campaign against me would have been far less vicious.

Going early meant that, due to a change in the rules, I had to offer my resignation as general secretary. Gail Cartmail stepped in as acting general secretary for the period of the campaign. There were three candidates—me, Coyne and Ian Allinson from the ultra-left. At the start of the contest I spoke to Ian and his team and said, "If this election is close you could split the left vote and hand Unite to the right wing." They said they didn't think Coyne would even get on the ballot paper.

In truth, I didn't think it would be close, either. Out on the road I got a good response. As always, I travelled the length and breadth of the country and held some fantastic meetings. The organisation was good on the ground, although we found it much more difficult to get into factories and workplaces to speak to members than in previous contests—the companies refused me permission. Word must have spread around establishment networks not to allow me in. But nevertheless, the nominations phase was a landslide for me. I was nominated by 1,185 branches—80 per cent of the total—while Coyne secured 187 and Allinson 76. Branch nominations are usually a good indication of the lie of the land. I remember the journalist Kevin Maguire tweeting, "They think it's all over, it is now."

But Coyne was fighting a different battle, pumping out lies through the media. I have never seen—and nobody else has ever seen, including other general secretaries who told me so—anything like Coyne's negative campaign in the whole of the trade union movement. I have been through many tough battles and observed plenty of sharp practices but even I was shocked. It was vicious. It was horrible. It consisted almost entirely of personal attacks and smears against me—nothing to do with my vision or performance in the job, just accusations about my life with the truth twisted and distorted out of recognition—and attempts to use my support for Corbyn to batter me.

To work, the strategy needed a willing media to amplify the innuendo and false allegations so that our members would hear them. Well, Coyne certainly had that. I expected no better from the likes of the *Sun* and the *Mail*, of course, but it was the supposedly left *Guardian* that led the charge, and the journalist Rajeev Syal in particular. The coverage was pure tabloid: partial, inaccurate, obsessive and disgraceful.

An extraordinary moment of the campaign came when Coyne appeared on the BBC's 'Question Time' programme. The panel show rarely had a trade unionist of any description among its guests, while there seemed to be an 'entrepreneur' in the line-up every week. Yet here was the BBC putting an unknown regional secretary in front of millions of people. It was a measure of the clout of those behind Coyne that they had sufficient power to pull that off—and a sign of the BBC's bias against Corbyn, which became undeniable as the months and years rolled on.

Coyne's campaign was awash with cash. We later learned a company called Black Swan was harvesting the data of more than half-a-million Unite members in an operation that brought to mind the Cambridge Analytica scandal.

I started to wonder, is all this having an impact? Are people falling for it? Sadly, the answer was yes. That was evident even at the moment of victory. The relief I felt when Steve told me "Congratulations" quickly gave way to disappointment as he added, "You've only won by about 5,000 votes, but you've definitely won."

It was a salutary lesson in how negative campaigning can work. Coyne's 53,500 votes was what we had expected him to get when we mapped out the contest at the beginning. I was predicted to win more than 120,000 votes based on previous experience, but only managed 59,000. Meanwhile Allinson, the ultra-leftist, picked up 17,000 votes that almost spelled disaster for the left. Effectively, my vote had halved, but it hadn't transferred to Coyne. Members hadn't been moved to vote for him, but they had been persuaded not to vote for me. The effect of the negative campaign was to suppress my vote.

I felt disappointed and hurt that the membership had been affected by such lies. But I was boosted by friends and supporters who told me, "Lennie, we've just defeated the whole right-wing establishment!" It was true. Despite everything the media and the establishment had thrown at me—most of it in order to get to Corbyn—I'd still beaten them. I took pride in that.

———————

Gerard Coyne is not a good loser. For a year-and-a-half following his defeat he refused to accept the result, challenging it through every legal means possible. He made all kinds of allegations that I had cheated—I'd used Unite data and facilities, I'd spread false information, I'd tried to nobble his campaign. None of it was true, but I had to live with this rubbish being pelted at me by the media day in, day out. Most of the press chose to believe the claims and constantly implied the election would have to be rerun and I wouldn't stand. The truly maddening thing was that I knew all along that Coyne's campaign was guilty of many of the worst accusations they were levelling at me.

Coyne's antics were so serious that, as soon as all the votes had been cast, he was suspended from his job for Unite, investigated, found to have misused data and sacked. It emerged his campaign had wrongly used data from the Labour Party to phone bank Unite members in a tie-up with Labour's Siôn Simon, a right winger who was running for West Midlands mayor. During the campaign Unite also discovered that a union officer, Margaret Armstrong, who I had previously liked, had sadly crawled into the gutter with Coyne and provided Unite members' data on a memory stick to his campaign. She was dismissed from her job.

Of course, Coyne's sacking was reported as a vindictive act of vengeance perpetrated by me. That was pure fiction. It was Gail Cartmail, the acting general secretary, who dealt with the matter. Gail, whose integrity is beyond reproach, wouldn't take orders from anybody. She carried out her duty impeccably. She had already had to take the Coyne campaign to task for spreading lies about me during the campaign and there were a whole host of other complaints and potential disciplinary matters pending. In fact, I know that senior members of staff at Unite favoured suspending Coyne much earlier, while the race was still in progress, as the breaches were so blatant. I'm glad Gail chose not to, as it would have been seen as a fix.

Coyne's Trump-like crusade to overturn the election result began with an attempt to challenge his dismissal. He first claimed interim relief, which is intended for workers sacked by their employer for undertaking trade union duties. He was laughed out of court. Then he went for unfair dismissal. He eventually had to withdraw that. In the meantime, he complained to the Information Commissioner's Office about data misuse by my campaign. He got nowhere, but the ICO did find that *his* campaign had obtained data originally given by Labour to Owen Smith in 2016, a possible breach of the law.

Coyne's last legal avenue, his grand finale, was to put 10 points of complaint about the conduct of the election to the Certification Officer, the statutory official who oversees trade unions, who had the power to cancel the result and order a new election. I don't mind admitting I was worried sick about that. I knew Coyne's complaints were groundless, but the outcome was now in the hands of a government-appointed official. It didn't calm my nerves when the Certification Officer announced she wasn't legally qualified to adjudicate the case so was bringing in a retired High Court judge as her assistant to hear it.

Well, talk about the establishment! Coyne, of course, had the resources to hire a top QC—his bottomless pockets made it possible to bring all these hopeless cases in a bid to cancel a democratic vote. I have never been so naïve as to believe the truth will out when it comes to legal proceedings. I knew I was in the right, but I was far from confident.

The ordeal dragged on for months. All the while, the media was assuming I would lose—almost gloating about it. It made this a strange, unsettled period of my life. Finally, in October 2018, His Honour Jeffrey Burke QC gave his view on Coyne's 10 complaints. I had been wrong to ever doubt the man—he was clearly a fine and distinguished judge. "For the reasons which I have set out," he concluded at the end of his ruling, "none of the complaints succeed; and they are, therefore, all dismissed." It was a comprehensive, crushing defeat for Coyne, but like a bad penny he would turn up again three years later running for general secretary in summer 2021.

———————

There is a postscript to the story of this grubby attempt to dislodge me using underhand means. I hadn't communicated with Tom Watson since the chicken coup in July 2016, when he called off our negotiations via press release. But I knew he'd been involved in Gerard Coyne's gambit throughout. That hurt me far more than his role in the coup. For friends to be on different sides of a faction fight in the Labour Party is one thing. It happens. But taking it to the next level, to a personal level, by intervening in the affairs of a trade union to try to remove me from my job, was an act of vindictiveness that I found difficult to get my head around. So, once the judge's verdict was in, I couldn't stop myself. I texted:

> Tom, you and your right-wing mates in the West Midlands failed in your little Coyne adventure. How sad that you turned on your friends who were always there for you in your darkest times. Your newfound friends wouldn't spit on you if you were on fire.

He came back:

It is better to conquer yourself than to win a thousand battles. Then the victory is yours. It cannot be taken from you, not by angels or by demons, heaven or hell.

I replied:

How philosophical, good luck.

He responded:

You probably know it's a quote from Buddha. I prayed for you. Prayed you can find peace and despite everything, I greatly care for you and often worry about you.

That was the last time I heard from him.

CHAPTER 18

WITHIN TOUCHING DISTANCE
OF POWER

The political world was abuzz with speculation. Theresa May was going to make an announcement. Was she going to call an election? "Please, fucking hell, no!" I thought.

It was Tuesday 18 April 2017. Jeremy Corbyn had survived the chicken coup but that destructive, indulgent folly had left its mark. Labour's polling hadn't recovered. Jeremy would need a few years to turn things around. His LOTO team had only just reached full strength. The hundreds of thousands of new members hadn't had time to work their way through the party and give it new dynamism.

It was too soon. Which was precisely why May was going to do it. OK, she had promised, on camera, not to call an election. But why wouldn't she? She had the task of passing difficult Brexit legislation with a small majority of 17 and a restive contingent of Eurosceptic MPs for whom she knew her deal with the EU wouldn't be hard enough. Her advisors and analysts were telling her she would crush a shambolic-looking Labour Party with ease. It was almost a free hit.

The news reporters' attention was focused on which plaque would be fixed on the podium the prime minister was due to speak from in Downing Street. If she was calling an election, it couldn't have a government plaque on it.

Perhaps May had something else to say. What if she was going to announce that Prince Phillip had died or something? He'd had a good innings. Anything but an election.

Out came the podium. It didn't have any plaque on it. "I have just chaired a meeting of the cabinet," May said, "where we agreed that the government should call a general election to be held on 8 June." Well, at least Prince Phillip was OK.

For me, the 2017 general election will forever hold one lesson: radical politics can succeed. Against all the odds, contrary to all the opinion polls, despite all the efforts of snide, treacherous snakes saying Labour would be obliterated, the country embraced the unashamedly radical prospectus put forward by Jeremy Corbyn and rewarded the party with its biggest increase in the popular vote since 1945.

I can already hear the sound of right wingers crying out in frustration, "But he didn't win!" to which I say we need to be a bit more serious than that. Given where Labour was coming from after the 2015 defeat, given the party had been torn apart less than a year earlier, given its dire position in the polls at the beginning of the campaign, and given the sheer ambition of what it was proposing to do, 2017 was an incredible result.

Labour won 40 per cent of the vote. Since 1970, only two Labour leaders have achieved that: Jeremy Corbyn and Tony Blair. Bar the latter's 1997 landslide, more people voted Labour in 2017 than in any election since 1966. In England the party won its second highest number of votes ever. Such statistics would usually mean an election victory. The reason that wasn't so was because—contrary to popular perception and despite a terrible campaign—the Tories actually did extremely well, securing their biggest vote since 1992. The smaller parties were squeezed out of the picture.

The British media and political class prefer to forget that 12.9 million people voted for a radical manifesto fronted by a left-wing leader in 2017. Labour's terrible performance in the Brexit election two years later allowed commentators and careerists to pretend the earlier result never happened. The left can't let them get away with that. We showed in 2017 that it can be done. We proved wrong all the experts and naysayers who said you can't win popular support with a left programme. We gave future generations reason to hope.

I would be lying if I said I expected it to turn out that way when the election was called. I thought we would be in serious difficulty. Jeremy's second leadership victory hadn't stopped the sabotage from members of his own party or improved Labour's standing. Labour had seen off UKIP and its fantasist leader Paul Nuttall in a by-election in Stoke-on-Trent in February 2017 but had lost one in Copeland. Some of the few supportive voices Jeremy had in the media were having serious doubts.

After the election was called, Owen Jones came to see me. I like Owen very much but he has a tendency to worry. He was convinced we were going to get wiped out and had stats and opinion polls zooming out of him going back to when Adam was alive. He said it wasn't too late to change leader. I said, "Owen, are you living on the same planet as me? That's ridiculous. We're in an election campaign." He told me I was the only one who could get Jeremy to stand down. I said, "I'm pleased about that because I'm not fucking doing it, so let's move on."

I was utterly convinced that I was doing the right thing in sticking by Jeremy. This was a man who had been overwhelmingly chosen by the membership to present an alternative to the country. He deserved his chance. But at the same time, I was under no illusions about Labour's position in the polls. I too thought we would be badly beaten.

Early in the election campaign I had a meeting with John McDonnell, Seumas Milne and Karie Murphy in Seumas' office in parliament. The topic of the meeting was 9 June—what would we do the day after a heavy defeat? I'm not sure why Karie was there because she disagreed with the premise. "I don't know what you three are talking about because we're going to win," she said. We all just looked at her.

The rest of us expected a drubbing. We had to prepare ourselves to defend the left's position. There were two things we needed to do: 1) prevent Jeremy being forced to resign immediately, to buy some time; 2) find someone to succeed him. I was given the task of speaking to the trade union general secretaries.

I went to see Dave Prentis of Unison and Tim Roache of the GMB at Unison's HQ in Euston. It was supposed to be a meeting of the Big Four unions but Dave Ward of the CWU was suffering from an illness. That put me at a disadvantage because I was very close with Dave—a great comrade, solidly on the left—and I relied on his support. The dynamic of these Big Four meetings depended on whether Unison and the GMB had a united position. When Paul Kenny was GMB general secretary, he and Prentis formed an alliance to counterbalance me. I knew that; I would try to find ways to play them off. Roache was a different proposition. He was more open to persuasion, a less reliable ally to Prentis. My aim was to draw out the differences between them.

As expected, Prentis thought Corbyn should resign immediately after the election. He made some jibe about how there would be so few Labour MPs they could meet in a telephone box. I argued that we'd been critical of Ed Miliband's decision to go immediately; Jeremy should instead stay on, call for calm and announce a process to elect a new leader in the first quarter of 2018. Prentis said that was ridiculous, far too long. So I played the Tom Watson card—I wasn't going to agree to Corbyn going right away because Watson would become interim leader. That provoked strong agreement from Roache, who said he wasn't having Watson taking over. I had an ally.

The conversation moved on to who might replace Corbyn. I said we would need time to decide among ourselves if the unions could unite behind a candidate. There was a genuine view in the party that it should be a woman, I said. Three jumped to mind—Yvette Cooper, Lisa Nandy and Emily Thornberry. Prentis immediately said his partner, Liz Snape, who was in charge of Unison's political team, was a huge fan of Cooper. Unison would likely be backing her. Roache said the only one of the three he wouldn't have was Thornberry. I said the only one of the three I would have was Thornberry. Although I believe she later lost her way over Brexit, at the time Emily was very much in the frame. She had given an excellent speech at the 2016 conference—pro-Corbyn and very warm and personal, in stark contrast to Watson's horrible anti-Corbyn contribution. Had the election gone as disastrously as predicted, I think there was a chance Unite would have backed her.

It was clear we didn't have a unified position and would have much to discuss after the election. Eventually, Roache said that while he didn't think Jeremy staying until the following year was a runner, he should be able to take his conference in September. I seized on that and pushed a bit further, saying, "OK, shall we talk about having a new leader by Christmas?"

Prentis was still resistant. I started to take the gloves off and asked, "What happens if Corbyn tells us to fuck off, he's not leaving unless he's challenged?" Prentis said Corbyn wouldn't do that. I replied: "I don't know what he'll do, but he'll have every right to do that, which is precisely why he needs to be treated with some respect and dignity. So we should support what Tim has come up with."

Finally, it was agreed: the Big Four would ensure Jeremy could stay on after the election, but we'd have a new leader by Christmas. I went back and reported to John, Seumas and Karie that I'd bought some time for the left to gather itself after the coming defeat. Karie was her defiant self, still proclaiming that victory would be achieved.

Labour's general election campaign got off to a flying start. The policy team under Andrew Fisher had some eye-catching ideas ready to go that encapsulated the "for the many, not the few" message that would become Labour's inspired election strapline—policies like giving primary school children free school meals paid for by taxing private school fees. Jeremy Corbyn gave an excellent first speech and looked up for the battle. The only blows that troubled the leadership came not from the Tories, but from their own side. Barrow and Furnace MP John Woodcock declared he would "not countenance" making Corbyn prime minister even while expecting to stand to be a Labour MP. He should have been deselected there and then, but the right still controlled the National Executive Committee and Tom Watson protected him. Woodcock was later given a peerage by the Tories for services rendered.

NEC officers also defied Corbyn by ruling that candidates would be imposed in every seat, cutting local parties out of the process entirely. I didn't agree with parachuting people in, but it was good for Unite as a decent number of our favoured candidates were chosen. I expect the right let the unions get our way in many seats because they thought they would need our money after the election, and most of the candidates would lose anyway.

That was certainly how it looked from the local elections held two weeks into the campaign on 4 May. Labour's performance was very poor, vindicating my pessimism about the coming general election. Those who vote in local elections tend to be older. Theresa May's "strong and stable" message and her determination to make everything about Brexit seemed to be playing well with them. Labour would need a game changer.

It came in the most unlikely form. On the evening of 10 May, newspapers reported that Labour's entire draft manifesto had been leaked, perhaps the most extraordinary act of sabotage in British political history. The press couldn't hide their glee. Not only could they present Labour as dysfunctional, but the radicalism of the draft programme meant they could terrify readers with tales of a return to the 1970s. The rich would be taxed and utilities nationalised. It would be socialism! There was just one thing they hadn't counted on: people wanted it.

The leaking of the manifesto turned out to be spectacularly counterproductive. You couldn't buy the coverage it generated. Labour's policies were all over the news, getting wider exposure than we could ever have dreamed of otherwise. The ideas might have been political taboos in the shrivelled imaginations of the political class, but they sounded like common sense to real people. Sixty-five per cent wanted to raise income tax for high earners; 71 per cent supported banning zero-hours contracts; about 50 per cent wanted to nationalise rail, mail and energy, with just a quarter opposed.

The following day was Labour's Clause V meeting, when the different parts of the party agree the manifesto. The atmosphere was charged. Emily Thornberry made a withering speech, implicitly attacking Tom Watson, suspected of being the source of the leak—it was fantastically powerful. Ironically, this was one of the few times Watson wasn't to blame—the finger of rumour later pointed strongly towards the office of Scottish leader Kezia Dugdale.

Some expected the right to put up a fight against the manifesto—maybe the leak on the eve of the Clause V meeting was timed to help their cause. But in the event, there was no resistance at all. I suspect they wanted to make sure the left was blamed for the rout they thought was coming, just as the 1983 defeat had been pinned on the left by the jibe that the manifesto was the longest suicide note in history. Their attitude was, "By all means, if you want to write an even longer suicide note be our guest, and we'll be here to pick up the pieces when you get smashed." But their silence also revealed that they had no ideas to offer. Despite all the turbulence of Corbyn's leadership, he and John McDonnell had successfully transformed Labour into an anti-austerity party. What was the right going to say? That we should have austerity? That public sector pay should be frozen? That investment banks were a bad idea?

The position on Brexit was crucial. The Tories were telling Leave voters they had to support Theresa May if they wanted Brexit to happen. But Labour neutralised the issue with a promise to respect the result of the referendum. The difficult topic of immigration was deftly sidestepped with the matter-of-fact line: "Freedom of movement will end when we leave the European Union." This was coupled with commitments to protect the rights of EU citizens and immigrants. It is fascinating to look back at how easily that Brexit position was reached in 2017, in light of the battles that defined Labour's 2019 election defeat. Shadow Brexit Secretary Keir Starmer was on board with it, along with the rest of the shadow cabinet (if only their integrity had been genuine).

The manifesto—a great manifesto skilfully pulled together by Andrew Fisher, expressing Corbyn's vision and giving working people hope—sailed through the Clause V meeting as smooth as you like. I wish my departure from the building had been as smooth. As I came out, I saw a bank of photographers at the bottom of a set of stone steps. Quickly darting sideways behind a column to get out of their viewfinders, I slipped and fell. I jumped back up as quick as I could, despite being hurt, hoping no one had noticed, and walked off down the street, trying to hide the fact my back was killing me. I eventually got clear and met friends including Jeremy's political secretary, Amy Jackson, who asked if anyone had seen me fall. "I may have got away with it," I hoped. Amy checked Twitter. "No, there's nothing," she said. Then, "Oh." Whoever got the photo must have made a fortune because it was on the front page of the *Sun* the next morning. On the same day, Corbyn's driver had run over a photographer's foot and so the headline was, "What a pair of wallies." Chris Evans called me Lennie Long Legs on his radio show because the angle of the photo made it look like I had enormous legs. It was very embarrassing. But at least my friend, Paul Flanagan (and others I hope), noticed I had my Paul Smith socks on.

———————

The manifesto allowed Labour members to knock on doors with a programme they truly believed in. There was a buzz about the party. Labour started to rise rapidly in the polls. Watching this, I made sure to pinch myself. Other people could float away, I told myself, I've got to keep my feet on the ground and be ready to protect the left project on 9 June. That's why, in an interview with *Politico* on 16 May, I said a successful campaign would mean Labour holding 200 seats. I was trying to lower expectations, especially within the trade union movement, to ensure our agreement to give Jeremy Corbyn some time would survive the shock of a rout. In private people were talking about Labour winning just 150 seats so I thought 200 might have been too optimistic. But the comment was ill-judged and was easily used against us.

Although I was expecting a bad result, I was doing everything I could to help secure a good one. Unite poured resources into Labour's campaign—£5 million, 70 per cent of the total donated by all affiliates. The other big unions, including Unison and the GMB, claimed they had been cleaned out by the 2015 election. I offered them loans but none accepted. I suspect they just didn't want to spend money on Corbyn and a doomed campaign.

From mid-May my chief of staff, Andrew Murray, was seconded to the election campaign. Karie Murphy, Seumas Milne and Andrew Fisher were under enormous pressure and had asked for some help. But another reason for seconding Andrew was that we knew Corbyn was being sabotaged. There's no doubt in my mind that there were influential people in the structures of the party who would have been happy for Labour to be not just defeated, but crushed, so they could get "their" party back. The situation was extraordinary—Labour's general secretary and his most senior staff gave every impression of wanting to lose.

We suspected money was being allocated unfairly to favour right-wing MPs—so much so that Unite's final donation of £500,000 was given on the strict condition that it be under the control of Karie and Andrew. But we didn't find out just how extensive and brazen this sabotage was until two-and-a-half years later, when Labour staff were searching through files while preparing evidence for the Equality and Human Rights Commission's inquiry into antisemitism. They uncovered reams of communication allegedly showing McNicol's team making abusive comments about LOTO staff, hoping for Corbyn and Labour to do badly, and being deliberately unhelpful and obstructive. Most shocking of all, the search revealed the existence of a secret election programme based in Ergon House, Labour's London regional office, from where a "key seats team" made up of staff hostile to the leadership apparently ran a parallel election campaign to push money into the constituencies of right-wing Labour MPs, including Chuka Umunna, Rachel Reeves and Yvette Cooper. All of this was hidden from LOTO, in breach of the Labour Party's rules, and possibly broke laws against fraud and false accounting.

The Ergon House Project was the most extreme example of the defensive election strategy being followed by McNicol's team and the party machine. They were only interested in keeping the seats Labour already held—they saw no point in putting effort into offensive seats the party had no realistic prospect of taking from the Tories. Their aim was no more than to weather the storm—shield their mates in the PLP while going down to a defeat that would sweep Corbyn and the left from the leadership. They maintained this strategy against the explicit instructions of LOTO, which needed a much better result in order to survive. LOTO demanded an offensive campaign, believing that by giving people something bold and distinctive to vote for they could mobilise new voters and defy political gravity.

To be honest, I understood the defensive approach early on in the election. History suggested it was impossible to move the polls dramatically during a campaign. But in the middle of May it became clear something unusual was happening in the country. Labour's campaign was taking off. The Jeremy Corbyn of the campaign trail was once again the man who had inspired the incredible surge of support in 2015. Thousands of people were turning out at short notice to hear him speak at every stop. There was real excitement around him. Musicians and actors were coming out in support. Young people were registering to vote in the hundreds of thousands. Momentum, the pro-Corbyn group, was doing the work of organising activists on the ground that the official party seemed unwilling to do. On social media, a whole community of Corbyn supporters was pumping out the party's messages and improvising their own, reaching millions of people on Facebook and Twitter and countering the relentless negativity of the mainstream press.

Labour HQ's defensive approach was behind the times. On 20 May Corbyn spoke at a rally on the beach at West Kirby in the Wirral. I knew the area; it's relatively affluent. I was astounded to see images of thousands of people clambering over sand dunes to hear the Labour leader. From there he went to Prenton Park, the home of Tranmere Rovers Football Club, in Birkenhead, to speak in front of 20,000 music fans at a Libertines gig—an astonishing thing for a politician to do in the middle of an election. Instead of jeering him, they sang "Oh Je-re-my Cor-byn" to the tune of 'Seven Nation Army' by the White Stripes, and a chant was born. That night, an opinion poll had Labour on 35 per cent, the same share of the vote that won Tony Blair the 2005 election. I started to think, "Oh my God, can this go on?"

Meanwhile, the Tory campaign fell apart. Their manifesto was a disaster, a dreary document memorable only for a policy immediately branded as a dementia tax, which bizarrely attacked the property-owning older generation who made up the Tories' core vote. Unbelievably, just four days after its launch,

With Tony Woodley. "You go first, Tony, and I'll follow."

With my great hero Jack Jones in 2004.

I've had the chance to meet some great people, and Anthony Joshua is one. These are Mohammed Ali's gloves, donated by Unite to the British Olympic boxing team in 2012. *Photo by Mark Harvey.*

A great friend and socialist, and a brilliant actor and comedian, Ricky Tomlinson. *Photo by Mark Thomas.*

"Bloody media." *Photo by Peter Macdiarmid/Getty Images.*

Marching against austerity, fighting for a better future.

Photo by Mark Thomas.

A woman's place is in her union. With locked-out Northampton Hospital
NHS workers in 2014. *Photo by Mark Thomas.*

"If you have no stomach for this fight, depart the battlefield"—my 2016 Labour Conference speech. *Photo by Mark Thomas.*

Leading the "Oh Jeremy Corbyn" chant at the Durham Miners' Gala.
Photo by Mark Harvey.

Never trust a Tory. *Photo by Mark Harvey.*

"Hello, is anybody home?" *Photo by Stefan Rousseau/PA Archive/PA Images.*

A decent, good man who changed British politics. *Photo by Mark Harvey.*

Theresa May had to U-turn on the flagship policy. I had never seen anything like it. Her contrived image as a "strong and stable" leader dissolved. The slogan became a national joke. She was exposed as a terrible candidate at the head of an awful, arrogant campaign. The Tories' celebrated strategist Lynton Crosby had been knighted for his work on the 2015 election; he should have been beheaded for the 2017 campaign. I couldn't believe how bad it was.

Just as I began to allow myself to believe things really were turning around, the election was brought to a violent halt. On the night of 22 May, 22 people, most of them kids, were killed in the Manchester Arena terror attack, when a bomb was exploded at an Ariana Grande concert. Conventionally, the political fallout from such an atrocity would be expected to benefit the governing party. That's certainly what I feared. The situation put Corbyn in a particularly difficult position. Here was a man relentlessly smeared as a terrorist sympathiser and a supporter of the IRA who would now have to chart a political path through the raw emotions and public anger provoked by a despicable act of violence. I thought he should keep his head down.

Seumas Milne had other ideas. He, Andrew Murray and Karie Murphy felt they could not sit back and allow the Tories to control the narrative. They hatched a bold plan to restart the campaign after a four-day pause with a strong speech on terrorism and security. Corbyn would condemn the terrorists but wouldn't shy away from putting the attack in the context of Britain's disastrous involvement in the War on Terror.

I was sceptical. I thought Jeremy shouldn't do it. It was too risky. The media would distort whatever he said—"Oh there's Corbyn, blaming the system instead of the bastards who did it." On the night before the speech the press did exactly that, reporting that he would say: "UK wars to blame for terror." MPs were letting it be known that Labour would be finished if he went ahead with it. I thought they had a point.

I was wrong. When Jeremy spoke the next day his speech was measured and well-crafted. He made the obviously true, yet somehow controversial, observation about "the connections between wars that we've been involved in... and terrorism here at home." But he was crystal clear that "no rationale based on the actions of any government can remotely excuse, or even adequately explain, outrages like this week's massacre."

The Tory response was predictable. Corbyn had said "terror attacks in Britain are our own fault," claimed Theresa May. The media were ferocious. It still looked like it could go horribly wrong. But a snap opinion poll by YouGov later that day turned the debate on its head. According to the pollster, 53 per cent agreed with Corbyn while only 24 per cent disagreed. The press had miscalculated again. It was a pivotal moment in the election.

Corbyn grew in stature following the speech. In a string of high-profile media appearances he excelled, getting the better of Jeremy Paxman in a set-piece interview and dramatically turning up at short notice to take part in a BBC leaders' debate in Cambridge. May was caught flat-footed by the move and looked cowardly for her refusal to debate Corbyn head-to-head. Jeremy's personal ratings shot up, while hers collapsed. The only sticky moment came on a BBC 'Question Time' leaders' special, when Corbyn was subjected to seven minutes of interrogation from angry old men in the audience demanding he should be prepared to push the nuclear button. Eventually, he seemed to grind to a halt and declined to respond at all to one man's point. I was holding my breath watching the TV. He looked severely wounded. But he was saved by a young woman in the audience who exclaimed to a huge cheer, "I don't understand why everyone in this room seems so keen on killing millions of people with a nuclear bomb!"

The polling was just getting better and better for Labour. A YouGov seat projection released on 30 May suggested the Tories were going to lose their majority. Commentators laughed at it. Not every poll was as positive, but on 3 June, with just five days to go, a Survation survey put Labour on 39 per cent, just one point shy of the Tories. I would not have believed that possible six weeks earlier facing a 25-point deficit; no one would, except Karie.

But then tragedy intervened for a second time. On the evening of 3 June— Saturday night—I was in Borough Market in London with friends. We were planning to eat at one of my favourite restaurants there called Black and Blue, but the Champions League Final was being played that night between Juventus and Real Madrid so it was decided that a takeaway back at my flat watching the match would be preferable. Just after 10 p.m., eight people were killed when a group of terrorists drove a van into pedestrians on London Bridge before going on a murderous rampage through Borough Market, including forcing their way into Black and Blue.

The impetus seemed to have been stolen from Labour again. But remarkably, when campaigning resumed, Corbyn managed to win the debate about security. His line, "You can't protect people on the cheap," put the focus on the cuts to police that May had made as home secretary.

The final stretch saw Corbyn addressing big, outdoor rallies in Gateshead and Birmingham, while May remained hidden away in warehouses talking to handfuls of Tory members. She could still rely on the press—the *Daily Mail* printed 13 pages of invective against Corbyn, John McDonnell and Diane Abbott on the last day of campaigning.

The final polls suggested Labour's progress had been halted or even reversed after the London Bridge terror attack. In Labour HQ, a senior member of Iain McNicol's team seemed overjoyed to report to LOTO staff that private polling had them 13 points behind. That, to me, encapsulated everything about the saboteurs.

It's a political cliché that there's only one poll that counts, but nowadays that tends to mean the 10 p.m. exit poll rather than the actual votes. I was waiting for the big moment with a group of comrades at the International Transport Workers Federation building in Bermondsey. I didn't think there was a chance of a Labour victory, but by then we felt it may not be a disaster, and if it was not a disaster that *would* be a victory. We had bottles of beer and wine ready to celebrate if needed.

The result flashed up on the big TV—hung parliament! Tories lose their majority! It was an incredible moment. I jumped around and hugged people.

More than anything, I felt a sense of relief that this decent man, Jeremy Corbyn, hadn't been humiliated.

Next morning I was up early, spick and span, to go down to College Green in Westminster where the media were camped out. I must have done 15 interviews, maybe more. I did everything—mention a station, I did it. My director of communications, Pauline Doyle, was saying, "Can we go now?" I would reply, "Well, have we done every one of them?" A crew would be interviewing someone with a little crowd watching and when they finished I would say, "Hi, do you want me next?"

I remember Andrew Neil asking, "Well, Mr McCluskey, you thought 200 seats would be a good result, what have you got to say about that?"

"If I thought 200 seats was going to be good, how do you think I feel on 262?" I answered. "Overjoyed, fantastic, what a smack in the eye for all you lot, including you."

"No, not me!" he said.

"Oh, Andrew, I think you as well."

After all the worrying I had done about 9 June, it turned out to be a great morning.

———————

There's a convincing argument to be made that had the election gone on for another fortnight, Jeremy Corbyn would have been prime minister—not with an overall majority, but as the only person able to form a government in a hung parliament. He took us to within touching distance of power. Just 2,227 votes, divided between the seven tightest Conservative holds, would have deprived Theresa May of the ability to scrape a majority by cobbling together a shady deal with the DUP.

In that scenario, Jeremy would have formed a minority government. He would have presented Labour's programme in a Queen's Speech and given the SNP the choice of either voting it through or going back to the people of Scotland and explaining why they were risking another Tory government. Of course, there may have been deals to make—I would have been in favour of promising the SNP another independence referendum if they won the 2021 Holyrood elections. But either way, the SNP would not have had the whip hand. I believe such a government could have lasted a full term and implemented its programme. But if not, Labour could have gone back to the electorate with confidence, saying: "Give us a mandate to finish all these things that are making your life better, like investment in your community and manufacturing, publicly-owned railways, water, mail and energy, and better wages."

We came agonisingly close to being able to do all of that. Had it not been for the campaign of sabotage and backstabbing from within Corbyn's own party, we would have succeeded. The resources diverted to the safe seats of right-wing MPs could have enabled us to win those extra 2,227 votes in the places where they were needed. Had Iain McNicol and Labour HQ wanted to look for a light at the end of the tunnel, had they *wanted to win*, it could have tipped the balance to Labour and Jeremy could have been in Number 10.

Painful as that thought is, the 2017 result gave the left a shining example that has to endure. All my life I've listened to people tell me you can't win support with a left programme. Now I know—we all know—that's not true. As the 2019 Brexit election fades into the past, it's 2017 that will stand as an inspiration to future generations. I'm proud of what we did.

CHAPTER 19

LABOUR'S ANTISEMITISM CRISIS

The ballroom was chock-a-block. Several hundred people were squeezed into every corner of the once-grand hall in a Brighton seafront hotel for the launch of a new organisation, Jewish Voice for Labour.

It was the 2017 Labour Party Conference. After Labour's miraculous comeback in the snap general election that summer, there was a sense of jubilation in the air. I had just come from another fringe meeting with John McDonnell about how we were going to govern from the left—those were the conversations we were now having.

Ever since Corbyn emerged as a serious contender in his first leadership campaign, he had been a target for his support of the Palestinian cause. The attacks came in waves. First, they focused on him, trawling his decades of pro-Palestinian activism for anything that could confer guilt by association. The second, more effective wave, in 2016, focused on Labour Party members, blaming the left-wing leadership for any antisemitic comments discovered on social media—even if they had been made when Ed Miliband was leader. Then the whole thing blew up when Ken Livingstone made his utterly bizarre and unnecessary comments on the radio.

After that, the issue of antisemitism became a constant rumble, but didn't play a prominent part in the 2017 election. It was clear that horrible antisemitic ideas were being expressed on social media by some among the vast Labour membership; it was baffling that the party's bureaucratic processes were so slow to deal with it; and it was obvious that many of Corbyn's opponents saw a political opportunity to damage the leadership.

The Jewish socialist Glyn Secker asked me along to the JVL launch. I was fascinated to hear what pro-Corbyn Jewish members had to say. Up to that point the party's official Jewish affiliate, the Jewish Labour Movement, had spoken on behalf of Jewish members, and had been consistently critical of the leader.

The JVL meeting was already in full flow when I arrived so I stood at the back and listened. It was riveting to hear Professor Avi Shlaim recount his days in the Israel Defence Forces in the 1960s and then take on many of the accusations levelled against Corbyn.

Just as I was leaving to go to another meeting, the chair, Jenny Manson, spotted me near the door and said into the microphone, "Can I welcome Len McCluskey..." A huge round of applause broke out. I hadn't planned to speak but what could I do? I moved into the aisle so I could be heard and said: "I just want to commend JVL and everybody here for keeping the fantastic, radical spirit and history of the Jewish people alive. And I can tell you, on behalf of Unite, we'll be looking to affiliate to JVL as soon as we possibly can."

The room erupted. I was going to say more but decided I didn't need to and made my exit. My spontaneous commitment was picked up by the media and was soon reported all over.

It's fair to say the JLM were less than happy about Unite supporting a group they considered not only a rival but an illegitimate force in the party. As a result, some months later a JLM delegation came to visit me, including Peter Mason, the JLM's secretary, and Rabbi Laura Janner-Klausner and Rabbi David Mason.

It was an interesting exchange. I said I would be happy to work with the JLM as the fight against antisemitism was an important subject close to my heart, but why were they so concerned about my remarks at the JVL event?

They rubbished JVL and explained how they felt under attack from Corbyn's supporters. I asked if I would be right to say the majority of JLM members would prefer Corbyn not to be leader. After some prevarication they agreed. I said Corbyn had been constantly attacked and vilified—so much so that his supporters saw people as being either for or against him. That may be regrettable but was inevitable given such hostility. If the JLM would prefer Corbyn not to be leader, was it any surprise his supporters saw their organisation as an opponent? Indeed, the very fact the JLM was perceived as being anti-Corbyn had given rise to JVL.

After a good discussion I said I was determined to engage with both the JLM and JVL. Assistant General Secretary Gail Cartmail, who has Jewish heritage, was given the task of liaising with both of them on education in the union, but I'm sorry to say little came of it. As for the two Jewish organisations, they became symbolic of a debate in which there was virtually no common ground.

What was the Labour antisemitism crisis? I put that question in the past tense because, although I have no doubt instances of antisemitism occur among the party membership to this day, the issue suddenly became invisible as soon as there was a change of leadership in 2020—except insofar as it related to the previous era. I'm not sure there has ever been anything like the Labour antisemitism crisis in the history of British politics. It was ferocious and relentless and extraordinarily painful for people on all sides.

It's important to be clear what Labour was accused of. The accusation was not merely that antisemitism existed within Labour. No sensible person claimed otherwise. It was not merely that some Labour members engaged in disgraceful antisemitic abuse. No sensible person denied that. It was not merely that Labour's disciplinary processes initially weren't up to the job. No sensible person argued they were. Highlighting these things was perfectly legitimate and necessary; they weren't smears.

But the accusations made against the party went much further. First, it was claimed that Labour was "riddled" or "overrun" with antisemitism; that this racism was not just present among the membership as in wider society, but was disproportionately concentrated there. Second, Labour was accused of being "institutionally antisemitic," a "racist party." Third, the leader Jeremy Corbyn was alleged to be at best tolerant of antisemitism, and at worst an antisemite himself. Finally, these separate allegations were folded together into the claim that Labour posed an "existential threat" to British Jews.

It's hardly surprising, given these claims were amplified with great enthusiasm and dedication by the entire media, that many sincere people became deeply worried. Real fear was felt by many Jews and genuine offence was taken. But there's no two ways about this: these lurid accusations weren't true. No evidence that antisemitism was more widespread in the Labour Party than in wider society has ever been produced. All the evidence that exists suggests the opposite. A tiny fraction of Labour Party members had complaints of antisemitism made against them. Research showed antisemitic attitudes were no more prevalent on the left—from which the Labour membership was drawn—than in any other part of the political spectrum. Of course, a party that bills itself as anti-racist should aim to eradicate prejudice within its ranks altogether, but there is no evidence that Labour was "overrun" by antisemitism; it wasn't.

Neither was the party "institutionally antisemitic." I reject out of hand the notion that Labour was a "racist party" under Corbyn. It had no rules or policies that discriminated against Jewish people. Despite the publication of the October 2020 report into antisemitism in the Labour Party by the Equality and Human Rights Commission (EHRC) being hyped up in advance as the moment the party would be officially branded "institutionally antisemitic," it was not. The idea that Labour represented "an existential threat to Jewish life" in Britain, as the three main Jewish communal newspapers declared in July 2018, was baseless.

As for Jeremy's own views, this was a man who despised racism, who fought it all his life, who had never expressed any hostility towards Jewish people in all his years of pro-Palestinian activism, who enjoyed excellent relations with his local Jewish community and with many Jewish activists, and who had been willing to put his own safety at risk when necessary to oppose antisemitic marches that aimed to intimidate Jewish people. The centre of his constituency, Finsbury Park, was a place where all religions and nationalities mixed in harmony, something Jeremy was very proud of.

Most prominent people associated with the Corbyn project could boast similar records. All my life I've considered antisemitism the biggest evil, ever since my dad spoke to me about the Second World War. I have always felt deep, deep sympathy with the Jewish people who have suffered so much throughout history. In my younger days I fought antisemitism physically, on the streets, taking and throwing punches. There were two occasions in the 1970s—one in Liverpool and one in Birkenhead—when I was involved in confronting anti-semitic National Front marches. The left had to stop them because the police wouldn't. We knew there would be violence. I remember grabbing anything I could use to hit the fascists because they were hitting us. It was frightening stuff. There was a lot of blood, a lot of pain taken and a lot of pain inflicted, but on both occasions we were successful in driving them off our streets. I took great pride, in more recent years, in seeing that tradition continued when fascists attempting to march in Liverpool failed to even get out of Lime Street station before being sent scuttling home by thousands of decent people who came onto the streets to block their way.

So when I, along with others, was accused of minimising, tolerating or even propagating a form of prejudice that has always revolted me, it was devastating. I found that defending Corbyn and the left opened me up to the charge of deny-ing antisemitism. The height of that came at the 2017 Labour Party Conference in Brighton. In an interview with BBC 'Newsnight' I said the issue of antisemi-tism had been used as "mood music" for the campaign to undermine Corbyn. I was heavily criticised, but my intention was in no way to question the serious-ness of anti-Jewish racism. What I was trying to get across was that there were unquestionably people on the right of the Labour Party, in the establishment, and in the media who had less interest in the issue of antisemitism than they did in using it to attack Corbyn.

Ironically, the same conference passed changes to the party rulebook to explicitly outlaw antisemitism, proposed by the JLM and supported by Unite. Although you wouldn't have known it from the coverage, the Labour leadership was making a genuine attempt to get to grips with the problem.

The leadership regularly took a battering for failures of the party machinery to act swiftly against sometimes grotesque examples of antisemitic speech originating on social media and mysteriously fed to the press. The trouble was, the leadership had little control over the machinery. Until spring 2018 the left was in a minority on the party's National Executive Committee, the body that appointed the general secretary. Iain McNicol remained in post. The party's disciplinary unit answered to him and was headed up by staff who were allegedly up to their necks in the sabotage against the leadership, including involvement in the Ergon House project to secretly divert party funds during the 2017 general election.

There are some who suspect the disciplinary unit of allowing antisemitism complaints to fester in order to cause the leadership problems. It's difficult to prove intent. But there were examples of cases stalled for years and instances of blatant antisemitism going uninvestigated, even when LOTO staff flagged them up. It was only once McNicol was finally ousted and Jennie Formby became general secretary in April 2018 that processes were overhauled and sped up, more staff were hired, and the backlog began to be cleared.

In the meantime, the Jewish communal leadership—in particular the Board of Deputies of British Jews and the Jewish Leadership Council—became prominent in the public debate, issuing demands to the Labour leadership. But it increasingly appeared they were not willing to take yes for an answer. They demanded Corbyn apologise for antisemitic views expressed by some members. He did. They demanded he apologise for some of his own actions, like failing to recognise a mural as being antisemitic. He did. They demanded he commit to the security of the Jewish community in Britain. He did. They demanded he make clear that any of his supporters engaging in antisemitic abuse did not do so in his name. He did. The response of the communal organisations? Intransigent hostility and a refusal to talk. The more Corbyn and Labour attempted to address their worries, the more extreme their rhetoric became.

There's no question that the issue of Israel–Palestine underlaid the Labour anti-semitism crisis. What changed with Jeremy Corbyn's election as leader was that for the first time there was the chance of a major Western power being led by someone who unequivocally supported Palestinian rights. That went hand-in-hand with the serious prospect of Britain diverging from its imperial role as a dependable US ally. Labour had to be brought to heel.

My support for the Palestinian cause is longstanding. I will never accept that it's antisemitic to criticise the government of Israel for its treatment of the Palestinians. The occupation, the settlements, the blockade of Gaza and the regular military assaults against a mostly defenceless people are obscene.

I do, however, accept Israel's right to exist. I know the history of the Sykes–Picot Agreement, the Balfour Declaration and the Nakba. It's essential to recognise the wrongs that led to the dispossession and ethnic cleansing of the Palestinians. I also believe that had I been a young Jewish man at the end of the Second World War, I would have fought and if necessary died to create the State of Israel as a safe haven for Jews after the horror of the Holocaust.

The result of that history is that Israel exists, and as a state it has rights. In my view it's a dead end to oppose its existence. It's true that Israel itself has been busy destroying the chances of a two-state solution, but the practical barriers could be overcome if the political pressure was strong enough to do so. If JVL had not recognised Israel's right to exist within the pre-1967 borders I wouldn't have been able to support them. I asked and they said they did. Similarly, I posed the question to the Palestine Solidarity Campaign, which Unite is affiliated to and active within. Their answer was that, as the Palestine Liberation Organisation recognises Israel's right to exist, so do they.

I had become pessimistic about a solution, but I remember the case being made by an unlikely speaker—Sir Malcolm Rifkind, the former Conservative minister—at an event organised by BICOM, the pro-Israel campaign group, in Portcullis House in November 2017. I was deeply impressed with his speech and told him so afterwards. I also attended the Balfour Project Centenary event in a packed Methodist Central Hall in Westminster where Lord David Owen made an impromptu speech and I congratulated him on an incisive contribution. This led to him visiting my office a week or so later to talk further. Sir Malcolm Rifkind and Lord David Owen—two people whose politics are far from mine—had given me refreshed hope that a just solution and peace in the Middle East could be achieved.

The thorny issues of history and identity came to the fore in summer 2018 when Labour was urged to adopt the International Holocaust Remembrance Alliance working definition of antisemitism. The pro-Palestine movement saw the definition as a means of censuring criticism of Israel by conflating it with antisemitism. In July 2018, Labour's NEC passed a code of conduct which incorporated the IHRA definition but elaborated on or amended four of 11 examples of purportedly antisemitic speech that accompanied the definition. All hell broke loose.

For six weeks during the summer, Corbyn and Labour were hammered. On one day in August, Corbyn's press team received inquiries from journalists about 17 separate antisemitism stories after 3 p.m.—plainly a coordinated attempt to overwhelm them. Marie van der Zyl, president of the Board of Deputies, later boasted, "Over the summer, we showed how we could keep this issue of antisemitism on the front pages day after day, week after week."

It's my view that Jeremy's reluctance to adopt the IHRA examples unamended at the outset was a mistake. I understood his reasoning. Here was a man who had been actively engaged all his life in the Palestinian cause and wanted clearer explanations of some of the examples relating to Israel to ensure there was no ambiguity that could be exploited to shut down legitimate criticism. But in the context of the politics of the time, that handed his opponents ammunition. Unite advised Labour to accept the examples immediately. Clarifications on how they applied to disciplinary cases could have been made further down the line. What mattered was getting Jeremy into Number 10. One of his first acts would have been to recognise the State of Palestine, achieving more for the Palestinian cause than all the endless weeks of debate about the IHRA definition.

Jeremy and his team were under relentless attack on incredibly difficult terrain, but I do think a stronger lead on the antisemitism issue could have lessened the damage. Instead, his and the party's response fell back on dry arguments about process. The truth (as the EHRC report later acknowledged) was that improvements to Labour's processes greatly accelerated under Jennie Formby. But that had virtually no impact on the public debate because by then Corbyn's opponents knew they had him on a hook.

Labour MPs were determined not to let him wriggle off it. When the party released figures showing progress on complaints in February 2019, they were rubbished by Margaret Hodge, an implacable opponent of Corbyn who became the leading voice in the antisemitism debate after allegedly calling him a "fucking antisemite" in parliament. "I alone put in over 200 examples, some vile, where evidence suggested they came from Labour," she tweeted, "so don't trust [the] figures." It turned out Hodge's 200 examples concerned 111 individuals of whom only 20 were party members. Don't trust the figures indeed. Unfazed, she continued the fight by penning an article in the *Daily Mail* of all papers—the very publication that in the 1930s had been sympathetic to the Nazis.

Another important intervention came from the BBC, through the 'Panorama' episode, 'Is Labour Antisemitic?' The "is" in the title was presumably wrongly placed—a typo, perhaps—since the programme didn't set out to answer a question but to prove a case. As journalism, I thought it fell well below the BBC's standards.

The gulf between the media's representation of Labour's antisemitism crisis and the known facts reminded me of the debate about benefits under the Cameron government, which was accompanied by a concerted campaign to demonise "scroungers," often using individual stories of appalling—but completely unrepresentative—behaviour. As a result, the public thought benefit fraud accounted for a quarter of the welfare budget, according to a 2013 poll, when the reality was 0.7 per cent. Similarly, a 2019 poll by Survation found the public thought complaints of antisemitism had been made against a third of

Labour Party members, when the best estimate was that just 0.3 per cent were subject to disciplinary investigations.

When allegations were falsely levelled or claims overstated, it made addressing the reality of the problem more difficult because it bred cynicism and denial. Worst of all, it stoked unnecessary fear among Jewish people, who were misled into believing Labour posed a threat to them.

Did any of this damage Corbyn electorally? I don't believe antisemitism was much of an issue on the doorsteps of Darlington or Doncaster in the 2019 general election. But it was part of toxifying Corbyn. It made it more difficult to re-conjure the hope and optimism of the 2017 campaign. It disheartened and divided our own members and supporters. And it demoralised Jeremy himself, a man with not a racist bone in his body. It struck at the heart of his politics, at its strongest point, not its weakest. But ultimately, it would be another issue, Brexit, that would bring him down.

CHAPTER 20

A SLOW-MOTION CAR CRASH

The beginning of the end can be dated precisely. It was 11.11 a.m. on 25 September 2018. At the Labour Party Conference in Liverpool, Keir Starmer, the shadow Brexit secretary, was addressing the hall.

"If we need to break the impasse," he said, "our options must include campaigning for a public vote, and nobody is ruling out Remain as an option."

Most Constituency Labour Party delegates—hundreds of them, representing the vast membership under Jeremy Corbyn—let out a roar and rose to their feet for a long ovation. Many trade union delegates did not. Dennis Skinner, the legendary MP for the Leave-voting former-mining community of Bolsover, sat motionless, face like thunder, on the front row. Beside him, Corbyn's LOTO staff wore similar expressions.

Starmer had delivered the line looking down at the printed copy of his speech. There was a reason for that. He had broken collective responsibility. He hadn't told anyone he was about to shift Labour's delicate position on Brexit to one that explicitly countenanced remaining in the European Union. He hadn't cleared that version of his speech. The line didn't appear on the autocue in front of him. LOTO wasn't expecting it.

Starmer had unilaterally sought to put Labour on a path to becoming a Remain party. What was just as significant, he had thrown down the gauntlet to Corbyn, rightly assuming the leader would prove unwilling or unable to stamp his authority on him and the party. The end point of that dynamic, a little more than a year later, was a crushing general election defeat and the destruction of the Corbyn project.

––––––––––––

It was like watching a vehicle hurtle towards a concrete wall. Labour's catastrophic defeat in the 2019 general election was a slow-motion car crash. The vote was lost months before campaigning began, as Labour careered off course on the Brexit oil slick.

It wasn't inevitable that Labour would come unstuck over Brexit. It did so due to a deadly combination of political naivety from some and opportunism from others that flourished in the vacuum where strong leadership should have been. Most Labour MPs had long been fanatical about the EU. For them, demanding Labour back a second referendum had a triple benefit: it was a cause they actually believed in; it was a position the leadership didn't want to adopt; and, unusually, it put them in harmony with the bulk of the party membership. But while most members were committed Remainers—which mattered to a leader who took his legitimacy from them—they were even more committed supporters of Corbyn and were, I believe, open to being won over by him.

It was a historical tragedy that at the very moment Jeremy's leadership was finally secure, an issue completely unsuited to his way of doing things consumed British politics and destroyed him. The Leave-Remain divide cut across the class appeal that underpinned his "for the many, not the few" rallying cry. He just wasn't excited or passionate about the issue. What got him out of bed in the morning was poverty, the climate crisis and peace, not trading arrangements and supranational law. On the issues that motivated him, he was capable of providing an inspiring lead. On those that didn't, he wasn't.

What's more, Jeremy's collaborative style of leadership—which had worked so well when his top team were all pulling in the same direction in the 2017 election—wasn't effective when his closest friends and advisors were on different sides of the debate. A noble quality proved to be a fatal weakness. Brexit divided Labour from top to bottom. Most Labour constituencies voted to Leave in 2016 but most Labour MPs were Remainers. Two-thirds of Labour voters had supported

Remain, but the party couldn't win without the third that voted Leave, who happened to be disproportionately concentrated in marginal seats. It was a terrible hand to be dealt. Jeremy wanted to hold his team together, the party together, and Labour's supporters together. But his method of doing so was to avoid open confrontation with either side, rather than chart a course and ask people to follow him. The resulting drift was an opportunity for ultra-Remainers, who had the balance of forces in their favour, to create unbearable tensions throughout the party. To the public, it just looked like Labour was a mess.

The story of how we arrived at that point begins in the aftermath of the 2017 general election. Labour's Brexit position in that contest was, in my view, exactly right: respect the referendum result, commit to leaving the EU, but pledge to negotiate a deal to keep us close to our neighbours and protect jobs and rights. That was the promise every Labour MP elected in 2017 made to their constituents. It was also a position Unite supported wholeheartedly. Even though we had argued for Remain in the referendum and had backed it with significant resources, we accepted the democratic result.

Following his brilliant 2017 election performance, Jeremy's leadership was, for the first time, under no threat. For six months he reigned supreme. It's clear to me he should have used that political capital to cement Labour's Brexit position. It was inevitable Theresa May would struggle without a stable majority in parliament; that would encourage the Remain cause. Jeremy should have got on the front foot and said, "Let me make something clear: I've just gone to the people and told them I would respect the referendum result and negotiate a deal to take us out, and that will remain Labour's policy and my position."

He should also have written to every Labour member with the message: "Stay with me. I know the majority of you want to Remain, but respecting the result is where we need to be politically to win the next election." I strongly urged Jeremy's team to arrange for such a letter in the first quarter of 2018, to no avail.

Of course, all of that is easy to say. It wasn't as clear at the time to those in the Leader's Office. In the immediate aftermath of the 2017 election the threat to

Labour's successful Brexit position wasn't obvious—the first mass march for a so-called people's vote, for example, didn't come until June 2018.

The focus was instead on how to ensure the UK got a good exit deal that protected what mattered to working people, not a bad deal that suited Tory free marketeers, and certainly not no deal, which Unite, as a manufacturing union, knew would be a disaster for our members. We were in contact with our sister unions in Europe who were reporting to us what their government ministers were telling them. That put me in no doubt that a Labour government could achieve the kind of deal we wanted.

The priority for us was to secure an economic relationship with the EU that meant there would be no tariffs at the border. The question then arose of whether that was possible while ending the free movement of labour. Stopping free movement had been a main reason a majority had voted Leave. But that didn't prevent the UK negotiating new labour mobility agreements giving EU workers preferential access as part of the talks. Unite argued that what mattered was protecting workers through labour market regulations. Proper regulation would end the exploitation and abuse of migrant workers, undermining the rationale for companies to deliberately recruit cheap labour from overseas. The numbers coming in would be reduced as a result.

I took some criticism from the left for promoting this view. I was accused of playing into a right-wing agenda by implying migrant workers were a problem. But I consistently argued that if we didn't address the issue of immigration, we would leave space for the right wing to peddle their poisonous filth, because the truth was migrant workers were being used to undercut rates of pay and undermine terms and conditions in certain industries—we knew because we represented them. I always went out of my way to say migrant workers were not to blame for anything in our country; the only people to blame were the greedy bosses.

Unite's focus on securing frictionless trade was shared by the Labour leadership. In February 2018, in a speech in Coventry, Corbyn came out in support of a customs union as a central part of the UK's post-Brexit relationship with the EU. It was reported by commentators as a move in a Remain direction, but Corbyn's Remainer critics merely banked it and moved on to their next demand: continued membership of the EU Single Market. A pattern was set.

———————

Two years before coronavirus, another contagion spread through the country: Remainitis. Its symptoms were a loss of judgement and perspective. The infection took hold in the Parliamentary Labour Party in spring and summer 2018, beginning with the rump of Blairite backbenchers and gradually moving through the ranks, ultimately reaching the shadow cabinet.

Emily Thornberry, the shadow foreign secretary, became severely afflicted, believing the pro-EU Lib Dems threatened her 24,000-vote lead over them in Islington South. Inoculation should have been swift. Emily was a very talented politician but if she wanted to take a position that was incompatible with Jeremy's she should have been asked to do so from the backbenches. Keir Starmer's insubordination at the 2018 conference should have been met with the same ultimatum. The trouble was, Jeremy couldn't sack people for defying him if he hadn't said precisely where he stood.

The public sensed growing incoherence in Labour's message. The headline from Starmer's 2018 conference speech was Labour raising the prospect of remaining in the EU; the headline from Corbyn's speech the next day was an offer to support a "sensible deal" to leave if Theresa May could deliver one.

Remainitis thrived on the ambiguity. Ultra-Remainers saw their pressure getting results and were emboldened. At the same time, encouraged by New Labour ghosts who cared much more about damaging Corbyn than staying in the EU, the People's Vote campaign directed their anger at Jeremy, portraying him as Brexit's midwife. It was staggering to hear them talk about the EU as if it was a panacea. I felt like saying to them, "Where the hell have you been for 40 years?"

Remainers came in different shades. There were many who were willing to accept the democratic reality, even if they didn't like it. I thought Jeremy needed to reach out to them, saying: "When we win power, we will come out of the EU but I'll negotiate a deal that will allay your fears. Right now, I want to understand what your fears are; I want you to explain them to me." But there were others who would brook no compromise. They needed to be strongly challenged. The irony was these ultra-Remainers sowed the seeds of their own destruction. Their success spawned the Brexit Party in January 2019. In taking an idea that was taboo—rerunning the referendum—and making it seem realistic, they generated the demand for Nigel Farage's resurrection after the slow death of his UKIP vehicle. Farage made no secret of his intention to appeal to working-class voters in traditional Labour seats who had voted Leave and felt Labour was betraying them. He may have been a "pound shop Enoch Powell," as Russell Brand once called him, but he was on to something—and it would prove fatal for Labour.

In November 2018, Theresa May secured a deal with the EU that pleased no one, then spent the first three months of the next year trying to force it through parliament. On her first attempt, she suffered the biggest government defeat in history, losing by 230 votes as the right wing of her party humiliated her.

That's when my phone rang. "Hello Len," said the prime minister down the line, "would you come and meet me?" It was apparently the first time she had spoken to a trade union leader since taking office. I was keen to go and put my members' concerns to her directly.

Within Unite we had a discussion about whether I should meet May alone or collectively with other trade unions. There were reports that Dave Prentis of Unison and Tim Roache of the GMB would also be invited, along with Frances O'Grady, the TUC general secretary. But Dave and Frances were full-on Remainers, and Tim was heading that way. Going in collectively would mean we spoke with one voice, but we didn't have one voice. Then there was the question of whether I'd go into Number 10 via the front or the back door. My team were saying we had to be careful not to be used by the prime minister for a PR stunt. She needed to be seen to be building wider support for her deal before trying again in parliament. I wasn't worried about that; this would be a PR exercise for

Unite and for trade unions who were never asked into Number 10 under a Tory government. I would go in through the front door.

When the day came, 24 January 2019, I walked up Downing Street, took my time knocking on the door, and smiled to the cameras before going in. Channel 4 News' Gary Gibbon described the spectacle of a "sworn enemy of the Tories and the establishment" rocking up for talks with the prime minister as "a new weirdness" in the Brexit process.

It was a weird meeting. May was flanked by her chief of staff Gavin Barwell and a few ministers, including Stephen Barclay, the Brexit secretary. "Hello Prime Minister," I said, and we sat down. She was often described as socially awkward, and that was my impression. I expected her to open the meeting by speaking for five minutes to set the scene. Instead, she spoke for about 30 seconds. I talked of the need for a customs union to protect manufacturing, saying, "If your deal goes through, we'd then have trade negotiations for different sectors, and I don't understand how you can have those negotiations without talking about a customs union, or customs arrangements—call it what you like." She looked towards Barwell whose face lit up. He said he couldn't agree more, we shouldn't get hung up on names, custom arrangements were what mattered. At that point, I thought, "Hang on, this isn't just a PR exercise." As I left, Barwell came running after me saying the Brexit secretary would be in touch to talk about some of the points I had raised. I knew then there was a deal to be done.

But May's proposals would have to be defeated twice more in parliament before the government began to negotiate seriously. Those months of Brexit deadlock were catastrophic for her, but what was less well-appreciated was how damaging they were for Jeremy Corbyn as well. Here was an anti-establishment outsider chained to the dispatch box in the House of Commons. Whenever the public saw him, he was making a testy late-night speech in the chamber, often broadcast live on BBC1 after a government defeat. To many who voted Leave, he became just another politician trying to frustrate their democratic choice and protect the status quo. This dragged on for months, with endless amendments and baffling procedural chicanery arousing contempt in much of the public.

With each parliamentary vote Labour won, a part of their support base was lost and Corbyn's credentials as an insurgent leader were shredded.

Like a condemned man being pulled apart by horses, Jeremy found himself heaved this way and that as different parts of his party bolted in opposite directions. In February 2019 a group of seven right-wing Labour MPs, a bunch of nonentities led by the future banker Chuka Umunna, broke from Labour to form the pro-second referendum Independent Group, which later became Change UK. Their departure surprised precisely no one, having been anticipated since at least the previous summer, but was greeted by the media with excitement verging on euphoria. The split was actually smaller than expected, and those involved were pigmies compared to the Gang of Four (the defectors who formed the SDP in the early '80s and secured Margaret Thatcher in power), but some in the Labour leadership were spooked and argued a bigger exodus had to be stemmed by shifting position towards Remain. In my view, if some of the most reprehensible MPs in the Labour Party wanted to deselect themselves, I didn't have a problem with it. Let them go.

At the other end of the scale were those on the backbenches and in the shadow cabinet who wanted to help ensure May's deal passed. I agreed with them. By this stage I didn't care whether we were in the EU or out, as long as we could get a decent deal. As general secretary of Unite I knew the strength of feeling on both sides—I was inundated with emails from our members. Many of them were pro-Remain, but I was struck by a meeting of 100 of our manufacturing convenors, from all the top companies, in March 2019. These were people with a lot to lose from a bad Brexit deal. They were fundamentally opposed to no deal but would have no truck with a second referendum either.

What I wanted was a Corbyn government that would help our people. As Tony Woodhouse, the chair of our executive, used to say, "Whether we're in or out, if we've still got a Tory government, we'll still be getting cut to ribbons." As far as I was concerned, obstructing Brexit was a dead end for Labour. May's deal might not have been a good deal, but neither was it a terrible deal or no deal. If it passed, Brexit would be behind us, the Tories would be in turmoil,

May would go under, Boris Johnson would take over but without the "get Brexit done" rationale to turbocharge his premiership, and I felt we would probably find ourselves in a general election by summer 2020, fought on domestic issues against a government that was split in all directions.

Some Labour MPs who wanted the deal to go through began to contact me. Lisa Nandy and Gloria De Piero, both of whom I like, came to my office. Apparently, between 30-40 of their colleagues held the same view, loosely organised as a Respect the Vote group. I was asked to go and meet them by Ian Lavery, a wonderful comrade who, along with Jon Trickett, was the strongest voice opposing a second referendum in the shadow cabinet. We met in Ian's office. About 15 MPs came. I thought that reflected their general problem—most of them didn't turn up, whereas the ultra-Remain MPs never missed an opportunity to push themselves to the fore. Those at the meeting weren't left wing, but the likes of Stephen Kinnock. They were looking for me to be their shield, scared that if they defied Jeremy and broke the whip to vote for the deal or to abstain, they would face deselection by their local party members. They wanted Unite's protection.

I met John McDonnell. Although he would later become the most powerful Labour advocate for a second referendum, at the time his attitude was the same as mine—he just wanted it over and done with. "Tell them to vote for the deal," he said to me.

Unfortunately, the Respect the Vote MPs seemed rather lacking in courage. They talked a good game but, whenever it came to the crunch, almost all of them fell into line with the whip.

———

The only way a version of Theresa May's Brexit deal was going to get through parliament was as a result of a cross-party agreement that ensured Labour's priorities were met. Following her third defeat on 29 March 2019, and after two rounds of 'indicative votes' in the House of Commons revealed there was no proposal—from a no deal Brexit to a second referendum—that could command a majority, May finally invited Labour to enter negotiations. Those talks rolled on for six weeks through April and the first half of May.

When Labour's team of negotiators, including John McDonnell, Keir Starmer, Rebecca Long-Bailey, Andrew Fisher and Seumas Milne, came face-to-face with their government counterparts, they found the Tory team was hopelessly split. The trouble was, so were they. The big question was whether Jeremy Corbyn could get away with doing any kind of deal to let Brexit through, even tacitly. He was afraid of being accused of keeping a Tory government in power. The organised Remain cause, which by this stage wasn't interested in a soft Brexit, only in stopping it altogether, would have screamed betrayal (indeed, Lib Dem and Green MPs had voted against a customs union in the indicative votes in order to kill off a threat to their prized second referendum).

I believe Seumas would have been in favour of doing a deal. He, Karie Murphy, Andrew Murray, Ian Lavery and Jon Trickett all saw the sense in getting Brexit out of the way if at all possible. I don't think McDonnell, who was really the key figure in this process, Starmer, Fisher and others were serious about coming to an agreement. The Leave-Remain breach had divided Labour's top team.

There's no question in my mind that there was a deal to be done had McDonnell wanted it. At a meeting in Corbyn's office with trade union general secretaries and Labour's negotiating team I said: "As a negotiator I can see that all the pieces of the jigsaw puzzle are on the table. If you sent me away over a weekend I could cut a deal. But I don't think you want to cut a deal." The arguments against were perfectly legitimate. I remember McDonnell saying to me, "Len, it's like negotiating with a company that's going into administration." May's authority was draining away by the day. It was clear Boris Johnson and the Tory Brexiteers wouldn't honour any deal made with Labour. The negotiations felt doomed.

The reason I was so sure a deal could be cut was because I had been having secret talks with the government myself. Following my conversation with the prime minister, I met the Brexit secretary, Stephen Barclay, in Number 9

Downing Street. It was useful, if for no other reason than allowing me to say I have been in Numbers 9, 10 and 11.

I had far more promising meetings with another cabinet minister, Greg Clark. As business secretary, he had dealt with me before. We had developed a good relationship that had produced positive outcomes in a number of cases involving manufacturing companies. He seemed to me to be the only Tory minister who understood the practicalities of the government's role in business. I also liked him as a man. He wanted to ensure a Brexit deal went through by a substantial majority. Basically, he was hoping I could persuade Corbyn to give Labour MPs a free vote, meaning those who wanted the deal to pass wouldn't have to break the whip.

I also saw an opportunity to get something out of this for workers and the trade unions. I had concerns about the way the TUC had approached Brexit because, in my opinion, Frances O'Grady—a good friend and great TUC general secretary—had overstepped the mark in pursuit of a Remain agenda. I remember saying to her, "Frances, instead of you banging the drum for Europe, we should be negotiating with the government to get something our people need." So I didn't involve the TUC or the other unions in my discussions with Clark. Those talks weren't about the Brexit deal itself, but simple, easy changes to the law unrelated to Brexit that would have a big benefit for trade unions—things the government could realistically concede. There was no ethical dilemma for me in this arrangement because I would have tried to persuade Jeremy to give a free vote anyway.

I settled on five demands: allowing workplace balloting for industrial action; allowing e-balloting for internal union elections; dropping plans to make compensation claims for workplace accidents prohibitively expensive by raising the small claims court limit; dropping the reintroduction of employment tribunal fees; and making unions eligible for the business rate property tax relief just as charities were. Clark, who had the ear of May, was very positive. I said I'd need something in writing so I could discuss it with my team. Since this was all being done under the table, he didn't want to provide that, but said he would send over his chief of staff with three copies of an agreement. She would stay in the room while we read the document, then collect up the copies and take them away at the end.

But when the chief of staff came to my office with the document, it didn't say what had been agreed. I rang Greg to find out why and there were some explanations—for example, where I had asked for unions to be eligible for the business rate property tax relief, he said that wasn't possible nationally, but local authorities could be given the power to make the change, and he pointed out that most properties owned by trade unions were in Labour-controlled areas. But his message, in not so many words, was that much of the agreement would have to be done on a nod and a wink. That would be difficult for me.

In any case, it became clear that within the Labour leadership, the Remain side of the argument had the upper hand, and the prospect of Jeremy agreeing to a free vote was unlikely. Labour broke off the negotiations with the government in mid-May, just a few weeks before the European Parliament election, which had to be held as the UK had failed to leave the EU.

That election on 23 May 2019 was humiliating for the two main parties, with Labour finishing third, polling 13.6 per cent, and the Tories doing even worse, coming fifth with just 8.8 per cent. The Lib Dems surged to 19.6 per cent, but it was Nigel Farage's new Brexit Party that was the big winner, topping the poll with 30.5 per cent. Things could have been worse: the Chuka Umunna vanity project Change UK sank without trace.

The result caused panic in the Labour ranks. Everyone was running around like headless chickens. I honestly couldn't understand why. I was saying, "Hang on, this election is totally irrelevant. Nobody gives a toss." All it had demonstrated was that the country was split down the middle on Brexit. Well, we knew that. It had no relevance to a general election. I sounded like a stereotypical Scouser telling people to "calm down, calm down."

The Remain side were acting as if the Lib Dems had swept the board, vindicating their position. Utter nonsense. But it helped the advocates of a second referendum to become dominant within Labour. This, I believe, is when John

McDonnell panicked and was lost to us. Diane Abbott had already been agitating hard for Labour to support a people's vote. Corbyn now had his two closest friends in politics, one in each ear, telling him to move on the issue—and that's what he did, committing to a second referendum in all circumstances.

Meanwhile, the collapse of her negotiations with Labour meant the end of the road for May. The day after the European election she resigned. Few doubted who her successor would be. In Boris Johnson, Labour would be facing a very different adversary.

CHAPTER 21

THE BREXIT ELECTION

"John," I said, "I couldn't care less whether we're in or out of the EU. If being a Remain party gets us into government, I'll shout it from the top of this building. Just tell me how that can happen. Tell me what I'm missing."

I'd gone to see John McDonnell in his office in summer 2019 because I couldn't, for the life of me, see how Labour could win a general election by appealing only to Remainers when the seats it most needed to gain—and those it was most in danger of losing—were almost all in Leave-voting areas.

I'd previously posed this question to Andrew Fisher, Jeremy Corbyn's policy chief who was urging his boss to embrace a second referendum. He hadn't been able to tell me how it would help Labour's chances. At least John now gave me an answer: Labour's members, its campaigning force, were Remainers. We couldn't run an election without our army, he said, and it was "crumbling." I told him I wasn't so sure. He said, "Len, I'm telling you, I go around the country, you don't. I speak to our members and that's the situation." "OK John," I said, "I'm not going to challenge you on that, other than to tell you that I do go around my union and that's not what I'm hearing. I'm being told that in our industrial heartlands, Unite members are furious about Jeremy bowing to Remain, and they're switching to the Tories."

We disagreed. As I left John's office I said, "I just hope you're right and I'm wrong."

———

There should be no doubt that the 2019 general election was the Brexit election. To those on the right of the Labour Party who try to pin the blame for the defeat on Jeremy Corbyn's left policies, I have only one thing to say: the Conservatives won 44 per cent of the vote and a landslide victory on the back of three words— "Get Brexit Done." People in Labour's heartlands didn't vote Tory because they disagreed with rail renationalisation or regional investment banks, they voted to make good on their choice from 2016. Labour's incoherent shift to supporting a second referendum was, in contrast, a disaster that led directly to its downfall.

After years of delay over Brexit, in Boris Johnson the Tories had a leader who could persuade people that political will was all that was needed to break the deadlock. I thought his buffoonery was a mask. This was a man who had won the London Mayoralty twice in a Labour city. Where Theresa May had been an awful campaigner, he was strong. He wasn't going to antagonise his core voters or give Labour easy attack lines on austerity. His strategy to pit the people against parliament was not only brilliant from his point of view, tapping into the anti-establishment sentiment in the country, but was devastating for Corbyn's insurgent project, already looking as if it had been captured by the forces of the status quo. A populist pitch from an old Etonian could easily have sounded phoney; Johnson and his team led by Dominic Cummings went out of their way to convince people he meant what he said. Every time he outraged the liberal commentariat, whether by proroguing parliament (unlawfully—it didn't matter) or withdrawing the whip from 21 Tory Remainer MPs, the public just saw someone who was determined to get things done—to get Brexit done.

Labour, on the other hand, was all over the place. I don't know if our leading voices knew the party line on Brexit, but if they did, they pretended not to. They pursued their own agendas, saying whatever they liked. There was no discipline. Leadership was absent. The only thing the Parliamentary Labour Party seemed united on was walking into Johnson's trap of appearing intent on frustrating the will of the people at every turn.

In the wake of the European election, a majority of Corbyn's shadow cabinet had come to the view that Labour needed to position itself as an explicitly

Remain party. At a showdown shadow cabinet meeting in June 2019, Corbyn's strategy director Carl Shoban argued that was the wrong conclusion, pointing out that the greatest swings against Labour had actually been in Leave-voting areas. "It remains the case that there are more target and defensive seats in the Midlands and North of England which voted Leave," his report read. "The recent elections don't suggest any change to this basic arithmetic... There is an evident risk that shifting to a more explicitly pro-Remain position would leave us vulnerable in seats we need to hold or win without enough potential seat gains in winnable Remain-majority areas."

These warnings fell on deaf ears. It became clear to me that we were drifting towards Labour not only supporting a second referendum, but declaring in advance that, whatever the circumstances, it would be fighting to Remain. I felt I needed to do something to stabilise the ship. The trade unions should step in and give a lead. In July 2019 I organised a meeting of the Big Four unions to thrash out a Brexit position statement that would serve as guidance to Labour. I wanted to give Jeremy something solid on which to stand his ground.

We met in Unison's HQ on 8 July. The discussions were complicated by the fact the unions were themselves divided on Brexit. The CWU had just had a policy conference that had rejected a second referendum out of hand; Unison was strongly for Remain; and the GMB was leaning the same way, although its position was more interesting. Tim Roache, GMB general secretary, believed that whatever deal was stuck with the EU should go back to the people, just as trade unions have to take any deal they make with an employer back to their members. By this time, I knew we couldn't put the "public vote" genie back in the bottle. My focus was instead on preventing the leadership from being bounced into adopting an out-and-out Remain position.

The statement we worked up envisaged two scenarios. In scenario 1, a Tory prime minister (who we assumed would be Johnson—he was elected two weeks later) had reached a deal with the EU or decided to leave with no deal. In that case, the statement read:

The Labour Party should confirm that whatever deal is negotiated by the new Tory prime minister or an exit based on no deal should be put to the people in a public confirmatory vote. The options must be:

1. Accepting the deal or a Tory no deal in the knowledge of its terms
2. Remaining in the European Union.

In this event, the Labour Party should campaign to remain in the European Union.

This position was somewhat theoretical, since Johnson was bound to go for a general election rather than a referendum. That led to scenario 2:

In the event that a general election is called, Labour's manifesto position should be:

Negotiating with the European Union to respect the Brexit vote from 2016, reflecting the negotiating priorities that Labour has outlined.

Any final Labour deal should then be put back to the people. The options on the ballot paper should be:

1. Accepting the Labour negotiated deal
2. Remaining in the European Union

The Labour Party's campaign position on such a ballot should depend on the deal negotiated.

As we were crafting the statement, a surprised Dave Prentis of Unison asked me, "Would you accept this, Len?" I said I would. He thought I would baulk at the idea of Remain being on the ballot paper in a second vote, but what mattered to me was getting the other unions to agree that Labour would negotiate a deal "to respect the Brexit vote from 2016." I believed Labour had to be able to tell the voters it accepted the referendum result and would negotiate a deal to leave. To bring Unison along with that, we agreed that Remain would be on the ballot when we took that deal back to the people. That was the compromise.

Now, in my mind Labour would negotiate a deal and then campaign for it in the subsequent referendum. That seemed self-evident to me, as I had total conviction that a Labour government would get a good deal. But the retort came back: "What If it's a bad deal? If we were negotiating as trade unions with an employer, we wouldn't recommend our members vote for a deal we thought was bad." I couldn't argue with that. If I wanted to achieve unity, I had to concede that Labour's "campaign position on such a ballot should depend on the deal negotiated." With a bit of discipline and political skill this was a workable position, but it left the door open for the likes of Emily Thornberry, Keir Starmer, Diane Abbott and ultimately even John McDonnell to publicly declare that, whatever the deal, they would campaign for Remain. I didn't envisage they would take a stance so ludicrous—the very people who would be negotiating a deal saying in advance they would tell the public to reject it. It was so stupid it beggared belief.

Once finalised, the statement hammered out by the Big Four was passed by TULO (the Trade Union and Labour Party Liaison Organisation) and presented to Labour. The position it outlined obviously wasn't ideal—it was a frustrating compromise. But I felt it was considerably better than the alternative at the time. The shadow cabinet debated it almost immediately. Unfortunately, that's where the unity ended. The politicians only agreed scenario 1. The more significant scenario 2 didn't go far enough for the Remainers.

———————

Labour remained all at sea on the Brexit issue for the rest of the summer. While Corbyn held talks with the SNP, Lib Dems and Greens about forming a temporary coalition government to depose the prime minister and stop no deal— which, however justifiable, reinforced the impression Labour preferred parliamentary stitch-ups to democracy—Boris Johnson set about his single-minded agenda from his new residence in Downing Street. Watching this slow-motion car crash unfold I could only think, "Can we have an election next week, please, before things get even worse?"

There was a chance for Labour to push for a general election in September 2019. At the time, Johnson's threat to leave with no deal was considered plausible. That happened to be the only outcome the entire Labour movement could unite against. If a Brexit election was unavoidable, then the least worst option was for Labour to be at the head of a groundswell of opposition to no deal. But, as had become usual, the shadow cabinet was split, with the Remain side—which sensed an opportunity to get a second referendum out of all the chaos—urging Jeremy against an election unless no deal was taken off the table. It was clear to me that some of them would have preferred a people's vote to a Corbyn government.

Meanwhile, efforts to cement Labour's Brexit position continued. A developed version of the trade unions' scenario 2 was adopted by TULO at the TUC Congress in Brighton in early September, setting the stage for it to be debated—despite the lack of shadow cabinet consensus—at the Labour Party Conference later that month.

Ultra-Remain party members (some of them backed by big money networks) had been organising for this moment for months, winning votes at Constituency Labour Parties to submit motions to Conference that would officially make Labour a Remain party. They had the wind at their backs as they arrived in Brighton. On Saturday 21 September a People's Vote march in the city was addressed by Emily Thornberry, whose Remainitis condition had become so severe she had taken to wearing a blue dress and a gold star necklace in an effort to look like a walking EU flag. "We must make sure that Labour campaigns for Remain," she announced, breaking collective responsibility for the thousandth time, "and not just that, but that we lead the campaign to Remain!" Keir Starmer spoke too, observing: "We've come a long way. This time last year we were talking about keeping the option of a people's vote on the table." Well, if anyone still believed he hadn't been pursuing a bigger agenda with the unauthorised line in his conference speech the previous year, that gave the game away.

The crunch came on 23 September, when Conference was given the option to vote for the leadership's position and a composite motion from Remainers committing Labour to "campaign energetically for a public vote and to stay in the EU in that referendum." Unite was instrumental in making certain the stance developed since the summer was put to Conference in the form of a National Executive Committee statement. "A Labour government would secure a sensible Leave deal... and within six months would put it before the people in a referendum alongside the option to remain," the statement read. "The NEC believes it is right that the party shall only decide how to campaign in such a referendum... following the election of a Labour government."

Despite the statement being based on an agreement between the unions, Unison then did the dirty on us and decided to back the Remainer motion instead. I thought that meant the NEC statement would go down to defeat. CLP delegates were expected to be overwhelmingly in favour of Remain, meaning it would take almost all of the trade unions' 50 per cent share of the vote on the conference floor to carry the day. Unison putting their sizable weight on the other side meant we were probably knackered.

But when I spoke at a number of fringe meetings in the run up to the vote, I started to think I might have miscalculated. These were some of the best fringe meetings I have ever done—packed to the rafters, electric. The response I got from the audiences was incredible. "We might be in with a shout here," I thought.

The debate on the conference floor was highly charged with fantastic contributions. The air was thick with tension and excitement. Then came the votes. Against the expectations of Unite and even LOTO, we won. The NEC statement was passed and the Remainer motion voted down. Extraordinarily, we carried most of the CLP delegates, cancelling out the desertions of Unison and, at the last moment, USDAW. The Remainers had been defeated and Emily and her dress had gone up in smoke. We had averted Labour becoming an out-and-out Remain party.

But the Remainers were not chastened by their defeat. Keir immediately contradicted official party policy on his own brief by saying he was disappointed by the result and would still campaign for Remain. "Would I have liked us to have gone a bit further and won that vote?" he asked, "Of course I would."

To be honest, it's difficult to feel aggrieved at Keir for such comments when there was no party discipline. Shadow ministers could say anything. Why blame

Keir, Emily, Diane or John, when what was needed was for Jeremy himself to tell them: "Step outside the line and you're a goner"? Had Jeremy come out publicly and asked delegates to support the NEC statement, the vote would have been more easily won. But he preferred to stay above the fray.

The ultimate example of this trait was seen in another drama at the 2019 conference: the attempted removal of Tom Watson as deputy leader. There's no question Tom should have been sacked from the shadow cabinet long before. Jeremy had the power to drop him as shadow culture secretary whenever he wanted, and Tom, in his quest to find ever more inventive ways to be disruptive, had provided him with any number of pretexts.

Tom's latest wrecking initiative was to reinvent himself as an ultra-Remainer. I don't believe there was an ounce of sincerity about it. This was someone who first responded to the referendum result by flirting with Trump-like protectionist rhetoric. But in 2019, seeking to drive a wedge between the leadership and the members, he gave a speech declaring: "Our members are Remain, our values are Remain, our hearts are Remain." It did beg the question: was Tom genuine about anything?

Unusually furious, Corbyn gave the instruction to sack Watson as shadow culture secretary but, in typical style, was talked out of it by McDonnell for the sake of party unity. Plan B was the considerably more difficult task of removing Watson as deputy leader. That would require a rule change at Conference to delete the position from the rulebook. Again, Jeremy gave the go-ahead to his chief of staff Karie Murphy to execute the plan, before backing out of it at the last minute. It was a self-inflicted wound. The plot broke cover and was then aborted, giving a delighted press the perfect soap opera with which to fill their reports as Conference opened.

The botched manoeuvre was unjustly blamed on Karie and became a key plank of a nasty campaign to oust her from her LOTO job. This was the culmination of the Brexit breach that forced apart the once solid team around Jeremy. The close alliance between the trio of most senior LOTO advisors—Karie Murphy, Seumas Milne and Andrew Fisher—had been the rock of the Corbyn project. That rock fractured over Brexit, with Karie and Seumas fighting a rear-guard battle to prevent Labour becoming a Remain party, while Andrew was increasingly drawn towards McDonnell. It all blew up when Andrew wrote a devastating letter claiming there was a lack of "human decency" in the Leader's Office. It was posted in a WhatsApp group of 12 people and inevitably leaked to the *Sunday Times*—as I'm sure was the intention. For someone who had been so close to Karie and Seumas, it was an extraordinary act of betrayal.

While Seumas was the real target of Andrew's letter, Karie was the one in the sights of John McDonnell, who was now unabashedly leading the Remain faction in alliance with Diane Abbott and other LOTO staff. They saw Karie as the final obstacle to Jeremy signing up unequivocally to the Remain cause. If she was removed, Seumas and the other advisors and comrades arguing Labour had to retain some connection to its Leave voters—Ian Lavery, Jon Trickett, Amy Jackson, James Schneider and others—could be sidelined.

In truth, it was less a principled policy battle than a naked power grab by McDonnell. In this he prevailed. On 7 October, just three weeks before the widely anticipated general election would be called, Jeremy removed Karie from her role in LOTO, sending her to Labour HQ to prepare the election campaign. The former head of the civil service, Bob Kerslake—an arch-Remainer who just weeks later would be on the front page of the *Daily Telegraph* saying Jeremy could be sacrificed to secure a deal with the Lib Dems—was brought in to conduct a review of LOTO. He wasn't even a Labour Party member. How disgraceful.

On 17 October Johnson secured a deal with the EU, upending the calculations of the ultra-Remainers in parliament who had thought the time for their beloved second referendum was nigh. The political terrain was transformed overnight. But that hadn't dawned on those at a People's Vote rally in Parliament Square two days later. This time, the full quartet of John, Diane, Keir and Emily appeared before the crowd, which responded by gracelessly chanting: "Where's Jeremy Corbyn?"

The Remainers didn't know it, but they had already lost. With a deal in hand, Johnson was now perfectly positioned to ask the country to back him in a general election and end the Brexit deadlock once and for all. Labour, in stark contrast, was promising more Brexit wrangling as it negotiated a new deal and put it back to the people.

Jeremy, the conviction politician, the man who promised straight talking, honest politics, was now widely perceived as sitting on the fence. The press was asking if he was planning to campaign against his own deal like his Brexit and foreign secretaries had pledged to do or break with most of his party to campaign for it. A few weeks into the campaign he and his team gave an answer—he would stay neutral. It went down about as well as you would expect. To me, it seemed obvious he should have said: "Yes, I'm 100 per cent confident I can negotiate a good deal and I will campaign for that deal." But to be convincing he would have needed his shadow cabinet behind him. By the election campaign it was too late to rescue any coherence in Labour's message.

When I visited our heartlands in the Midlands and the North during the campaign, I found the very people who two years earlier had embraced Corbyn as something fresh now thought he was betraying them. It was terrible to hear the way they talked about him—it wasn't nice at all; hatred isn't too strong a word. While people would mention the full range of ways in which he had been toxified, make no bones about it, the issue was Brexit.

I went to Jaguar Land Rover in Solihull, our biggest workplace with 15,000 workers, and met the convenors and shop stewards. The senior convenor, Mick Graham, a strong and impressive man, said to me: "Len, I hate to tell you this, but we couldn't get our stewards to go onto the shop floor and tell people to vote Labour. They said to us, 'Please don't ask us to do that because we'll get slaughtered.'" At a meeting of the stewards I was told: "Jeremy is regarded as a traitor over Brexit." That was it, done deal.

The irony is Jeremy's line that he wanted to bring the country together rather than dismiss one or the other side of the Brexit divide was statesmanlike. It might have worked for a typical Labour leader—it's not difficult to imagine the press rallying behind Tony Blair if he had talked about uniting a divided nation. But that kind of coverage wasn't available to an anti-establishment political project.

Instead, Corbyn's treatment at the hands of the media, including the supposedly impartial BBC, was shameful. Never in my life have I seen a character assassination of such ferocity and cruelty. For the crime of wanting to make the country a more tolerable place for workers and the most vulnerable, the man was painted as something alien to Britain. Researchers at Loughborough University found press hostility to Labour doubled compared to the previous election, while criticism of the Tories halved. "This level of negativity towards Labour was far from 'business as usual,'" they concluded. The imbalance was reflected in broadcast news coverage. It was typified by the political editors of both the BBC and ITV casually reporting that a Conservative advisor was punched by a Labour activist—an incident that never happened, invented by Tory spin doctors, and repeated by journalists so keen to do Labour in that they didn't even have the professional integrity to check the facts.

In interviews Jeremy looked frustrated and unhappy, bogged down in questions about referendums and antisemitism. He wasn't the same man. I had no hope that the magic of 2017 could be rekindled. A winter election meant there were few outdoor rallies. In an effort to move the agenda off Brexit, Labour overcompensated with a stuffed manifesto. It didn't work. Meanwhile, Nigel Farage's Brexit Party stood down its candidates in Tory-held seats, consolidating the Leave vote behind Johnson.

Unite put considerably more money into the Labour campaign than anyone else, as usual, but we knew it was faltering. Our desperation was clear from the "Come home to Labour" advertising campaign we ran in the heartlands in the final weeks. That was the most effective line we could put forward.

The exit poll moment couldn't have been more of a contrast to the jubilation of two years earlier. I watched it in a bar near Labour HQ. The result that flashed up on the screen was even worse than I expected. I just left the bar and went home.

I felt angry and let down. I blamed Jeremy and John—the former for his lack of decisive leadership on Brexit, the latter for his poor judgement. The two of them created a golden opportunity for the left—for which the credit is all theirs. They then wasted that opportunity—for which the blame must be theirs too.

The tragedy was that had Labour committed early to respect the referendum result and not been blown off course, it would have found itself in a far better place. Apart from the ridiculous confusion around whether a Labour government would campaign for its own deal, the actual position it stood on was preferable to full support for Remain. The trouble was, whatever it said in the manifesto, after months of looking as though it was trying to frustrate Brexit in parliament, and without giving a clear message to the contrary, Labour was perceived as a Remain party anyway. Given that, the obvious question is whether it would have been better for Labour to cut its losses and commit unequivocally to Remain. The answer is that it wouldn't have changed the maths: there weren't enough winnable Remain seats, but there were plenty of losable Leave seats.

As it was, Unite's position was vindicated in the most painful way possible. Of the 54 seats that Labour lost to the Tories in 2019, 52 had voted Leave. There was a 10 per cent swing to the Tories among Leavers, compared to no swing to the Tories among Remainers. A post-election poll by JLPartners of voters who abandoned Labour in 2019 having backed them in 2017 found Brexit was the number one reason for their change of allegiance.

Ironically, the most compelling evidence for the damage done by Labour's flirtation with the Remain cause was the subsequent behaviour of the man who kicked it all off back at the 2018 conference. When Boris Johnson finally secured a trade deal with the EU in December 2020, the new Labour leader Keir Starmer pledged to vote for it before even having read it, so keen was he to signal to voters in our heartlands that Labour wanted to get Brexit done.

CHAPTER 22

NEW MANAGEMENT

He was saying all the right things. Radicalism, unity, winning back the so-called red wall. The man speaking was Keir Starmer. It was the eve of his leadership election victory. The result wasn't yet known but the winner was. Keir had walked away with it. "Congratulations! You're going to be elected leader," I said.

I had phoned to assure him he should not see me or Unite as an enemy. "Absolutely not," he said. "I tell my team that you and I have a good relationship." In fact, I had been careful not to attack him during the contest. Unite had backed his opponent, Rebecca Long-Bailey, and I had come under pressure to launch some missiles at Starmer. I refused, not least because I thought he was going to win, but also because I didn't see him as a right winger.

"Keir," I said, "there are those that regard you as a Blairite. I don't. There are those that regard you as a right winger. I don't. But what will define your leadership is if you're strong enough to resist the pressure that you will come under from the right of the party, the establishment and the serious right-wing media."

"I will be able to resist that," he replied.

Our phone call lasted more than an hour. He set out what he was planning to do with his leadership, told me he would retain the group set up by Jeremy Corbyn to liaise with the unions and said he wanted a personal channel of communication with me. All very good, I said.

I praised the radical platform he had stood on. "The vast majority of Labour Party members want that radical edge," I told him. He said he did too; he had no intention of moving away from it.

Unity was his objective within the party, he stressed. "Keir, you'll be in a really good position to deliver that," I replied, "because people are tired of the divisiveness that Jeremy had to live with. Everyone wants a united party." He told me he liked Jeremy and that many of the policies developed under him were good.

"I think you can become the next prime minister in 2024—not with a majority, but as leader of the largest party in a hung parliament—by winning back our red wall seats," I predicted. "But to do that you will need the left because you will need a united party. It's the unions and the left economic policies that will help you win in our heartlands. If you ditch the radicalism and lose the left, then you won't have a united party, and you won't win those red wall seats back."

"Oh no, I want a united party," he said.

So much for all of that.

Who is Sir Keir Starmer? A babe in the woods, new to politics, fallen prey to his advisors? Or someone altogether more calculating, following a plan to marginalise the left? I try to take people at face value and give them the benefit of the doubt. Initially Keir seemed a decent man with the correct values. Six months later he had suspended his predecessor and was systematically attacking my wing of the labour movement. He had won the leadership promising unity around an unambiguously radical platform. The question was, did he believe any of it?

That Starmer won such a commanding victory was more down to the devastation of the 2019 general election defeat than anything he put forward. It was clear to everyone that the great idealist project on which the Labour Party had set sail in 2015 had hit the rocks. The only question was whether the ship had been holed below the waterline.

The left, having been under fire for nearly five years, had not had time for succession planning. Who would be the standard bearer? I thought it should be John McDonnell. We had disagreed strongly—sometimes, in private, viciously—over Brexit and the shenanigans in the Leader's Office. But for me, he was the one with the authority to carry forward Corbyn's policies. He could communicate a clear vision for the next stage. And if it was a radical platform with slicker leadership that the membership wanted, he would have their trust. I still believe he would have won. I urged him to stand; he declined, saying he had already announced he would step down with Jeremy.

Rebecca Long-Bailey was the name to emerge instead. She was very intelligent, competent, a rising star, but she was slow out of the blocks. While Starmer's campaign was up and running a week after Labour's 12 December defeat, Becky took an age to officially declare. Vital time was lost as, behind the scenes, people argued about the composition of her campaign team. By the time she came to see me shortly after Christmas, there were already doubts about whether she was up for it. "Becky, the first thing I've got to ask you is do you want this job?" She said she did. "OK," I said, "then there's every likelihood you will get Unite's support."

When the race got properly underway it was evident that most of the contenders realised the party membership weren't looking for a dramatic change in direction. The exception was Jess Phillips, the choice of the hard right. As in 2015, it was extraordinary to see this once dominant strand within Labour so diminished. Whenever they put their proposals before the membership openly, instead of pulling strings behind the scenes, they got nowhere. In the 12 years since the crash of 2008, they had come up with no policies and no vision. They were bankrupt of ideas. All they offered was nostalgia for the New Labour years. Jess herself was quickly found to be utterly vacuous, which many of us on the left already knew. She was a loud hailer with nothing to say. After giving what was, in her own words, an "awful" hustings performance, she dropped out on 21 January 2020.

The remaining candidates—except Starmer because of a terrible family tragedy—came to speak at a Unite hustings in front of our executive on 24 January. Emily Thornberry, once my tip for future leader, spoke well, but she had destroyed her chances over the previous year and would drop out of the race a few weeks later having failed to secure enough nominations from constituency parties. Lisa Nandy, who had come to see me seeking my support, was polished and authoritative. But it was Long-Bailey who had the politics that would do the most to improve the lives of Unite's members. She received our nomination, along with Richard Burgon for deputy.

Becky's campaign wasn't firing on all cylinders, however. From the very beginning it wasn't right. Nobody was quite sure who was doing what. There was no real direction, no energy. And the foot soldiers of the left were exhausted and demoralised, incapable of recreating the movement buzz of the Corbyn campaigns.

Starmer's operation, by contrast, was powerful and perfectly pitched. He promised to make "the moral case for socialism." He had clearly been busy preparing his lavishly funded leadership run while the rest of us were fighting a general election, reportedly meeting Corbyn supporters turned Remainitis super-spreaders Paul Mason and Laura Parker to refine his stance. Far from trashing the previous leadership, he argued, "we must continue to be the party that opposes austerity, supports common ownership and champions investment in our public services." In a slick campaign video, well-chosen episodes from his previous life as a lawyer were used to paint a picture of a lifelong crusader for justice.

"My promise to you," Starmer wrote above a list of 10 pledges to the Labour membership, "is that I will maintain our radical values." He would tax the rich and raise corporation tax—"no stepping back from our core principles." He pledged to scrap universal credit and tuition fees, "put the Green New Deal at the heart of everything we do," and "put human rights at the heart of foreign policy." He would "support common ownership of rail, mail, energy and water," and end outsourcing in the NHS. Appealing to his Remain base, he promised to "defend free movement as we leave the EU." He pledged to strengthen workers' rights and "work shoulder to shoulder with trade unions." He would devolve power and wealth, strive for equality, and provide "forensic" opposition to the Tories.

It was an unmistakably Corbyn-esque programme, albeit less bold and couched in vaguer language to leave wriggle room ("common ownership" instead of "public ownership," for example). With all three of the final candidates—Starmer, Long-Bailey and Nandy—explicitly positioning themselves inside this new policy consensus, Labour was united on a radical platform. The Labour selectorate only had to choose who would best put it across to the public. Overwhelmingly, they opted for Starmer.

Keir won on the first round with 56 per cent of the vote—less than Jeremy achieved in either of his victories but resounding nonetheless. Becky was a distant second on 29 per cent. Surprisingly, among affiliated members Lisa pipped Becky to second.

There was soul searching on the left about how such a solidly pro-Corbyn party membership could have produced such a result. Of course, the shock of defeat had changed the weather, but it was apparent that many had mistaken all Corbyn supporters for fully-fledged socialists, when in fact a large chunk of the membership simply liked Jeremy and identified with him on important moral issues like climate change, homelessness, mental health and nuclear weapons. There was also a more straightforward explanation: members just believed what Starmer told them—that he stood for the same things they, and Jeremy, stood for.

———————

I developed a very good relationship with Keir Starmer in the early months of his leadership. We met on three occasions despite the Covid restrictions and had at least a dozen telephone conversations. Contrary to what might be expected, I spoke to him far more than I ever did Jeremy Corbyn.

But a curious pattern developed. Our conversations would be very positive only for Keir to then do something completely at odds with the spirit of our discussion. I would report back to Unite's political team that we should give him a chance, and they would tell me I was being taken for a ride. On one occasion I said to Keir directly that my team thought he was taking the piss out of me. "Of course I'm not, Len," he said.

It was inevitable that Starmer would begin his tenure by telling the public, "I'm not Corbyn." All leaders differentiate themselves from their predecessors, and the media had toxified Corbyn to such an extent that Starmer had no option. That simple message won him the support of the soft right and soft left in the party as well as the liberal media. The unity he had promised was his, provided he could reach out and keep the left on board.

But for all his talk of unity, Starmer's shadow ministerial appointments suggested that was not his priority. While there was a smattering of left-wing figures in his team—most of whom would soon be gone, including Rebecca Long-Bailey who was sacked in June 2020—the junior ranks were flooded with right wingers like Wes Streeting and Pat McFadden. Starmer evidently calculated that he could get away with sidelining the left if he promoted the soft left—for the most important position of shadow chancellor he opted for Anneliese Dodds, a soft-left MP, although it was concerning that his alternative choice was right winger Rachel Reeves. Those concerns proved well founded when, after just a year, Dodds was shunted aside to make way for Reeves.

More revealing was the team Starmer gathered around him in the Leader's Office. While he did hire Simon Fletcher, who had worked for Corbyn, most of the senior positions were filled by people from the right—the likes of Director of Communications Ben Nunn and Chief of Staff Morgan McSweeney, who according to authors Gabriel Pogrund and Patrick Maguire masterminded Starmer's strategy to "convince a pro-Corbyn membership to marginalise Corbynism without their realising it." Even if, as was sometimes claimed, Starmer's own policy preferences were vaguely soft left, he wouldn't be able to resist the pull of the right when surrounded by advisors who were joining in the heaving.

So when, a week after becoming leader, Starmer faced his first challenge with the leaking of a dynamite internal report exposing the vicious factionalism of the Labour right bureaucracy under Iain McNicol, he and his team's only concern appeared to be who had leaked it. I later said to Starmer, "I don't give a fuck who leaked the report. In fact, if we ever find out who did it, they'll be getting a special medal from Unite."

What bothered Unite was the disturbing and outrageous contents of the report. This was evidence that allegedly showed antisemitism complaints had been appallingly handled before Jennie Formby took over as Labour's general secretary; senior HQ staff had shared abusive messages about MPs, LOTO colleagues and party members (including hoping that one young man, a Unite member known to suffer from poor mental health, "dies in a fire"); and that McNicol's team were "stunned" and "reeling" after Corbyn's better-than-expected 2017 election result, which was, according to one of them, "Opposite to what I had been working towards for the last couple of years!!"

The revelation that, during the 2017 election, senior staff had apparently diverted funds to a secret parallel campaign to protect right-wing MPs was a direct affront to Unite. Since we were by far the biggest donor, it had most likely been our money that was abused in this potential breach of the law. I demanded answers from Starmer; my letter was ignored. I raised it in person; again, I received no response. The party offloaded the whole issue of the leaked report to an inquiry led by Martin Forde; that was kicked into the long grass. Eventually, Unite threatened to take legal action against the party if we continued to get no answers.

Keir's tendency to ally with the right was most evident in his choice of general secretary. It was legitimate for a new leader to want to stamp his authority on the party machine by replacing senior staff, including Jennie Formby. She didn't deserve to be pushed out in the way she was, but in truth she wanted to go. Keir's initial choice to replace her was Anneliese Midgley, who worked for me at Unite and had previously been in Corbyn's LOTO. That was a welcome move. Anneliese was given the impression she would get the job. I agreed to release her but then, just like that, Keir changed his mind. David Evans, a former assistant general secretary in Tony Blair's Labour Party and more recently McSweeney's boss at a political consultancy, was given the leader's blessing. The left suspected Evans of being a factional warrior. They were right.

New Labour-style bureaucratic manoeuvres were back with a vengeance. The examples kept racking up. The most flagrant was the neutering of the party membership on the National Executive Committee by changing the voting system to one that prevented the left from ever winning all nine elected seats. When I asked Keir about reports of this plan before the meeting, he feigned ignorance. Then he pushed it through despite objections that such a change should be voted on by Conference.

This, and other moves like it, were extraordinary. Not even Tony Blair at the height of his power was so brazen. But unlike Blair, Starmer didn't replicate such ruthlessness when it came to opposing the Tories. His Labour was risk-averse and weak in parliament, afraid to attack the government over its failings during the Covid pandemic. 'Keep quiet, say nothing' seemed to be the strategy. Starmer earned a reputation for abstaining on contentious votes—including on the dangerous Covert Human Intelligence Sources, or 'spy cops,' Bill, despite the long history of state surveillance of trade unions.

In summer 2020, I went to see Keir with Dave Ward, general secretary of the CWU, to deliver a message that the left was feeling increasingly marginalised. I told him I was going to frame a copy of his 10 pledges and send it to him. How was anything he had done since winning the leadership conducive to party unity? Again, we were told we had got it wrong; Keir did want unity.

In July 2020, Labour paid out a six-figure sum and gave an apology to seven ex-staff who a year earlier had made allegations in the BBC 'Panorama' episode, "Is Labour Antisemitic?" They had sued the party for defamation after Labour had called them "disaffected former officials" who had "worked actively to undermine" Corbyn and had "personal and political axes to grind." I knew that Labour's barristers had advised the party it would win the case, but Starmer chose instead to settle in an attempt to draw a political line under the antisemitism issue. It cost the party a fortune; an abuse of members' money—much of it from Unite. If it had been Starmer's own money, I dare say he would have been rather more interested in the barristers' advice. It was a huge miscalculation that effectively hung up a sign outside the Labour Party saying: "Queue here with your writ and get your payment over there." It was especially outrageous as some of those who sued the party had since featured in the leaked report which detailed their allegedly factional behaviour.

I said at the time of the settlement that it would meet a reaction from Unite. In October 2020 that came, as our executive voted to reduce by 50,000 the number of members we affiliated to Labour, with the money saved invested instead in grassroots left organisations. Keir responded by telling the media he and I still had "a very good relationship." Later that month he would blow it up.

The Equality and Human Rights Commission report into antisemitism in the Labour Party had been long anticipated. When it was finally published on 29 October 2020, it did not conclude that Labour was institutionally antisemitic as some had insisted it would; it did not demonstrate that antisemitism was widespread within the party; and it did not accuse Jeremy Corbyn himself of being antisemitic. It did, however, find two specific cases among the many it investigated in which "agents of the Labour Party" (an NEC member and a councillor) had made comments that, it said, constituted unlawful harassment; and it found instances of political interference in antisemitism complaints (often in order to speed them up) and inadequate training of complaints staff that both amounted, in the EHRC's judgement, to indirect discrimination against Jews.

On the back of these findings, the EHRC made perfectly reasonable recommendations, the big one being the requirement for Labour to make its complaints process independent until trust could be restored. My view was that Labour should accept all the recommendations without equivocation. I already supported the idea of an independent complaints system—I thought the previous leadership should have embraced it to take the heat out of the issue. I expected Keir Starmer to welcome the report and take the opportunity to apologise so that Labour could move on from this painful saga, which is precisely what he did in a speech on the morning of the report's publication. His words were fine, in the main, and he resisted journalists' attempts to goad him into attacking his predecessor.

Then, about an hour after the speech, Keir called me to tell me he had suspended Jeremy Corbyn from the Labour Party. I had to pinch myself to make sure it wasn't a bad dream.

Now, it's important to get something straight. Later that day, Labour briefed journalists that Starmer hadn't personally suspended Corbyn; the general secretary, David Evans, had. This mattered because one of the EHRC's main lessons was that there must be no political interference in disciplinary cases—indeed, that such interference could be unlawful. It would have been highly embarrassing if Starmer himself had contradicted the EHRC's central stricture within hours of the report's publication. Starmer was careful to tell the BBC 'Today' programme the following morning: "Appropriate action was taken yesterday by the general secretary in suspending Jeremy Corbyn."

But that's not what he told me on the phone. His exact words—and I know this to be accurate because a member of my staff was with me in my office as I listened to the phone on loudspeaker—were: "He put me in an impossible position and I had no choice."

Keir had been enraged by a statement Jeremy had put out in response to the EHRC report that morning. In it, Jeremy had said:

Anyone claiming there is no antisemitism in the Labour Party is wrong... One antisemite is one too many, but the scale of the problem was also dramatically overstated for political reasons by our opponents inside and outside the party, as well as by much of the media. That combination hurt Jewish people and must never be repeated.

In his speech, Keir said if there was anyone who thought "there's no problem with antisemitism in the Labour Party; that it's all exaggerated, or a factional attack, then, frankly, you are part of the problem too, and you should be nowhere near the Labour Party either."

Keir was telling me down the phone that Jeremy had deliberately undermined him. "I didn't want to be in this position," he said. "I spent a week trying to make sure this isn't where we ended up. I spoke to Jeremy last night, Angela [Rayner] told him what I was going to say. It's as if he's gone out of his way to contradict that line in my speech. So I'm beyond angry with Jeremy."

There is no doubt in my mind that Keir overreacted. In actual fact, Jeremy hadn't said there was no problem with antisemitism in the Labour Party, or that it was *all* exaggerated. I told Keir: "I don't know why you said that in your speech in the first place if the whole purpose was to try to calm this down and move on."

I could not believe what had happened. After the call I listened to the audio of an interview Jeremy had done for broadcast news. In it he substantiated his claim that "the numbers have been exaggerated" by pointing to polling evidence. "The public perception in an opinion poll last year was that one third of all Labour party members were somehow or other under suspicion of antisemitism," he said. "The reality is, it was 0.3 per cent of party members had a case against them which had to be put through the process."

I phoned Keir back and left an answerphone message. "I urge you to listen to the full interview," I said. "I think it's been a kneejerk reaction, I've got to be honest with you." I suggested he take a step back, meet Jeremy personally and try to sort this out. "If not, this will spiral completely out of control, the total opposite of what you wanted to do," I warned.

That evening, a 'war room' conference call of the left was held via Zoom with Jeremy, Karie Murphy, Seumas Milne, John McDonnell, Ian Lavery, Jon Trickett, representatives from left trade unions, Momentum and others. It was agreed that before mobilising the membership against the suspension, with the potential of splitting the party, we should first see if a negotiated solution could be reached. Jon Trickett and I were delegated to sound out LOTO.

The leadership, it turned out, was keen to talk. The following afternoon, Friday 30 October, Jon and I went to parliament for a meeting with Keir, his chief of staff Morgan McSweeney, and deputy leader Angela Rayner. Angela began by requesting our discussion be confidential. Given what happened subsequently, I no longer feel bound by that.

Jon and I warned that Keir's decision to suspend Jeremy could lead to a major split. We asked if there was a way to negotiate a settlement to avoid an internal war. Keir replied that he didn't want a war and was happy to talk about ways to reach a solution.

Keir indicated that a clarification statement by Jeremy could be a way of resolving the issue. I then asked a specific question: "Are you saying that if we could reach an agreed form of words that both Jeremy and you, Keir, are happy with, then the suspension could be lifted?"

Keir said "Yes." Morgan and Angela also agreed.

An NEC panel would need to be convened to take care of the formalities and avoid the appearance of political interference. Angela suggested: "We can all come out and welcome his statement and that will set the climate."

Morgan then said he had asked his LOTO colleague Simon Fletcher to draft some words. Jon offered to help, as he knew Simon well. I proposed we allow them to work on a statement for the following day. That was agreed.

By the afternoon of Saturday 31 October, we had a draft. I joined a conference call with Jon and Morgan. I said (and I quote verbatim): "Morgan, as far as we are concerned it is our expectation that if Jeremy agrees to the statement then that is the end of the matter and the suspension will be lifted, after due process, and Jeremy will be back to normal."

Morgan's response was: "Yes, that is our expectation, also."

"And you speak on behalf of Keir?" I asked.

"Yes," came his reply.

That was the deal for Jeremy's reinstatement. A month and a half later, on 9 December, in response to questions from Sky News journalist Tom Rayner, Keir Starmer's spokesman would say: "There was no deal on reinstatement, no." When pressed on whether senior LOTO staff had advance sight of Jeremy's second statement (which they had in fact co-written), he would respond: "We are not going to comment on private conversations."

Well, I am perfectly prepared to comment. In fact, I am so confident of the account I have given here that I have submitted it for use in legal proceedings and will stand by it in court.

Back on the conference call, with the statement finalised, Morgan put a further suggestion to Jon and me. "If you could get Jeremy to publish this statement today," he said, "Keir is on Marr tomorrow and he will publicly welcome it."

Unfortunately, Jeremy wasn't prepared to move that fast. He was away; he didn't trust the other side to stick to the deal; and he thought releasing the statement long in advance of an NEC panel hearing would give the right too much time to ratchet up the pressure on Keir and scupper the arrangement.

So it wasn't until 17 November, on the morning of the panel hearing, that the statement was published. "To be clear, concerns about antisemitism are neither 'exaggerated' nor 'overstated,'" said the key passage (referring to "concerns" about the problem rather than the scale of it). "The point I wished to make was that the vast majority of Labour Party members were and remain committed anti-racists deeply opposed to antisemitism."

The five-person NEC panel (only two of whom could be described as pro-Corbyn) decided unanimously to readmit Jeremy to the party. The right reacted with rage. Margaret Hodge tweeted that it was "a broken outcome from a broken system." The Jewish Labour Movement blamed a "factionally-aligned political committee."

I don't know if Starmer was taken by surprise by the backlash, but it soon became clear he was going to crumble. It was reported he was given an ultimatum by Hodge—she would resign from the party if Corbyn remained a Labour MP. Starmer was also apparently "infuriated" by a tweet claiming the leadership had climbed down.

At no time in any of our discussions had there been any mention of the Labour whip being withdrawn from Corbyn. The objective of both sides had been to reach an agreement that would bring matters back to normal. But Starmer now reneged on our deal. He withdrew the whip, leaving Corbyn in the absurd situation of being an MP and a Labour member, but not a Labour MP.

Corbyn was told that if he wanted the whip restored he would have to make an apology—which begged the question: if an apology was so important to LOTO, why didn't they include one in the statement they wrote?

I'm a trade unionist. The one thing you never do is renege on a deal you've negotiated. Livid, I released what one *Guardian* journalist described as an "absolutely blistering" statement. "This is a vindictive and vengeful action which... shows marked bad faith," it said.

That was when I lost my personal relationship with Keir. I could no longer trust him.

———————

It was extraordinary that Keir Starmer was able to suspend a former leader and face so little resistance from within the Parliamentary Labour Party—including from the left-wing Socialist Campaign Group, half of which, despite the best efforts of its secretary Richard Burgon, proved to have a poor understanding of the word solidarity. It brought home how little had been achieved in the Corbyn era to reshape the PLP.

I thought back to a missed opportunity at the 2018 Labour Party Conference. There, activists were campaigning for the party to adopt 'open selection,' otherwise known as mandatory reselection—every MP facing a fresh selection contest before each general election. This was a way of making MPs accountable to local party members. Especially in safe Labour seats, MPs could otherwise become completely unmoored.

Mandatory reselection had long been a democratic demand of the left, fiercely opposed by the right and by most MPs. But now in charge, the left leadership worried the change would provoke a split in the parliamentary party at a delicate time. They favoured a compromise: a reformed 'trigger ballot' system allowing a selection contest to take place if a third of an MP's constituency party branches or a third of locally affiliated trade union branches wanted one.

I was asked by Jeremy Corbyn to support the compromise and get the other unions to agree. That was an uncomfortable position for me because Unite's policy was to support mandatory reselection. But on the basis that this was what the leadership wanted, and after being told Momentum was on board, I worked hard to get the other unions signed up.

There wasn't a stand-alone vote on open selection at the 2018 conference; only the compromise was put forward in a package of other reforms. When this agenda was voted on, wow—more than 90 per cent of Constituency Labour Party delegates rejected the agenda in protest at being denied the chance to vote for open selection, while all the trade union delegates, with the exception of those from the FBU, voted in favour of it and backed the compromise. The split between party members and trade unions was visible and the anger directed at us was palpable. There were shouts of "Shame on the unions."

Immediately afterwards I spoke at a number of fringe meetings. I emphasised that "What comrades need to understand is that Jeremy is asking us to accept this alternative." I was furious that the unions and I were getting the blame for something the leadership wanted.

That's why I lost my temper with the left-wing MP Chris Williamson when I saw him in the conference centre the following day. He had written an article in the *Morning Star* accusing Unite of voting against our own policy. I took his head off. I actually lost my own head a bit which I shouldn't have done, and I was overheard by reporters, which only made me angrier.

After all that, the trigger ballot system that was adopted proved to be a failure. Despite the bar having been lowered significantly, for the 2019 general election no MPs were successfully triggered, squandering a golden opportunity to change the PLP. Campaigners for open selection had argued that for an ordinary party member to put their head above the parapet to trigger their MP was much more daunting than choosing to back an alternative candidate in a selection contest that was happening anyway. I now think they were right.

If I could turn back the clock to the 2018 conference, I would push for open selection. But I wouldn't call the decision not to do so a mistake, more a missed chance. Politics is a game of chess. Every move you make meets a response from your opponents. At that time, with the party in disarray on Brexit and an evident split developing over a second referendum, there was a reasonable argument for the course that was taken. But two years later, as the abject state of the PLP was exposed again in the lacklustre response to Corbyn's suspension, the consequence of that decision was laid bare.

———————

In the wake of Jeremy Corbyn's suspension, Labour's general secretary David Evans launched an anti-democratic crackdown on the left, suspending at least 74 local party officers for allowing motions expressing solidarity with the former leader. Constituency parties were banned from even discussing the matter. Left-wing candidates were excluded from democratic selections up and down the country.

Meanwhile, Keir Starmer seemed to feel little obligation to honour the 10 pledges on which he had won the leadership, even arguing against raising corporation tax in advance of the 2021 budget. Struggling to inspire the public, his team fell back on vapid New Labour clichés, promising to be "unashamedly pro-business."

I still hoped and believed that Keir Starmer could be prime minister, but I was fearful that if he continued on the course set in his first year of leadership, he would not win back the red wall seats. The disastrous by-election defeat in Hartlepool in May 2021 seemed to vindicate my fears, and scraping home by the skin of our teeth in Batley and Spen two months later didn't make me feel any better. If a general election was called early, which seemed possible, Starmer would have little time to rectify his mistakes. He still had the opportunity to change course, unite his party around a radical platform, and make the promised "moral case for socialism." But he needed to realise that if the ship he was captaining listed too far to the right, it would go under.

Faced with the leadership's hostility, many left wingers have given up on Labour. I understand their despair. But I have been a member for many years and lived through far darker times. I still see infinitely more potential on the left of the party today than existed for long periods of my lifetime. Labour remains best placed to give working people a political voice. But if the future is a return to the sour recipes of New Labour the party will be over.

I believe Momentum has a vital role to play in sustaining the Labour left. During the Corbyn era Momentum had its troubles, no doubt, but it proved incredibly influential—just as the Campaign for Labour Party Democracy had before it. With the danger now that the left fragments and scatters, a rejuvenated Momentum, freed from the obligation to defend the leadership, must rebuild from the bottom up. I hope Unite will be able to help in that endeavour.

However, it is my lifelong conviction that organised labour is the rock on which progress is built. In the heat of Corbyn's suspension, a new alliance was forged between seven Labour-affiliated trade unions that rallied behind him: ASLEF, the Bakers, CWU, FBU, NUM, TSSA, and Unite. These unions are now fighting for a socialist future through a new organisation that will bring together trade unions, grassroots groups, radical movements and left MPs, giving the left the structure and coordination to press home its power and influence. This body will campaign for socialist policies and defend the democratic rights of members under attack by an over-mighty bureaucracy. The media will inevitably declare us anti-Starmer; in fact, we are simply pro-socialist.

Reports of the death of the left have been greatly exaggerated. I firmly believe Jeremy Corbyn changed the Labour Party and British politics for good. His leadership may have foundered on the rocks of Brexit, but on all the big questions for the future it is only the left that has answers that are both equal to the task and popular. Our economy and society are being reshaped in the wake of the Covid-19 pandemic. Technological advances are enforcing change on the workplace. Working people can't afford for us to abandon the radical agenda that we know in our hearts is right.

When Jeremy claimed after the 2019 general election defeat that Labour had nonetheless "won the arguments" on austerity, inequality, corporate power and the climate emergency, he was ridiculed. But he was right. The 21st century is not ringing out the death knell of the labour movement; it is sending out a call to arms. Our response must be a cry of hope. We are the ones with convictions and the courage to go with them. Our values are eternal. Never forget it.

CHAPTER 23

'FIGHTING BACK' TRADE UNIONISM

I remember how it felt to be out on strike for six weeks. It was 1972, I was 22 years old and working on the docks. I had been on strike before, but most disputes were settled quickly. This one was different.

No worker wants to be on strike. It pushes your resolve to the limit. Running desperately low on cash, with a wife and baby boy to support, I was forced to sell my car—my beautiful mint green Hillman Imp, the best car I ever had. Losing it was a massive wrench.

There was no strike pay; no solidarity fundraising appeals; nothing. We were on the bones of our arse. I slipped into debt, fell into arrears on my mortgage, and ultimately had to sell my house. It was horrible.

The hardship I went through was far from unique. Many workers before and since have experienced the same or worse. For as long as there are workers and bosses, there will be struggle and sacrifice. The odds can only be shifted in favour of our class if we stand together and help each other when in need.

That's the essence of trade unionism. But the history of the labour movement is littered with examples of disputes that could have been won, and workers whose lives could have been improved, if trade unions had been better prepared for battle.

Experiences like those six weeks meant that, as I moved up through the union ranks, I vowed that if I was ever in a position of power I would build a strike fund so large that workers would no longer have to sell their car or lose their house. I vowed that I would never abandon members on strike. And I vowed that I would not be browbeaten into accommodation with the bosses.

If there's one thing I hope people will recognise about my career, it's that I kept to those vows and, in proving they can bring success, provided an example for the trade unionists of tomorrow.

Politics impacts on every element of the lives of working people. My involvement in the maelstrom of events encapsulated in the previous chapters is an indication of how essential I believe politics to be. The working class can never afford to sit back and leave politics to others who don't have our interests at heart.

But Unite is a trade union representing workers in the industrial arena. The vast majority of my time as general secretary—90 per cent of it—has been spent away from politics supporting our members' struggles and dealing with the continued construction and evolution of my union.

Running Unite is a massive task. An awful lot of the work is mundane, day-to-day administration—not the kind of stuff that makes for a page turner. But every day, the diversity of Unite takes my breath away. I often ask people to name an occupation that doesn't have a Unite member doing it. Nobody can ever come up with one. Journalists, doctors, librarians, sewage workers, bio-chemists—Unite has them all. And there isn't a single town in our nations without a Unite presence.

I have recounted stories of high-profile industrial action in the aviation industry, the manufacturing sector and the docks. But I have been personally involved in a whole range of other disputes, from supporting ambulance crews in Yorkshire to offshore oil rig workers in Aberdeen. I have stood on picket lines with workers of all ages and backgrounds, from Oxford bus staff to young British Airways 'mixed fleet' cabin crew, whose passion, energy and resolve to win gave me fresh inspiration.

In Unite we have built a union with a distinct philosophy and culture—a 'fighting back' union, regarded as the most formidable and powerful union in our country. Of course, we deal constructively with thousands of good companies. We don't go looking for conflict, but neither do we back away from any fight if our members are being attacked. I'm very proud that we have developed that culture, because it didn't happen by accident. It has its origins in the history through which I have lived.

Being a 'fighting back' union has implications. If you're going to step into the ring, you need to be prepared. Employers will exploit weakness. The only response is to show them you are strong. That has led Unite to develop a number of innovations in the way we operate that are already being copied by trade unions around the world and which I hope will be taken up by many more. I believe they are essential to the future of trade unionism. We hear a lot about how the changing world of work means trade unions will become less powerful and less relevant, but I am not fatalistic. Unite has shown during my time as general secretary that it doesn't have to be that way, that a strong union makes for confident workers and vice versa. There's a truism that Bob Crow, Tony Woodley and I have often repeated, and which serves as my guiding star: "If you fight you may not always win, but if you don't fight you will surely lose."

Three of Unite's innovations are worth particular mention. The first is a very large strike fund. Throughout the history of the trade union movement, many a dispute has been lost because bosses were able to hold firm and starve workers back to work. Trade unions responded by providing financial support to their members, but too often this was paltry or soon dried up. This has been a persistent failing in our movement that I was determined to fix.

Before I became general secretary, Unite didn't have a strike fund (neither did its predecessors, the T&G and Amicus). There was strike pay, set at a low rate, but it came out of the general fund and involved a lot of bureaucracy. Early on in my tenure, I established our dedicated strike fund with a hefty lump sum to kick it off. While previously 10 per cent of members' dues were allocated to the union's branches, I persuaded the executive council to require 2.5 per cent to be returned for the strike fund. That alone brought in £1 million a month. With more coming in than going out, the fund soon built up. I'm particularly proud that it has become the largest strike fund in Europe, standing, at the time of writing, at £45 million.

The rate of strike pay for Unite members was initially set at £30 a day, or £150 a week—which was not too bad. It was substantial enough for striking workers to be able to feed themselves and pay bills. But, as general secretary, I had the discretionary power to double it to £60 a day if certain criteria were met—for example, if the strike was to defend a sacked shop steward.

An early test for this system came when our members at Argos went on strike. I had looked after Argos workers as a national officer and had negotiated the agreement they operated under. I wanted to see them win and, as the dispute met the criteria, I doubled the strike pay to £60. A while later, I picked up an email from a shop steward who I knew wasn't keen on the industrial action, complaining about the strike pay. I gave him a call. "Why are you moaning?" I demanded. "Don't you remember the days when we got nothing? I hear the company has made an offer. Is everyone going to accept it?"

He said: "They might, if you keep your nose out, Len."

"What do you mean?" I asked.

"Lennie, you've doubled the strike pay. Our people are getting £300 a week."

"And?"

"Len, we only take home £270 a week when we're working. They'll stay out until Christmas."

The Argos workers won, of course, but we later had to make a rule that strikers couldn't get more than full pay. Still, it was very powerful. During a dispute at St Mungo's, a homelessness charity in London, I told a mass meeting that I was doubling their strike pay, which by then meant they would get £70 a day. A manager reported back to one of our stewards: "As soon as we heard that, we knew we were never going to beat you." The dispute was settled immediately.

The discretionary arrangement to double strike pay eventually ran into difficulties, with members whose pay wasn't doubled regarding it as unfair, so at my suggestion the executive replaced the system with a single rate of £50 a day, or £250 a week. We also developed other tactics, such as taking out a limited number of strategically important workers on full pay, rather than an entire workforce on strike pay, leading to quick victories. I encouraged branches to create their own strike funds. When Rolls Royce workers were in dispute over job cuts at the Barnoldswick factory in 2020-21, they won a fantastic victory in part because their own strike fund allowed them to take action on virtually full pay. What tremendous power that gives workers.

Throughout my stewardship, Unite has been involved in four times as many industrial action ballots as every other British trade union combined and we have been successful in almost every one. We have frequently heard anecdotal evidence of employers conceding before any action was taken because of the power of the financial support on offer to our members.

The second innovation developed at Unite is the most exciting: leverage. The idea of leverage is to show a hostile employer that we can impose consequences on them that will cost more than whatever they're hoping to gain by screwing their workforce.

Our leverage uses highly sophisticated methods to identify a company's weak spots and press on them. We ask three questions about the employer: who is the real decision maker? How does the company make money? What consequences can we inflict? A vast amount of information is gathered to answer these questions and plan a campaign that may last up to a year.

Leverage is an explosive tactic that is not to be used lightly. It's for when an employer is already in an aggressive posture. It isn't a replacement for strikes—nothing can be more powerful than collective action by the workers. But in some cases strikes are impossible or unsuitable. That's when leverage comes in. These are muscular campaigns, very different to usual industrial relations. They are not negotiations; we make demands—reinstate a sacked shop steward, recognise the union, stick to a national agreement. The company needs to know we're serious and that our campaign will escalate, making each day worse for it than the one before.

Leverage was pioneered by Unite's organising department, headed by Sharon Graham, regarded as the best organiser in the whole of Europe. It developed out of our organisers' experience of fighting companies for union recognition when, of course, strike action isn't yet possible. From these conflicts different ways to pressure employers were developed and leverage was born.

We first used leverage in a concerted way in a dispute with Honda in Swindon in 2011, soon after I became general secretary. The company wanted to rip up our recognition agreement and suspended our senior shop steward. Taking out a steward crosses a line—if we can't defend our stewards, we're nothing. But there was too much fear among the workforce to strike, so we decided to try leverage. Before long, Honda executives were flying over from Japan to meet me. The result of the dispute was that our steward was reinstated and the managing director of the plant was sacked. Along the way, we gained 1,200 new members who were attracted by a union fighting for them.

The actions we take as part of a leverage campaign range from, at the lighter end of the scale, stunts to get the decision maker's attention—such as showing up at a CEO's golf club or protesting outside a company's HQ—through to heavier financial initiatives—such as pressuring a company's contractors or speaking to industry analysts and credit ratings agencies about our plans. In the early days of leverage it was difficult to get such analysts in the room. Now they queue up for information because they know our actions will affect the industry they monitor. The information they put in their reports is then read by investors and can impact the value of the company. During a dispute with British Airways in 2020, 48 industry analysts and two of the big credit rating agencies joined a conference call with Sharon to hear what we were planning to do.

Often, the best way to make an employer reverse course will not be to hit the company itself, or its biggest shareholders—because they are the hardest to move—but the clients from whom it generates its income. One of the best wins we've ever had came after seven construction companies, led by Balfour Beatty, announced in 2012 their intention to withdraw from a long-standing national agreement between employers and unions and create their own agreement known as BESNA. In response, we launched a leverage campaign that shook them to the core. We spoke to potential clients of Balfour Beatty and told them that if they went with the company they would have us in their hair all day long; if they didn't, we would go away.

We also called in the help of the Teamsters union in North America to send dozens of their members to occupy Balfour Beatty's US offices. I like to imagine their American CEO exclaiming, "Goddamn it, what the hell's happening here?" It was reported to me that he really did say he wasn't having some poxy dispute in the UK disrupting his life. That led to a memorable moment when Balfour Beatty's UK managing director rang me in my office at about 8 p.m. one evening. His words were reminiscent of a scene from a favourite film of mine, 'The Godfather': "Len, how did we get this far? We didn't want this. How can we put it right?" I replied that it was easy: simply email straight away to confirm that Balfour Beatty would stick with the national agreement. Ten minutes later the email arrived and the following morning the other six companies capitulated.

The following year, we won another big construction industry dispute after one of our stewards working on the Crossrail project in London was sacked having raised safety concerns (more than half our leverage campaigns have been in response to the sacking of stewards). We launched a fantastic campaign that included occupations of the offices of major corporate investors, the rail regulator, and even Google; the blocking of Oxford Street, Park Lane and Earls Court; and international solidarity protests in Holland, France, Spain, the US and Canada to pressure clients not to do deals with blacklisting companies. That led to a funny episode when I was in Toronto for a meeting with the United Steelworkers. One of the Crossrail contractors, a Spanish company called Ferrovial, operated a toll bridge in the city. Someone at the meeting said to me, "Hey Len, what's this about your people shutting down the bridge?" It was news to me. It turned out Sharon had somehow managed to close a bridge in Toronto over a dispute in London.

When the passenger transport company Go Ahead sacked a steward working on the buses in Manchester, we discovered its growth plan was to move into the Norwegian rail market by winning a contract worth £3.8 billion. We dispatched a team to speak to Norwegian politicians and the press, armed with a dossier detailing how this company dealt with rail contracts in the UK. The company was forced to weigh the benefit of getting rid of the steward against the threat to a multi-billion-pound contract. Soon enough, the steward was back at work.

Companies that sack our stewards always seem surprised when we don't play by the Queensberry rules. Of course, they make threats. If we haven't received a legal letter promising hell and damnation after two weeks of a leverage campaign, we start wondering if we're doing something wrong. The greatest compliment our techniques have ever received came in the form of a summit of CEOs in Paris in the aftermath of the big construction disputes. The meeting had just one item on the agenda: "Is Unite's leverage legal?" Unfortunately for the attendees, the answer, delivered by two QCs, was "Yes." Inevitably, the employers' next move was to try to make it illegal. There was talk of the Cameron government classifying leverage as secondary picketing, but nothing came of it.

So far, Unite has used leverage defensively. An exciting prospect for the future is to use it to advance as part of a strategic push to gain union recognition from the biggest players in each sector of the economy, especially from fiercely anti-union companies like Amazon.

Leverage is not easy to do. I don't know of any trade union in Europe that operates leverage in the focused and sophisticated manner that Unite does. For it to be effective, a trade union has to be prepared to make a big investment—we can have 40-50 staff on a single leverage campaign. It takes a lot of resources and a lot of guts. But I have no doubt that leverage is going to be a vital part of the trade union movement's armoury in the future. That's why unions from across the world, as well as here at home, have come to Unite to learn the methods Sharon uses. Leverage is not a silver bullet, but all I can say is that every time Unite has used it, we've won.

The third innovation is the creation of Unite Community—a section of the union for people not in work, whether for reasons of health, unemployment, education or retirement. Established in 2014, this is one of my proudest achievements as general secretary. It is unique—no other union has anything similar.

While all trade unions give a voice to workers in work, I wanted to give a voice to ordinary people in their communities who don't work. As well as running political campaigns on austerity, universal credit, the bedroom tax and other issues, I saw an opportunity for Community members to assist us in industrial disputes. Tory trade union laws severely restrict the ways in which workers can stand up for themselves, but they say nothing about non-workers.

The idea of Unite Community sprang from trying to organise contract cleaners as a regional officer in Liverpool in 1980. It was difficult—they were in a precarious position. But they had a brilliant union officer helping them, a friend called John Farrell. He set a Merseyside-wide minimum rate of pay and demanded the contractors meet it. They would tell him to get lost, so he would organise demonstrations outside the offices cleaned by the women (they were all women) and get everybody and anybody to come and assist in their struggle—a rudimentary version of leverage. Soon the companies in the offices would be onto the contractor asking, "What's going on?"

The contractor would say, "Well they want an extra 50p an hour, are you willing to pay it?"

"Yes, yes, we'll give it to you."

On more than one occasion, including when we occupied a hotel, the police would turn up saying, "Hang on, how come you've got all these people here? They don't work here."

John would reply, "No, that's so-and-so's husband, that's her brother, his uncle. They're nothing to do with the union, they're family members, don't be asking me about them."

John handled 54 disputes in a 12-month period and won every one, establishing an unofficial minimum wage for cleaners on Merseyside. I learned then that linking community activity with industrial organisation could be a powerful strategy for a trade union.

Years later, Unite Community would prove me right by leading the brilliant campaign to force Mike Ashley to scrap zero-hours contracts at Sports Direct. It was Unite Community members who did banner drops from bridges, protested outside Sports Direct shops and unfurled banners at Newcastle United football matches (the club owned by Ashley). The workers themselves couldn't take action because the vast majority were precarious zero-hour or agency workers who weren't in the union. Unite Community stepped in to expose an injustice.

Having Unite Community members supporting workers in industrial disputes adds another layer of pressure on the bosses. Whether Community members are taking direct action, protesting, collecting petitions, leafleting, supporting pickets or spreading the word on social media, their efforts help open up workplace struggles to the wider public and strengthen the workers' hand.

Trade unions should always be a visible part of society, not just a vested interest in work. The workers who make up our unions also make up our communities. But, despite being the biggest voluntary organisations in society, trade unions are often treated as if we don't exist. I have done what I can to change that.

For example, children don't learn about the role of trade unions as part of the national curriculum, even though so many social advances—equal pay, the minimum wage, pension rights, maternity and paternity leave, holiday pay, holidays themselves and much more—were won by the labour movement. That's why I launched our Unite in Schools programme in 2014 with the ambition to send speakers into all schools to talk to 15 and 16-year-olds about what trade unionism is.

Inevitably, the *Sun* newspaper ran a vicious attack on the scheme, accusing me of trying to brainwash kids and claiming it was just a way to recruit members. In fact, we simply wanted to explain what trade unions are and how collectivism works. I would rather the government made that a standard part of the curriculum, or the TUC took on the task, but in the absence of either Unite has stepped up. Young people are the most likely to be exploited at work and yet they begin by knowing next to nothing about how unions can protect them directly, let alone our broader role.

The creation of the think tank Class (the Centre for Labour and Social Studies) was another way Unite sought to influence wider society. There wasn't a left think tank that could fill in the substance behind the slogans and policies we espoused. It's all very well saying we want a more equal society, but how? So, along with others, in 2012 I set up Class to contribute to that work—not to be a voice of Unite or the trade unions, but to develop ideas that provoke debate. It was important to be hands-off, to allow Class to grow organically and ask questions for which Unite might not always have a comfortable answer.

It's because I believe trade unions should be visible that I insist on going in the front door of Number 10 rather than sneaking around the back, contribute articles to the national press and make myself available for media interviews. I see engaging with the media as an integral part of my job not only because our members want to see me articulating their concerns, but to give the wider public a sense of what trade unions stand for. Of course, there are limits. I would never do an interview with the *Sun* because of its lies over Hillsborough.

I enjoy broadcast interviews. I would rather do them live so that I can't be edited. I prefer interviewers who give their guests time to make a point, like John Pienaar, to those who don't, like Andrew Neil. But they're all the same—always on attack mode waiting for a slip up or a controversial remark. They have me on because I'm happy to give them controversy. That always worried my influential director of communications, Pauline Doyle. Eventually, she said: "I've realised that the controversial things you say aren't mistakes, are they?"

It's necessary for trade union leaders to go on the airwaves but it's not an answer to the decades-old question of how the labour movement can counter the vicious bias against workers that saturates the media. We know this isn't an accident, but part of what the corporate media exists to do. The British press, dominated by billionaire-owned, right-wing, Conservative-supporting newspapers, sets a narrative that treats all strikes as bad and almost all bosses as plucky entrepreneurs. The only daily newspaper that is consistently on the side of workers is the *Morning Star*, but its circulation is small. Even the left-liberal press seems to be willing to fight for the poor and vulnerable only so long as the poor and vulnerable don't fight for themselves. When push comes to shove, it invariably sides with the establishment. That allows the rest of the press to run wild, peddling lies to undermine workers. The broadcast media is no better, with vastly more airtime given to voices from business than trade unions.

Part of the answer is to make sure there are alternatives. Unite provides funding to the excellent *Tribune* magazine and *LabourList* website, helping to better inform trade unionists and left activists about developments in politics and the labour movement. For as long as I can remember there has been talk of the unions funding a national newspaper or TV channel, but a viable plan has never been produced. There is, however, a bright spot on the horizon: social media. While I'm aware of the dark side of this medium, it has proved itself essential for challenging the mainstream media. Trade unions, including Unite, are increasingly making use of digital platforms like YouTube, which allow us to speak directly to members and the wider public. When, in January 2021, Boris Johnson's government wanted to reopen schools as Covid-19 was surging, the NEU teachers' union held an online Zoom meeting that attracted 400,000 people—an incredible way to counter government spin. New media outlets with the potential to reach hundreds of thousands are popping up all the time—following the examples of *Novara Media*, *Skwawkbox*, *Double Down News*, the *Canary*, *Socialist Telly* and others. Individual left-wing figures have huge online followings. These means of getting our message across simply didn't exist in the past and fill me with optimism for the future.

The need for trade unions that aren't afraid to be combative, visible and inventive couldn't be more urgent given the historic challenges workers are now facing. We are already in a period of dramatic change in the workplace. Automation and the spread of insecure work threaten the very basis of collective organisation. But that doesn't mean the battle is lost—far from it.

The backdrop to these challenges could hardly be less favourable. The Covid-19 pandemic that took hold in 2020 dramatically weakened the power of workers. Many employers exploited the virus to shed jobs and claw back gains made through years of collective bargaining. Our members came under attack as bosses imposed changes their workforces would never have accepted in normal times. The ugly face of capitalism was revealed, but so too was the importance of trade unions as the only means for workers to defend themselves.

I was very proud of Unite's role during the pandemic. We helped convince the government to protect jobs by introducing the job retention scheme and then successfully argued that it should be beefed up and extended. We proved ourselves capable of dealing with the worst excesses of the bad bosses even in the most difficult circumstances, showing that a 'fighting back' union gets results for working people. Even the media was occasionally forced to acknowledge our positive role.

Unite was on the frontline of the fight against the most obscene tactic used by employers: 'fire and rehire,' whereby companies sack their entire workforce and reemploy them on grossly inferior contracts. Bosses have tried similar tricks in the past, but the callous way some employers exploited the pandemic to 'fire and rehire' their workers led to an outcry that prompted government ministers to condemn the tactic and Keir Starmer to say it should be banned.

'Fire and rehire' was pioneered by none other than British Airways, a parting shot from the despicable former CEO Willie Walsh. In April 2020, the airline declared 12,000 job losses, with the remaining 30,000 employees threatened with 'fire and rehire.' Unite launched a magnificent fightback through limited industrial action and a brilliant 'crisis leverage' campaign that included getting 301 MPs to sign up to the idea of redistributing the company's lucrative Heathrow landing slots. As a result of our fight, a cross-party parliamentary committee branded the airline's behaviour a "national disgrace." British Airways backed down, but the 'fire and rehire' tactic was taken up by other companies with less organised workforces.

'Fire and rehire' poses a serious threat to workers. It's up to the trade unions to defeat it. That means devoting our resources to stamping it out before it takes hold, to send a message to other companies that they better not try it. Unite is using every tool available, including higher strike pay in 'fire and rehire' disputes and leverage techniques, to see it off.

A worker who fears they can be thrown on the scrapheap at any moment is in no position to fight. There has been an explosion of insecure work in recent years, most famously in the so-called gig economy (a term that angers me because it sounds sexy when it is anything but). Casualisation, zero-hours contracts, agency work and bogus self-employment are other ways bosses can get the labour power they need without having to honour the rights previous workers have won for our class.

Some of these exploitative arrangements are easier to combat than others. Trade unions have had some success in organising agency workers, for example, but the gig economy is a much tougher nut to crack. While there are possibilities to tackle the problem at the top by deploying leverage and other techniques on the companies that own the businesses using these practices, and while small trade unions like the IWGB are attempting to organise at the bottom among hard-to-reach workers, ultimately stopping these abuses will require legal and political intervention. It's a question of what kind of society we want. As Unite has often said, we don't want a race to the bottom society, we want a rate for the job society.

Automation presents an even greater challenge to workers and trade unions. It's estimated that 35 per cent of jobs in the UK will be automated by 2035— equating to more than 10 million workers replaced by robots and computers. This is clearly a massive issue for everyone.

Automation in various forms has been a constant since the Industrial Revolution. Visit any of our manufacturing plants and you will see automation. Robots are favoured by management because they don't answer back, get sick or take holidays. I have mentioned my experience of working on the Liverpool docks as containerisation revolutionised the shipping industry, drastically reducing the number of dockers needed to do the work.

But the so-called 'Fourth Industrial Revolution' that's now underway is different because of the use of Artificial Intelligence. The range of tasks that can be performed by machines has greatly expanded. The Covid-19 pandemic has actually accelerated this trend. For example, Stagecoach, the biggest investor in automation in the passenger transport sector, has upped its development of driverless busses. Artificial intelligence can't catch Covid.

Automation is a huge concern for Unite because it is hitting the transport and manufacturing sectors hardest, where we are the biggest union. If there are going to be less roles, the task of trade unions is to ensure the remaining work is shared out fairly and workers don't lose money. That might mean, among other measures, a four-day week with no loss of pay. The issue is how we summon the power to push through such solutions.

We have done a lot of work to understand the impact of automation and how we can respond through our recently established research arm, Unite Investigates—because no one else will analyse these trends from a workers' perspective. We are providing those at the sharp end, our stewards, with the knowledge to be forearmed. We have drafted a new technology model agreement that stewards can take to companies—preferably across an entire sector to prevent undercutting—to allow workers to gain some of the benefits of automation without having to bear the costs.

It's not defeatist to say that automation, like insecure work, is an issue too big for trade unions alone to solve. We're talking about nothing less than the way we choose to organise our economy and society. Business profits will skyrocket as jobs are automated. Government will have to grapple with how a society can function when wealth is even more concentrated at the top while potentially millions of people have no work.

There is no clearer example of how it's a fantasy to think the industrial can ever be divorced from the political. Yet we don't have the luxury of being able to wait until the political situation improves before acting. That's why trade unions need to be visible players, prepared to fight. If we don't currently have the political power through the Labour Party to ensure workers get their fair share, we must exert our industrial power.

———————

I lived through decades when the trade union movement was on the back foot. Under sustained attack in the 1980s we battened down the hatches. Our membership was decimated. We had all kinds of ideas for how to resist, but they got us nowhere. Weakened, trade unions embraced a partnership model, accommodating ourselves to business. In place of providing a strong collective voice in the workplace, we offered our members insurance schemes and employment advice, as if we were an industrial version of a car breakdown service. I never bought into that.

What I wanted to do was show that trade unions could fight on the front foot. At a conference in New York in 1992 I heard a speech by Andy Stern, leader of the American union SEIU, about a method of organising based on empowering the workers on the shop floor. I was inspired. I became a champion of that organising ethos and later encouraged Tony Woodley to embrace it. Under his leadership—largely thanks to his bravery and willingness to try something new—we were able to set up an organising department that has since become an integral part of Unite.

My union now employs 130 organisers whose job is to go into workplaces and build a collective that's ready to take strike action itself if necessary. Any other British trade union would consider that number extravagant, but for me it's not enough. If our income would cover it, I would employ twice as many because I don't believe trade unions can win using the car breakdown service model. We can only win by empowering the rank and file and giving them confidence.

Trade unionism should be something workers do, not something that's done to them. Our organisers see the shop stewards as leaders and teach them that the most important thing they have is the workers' own collective strength. Employers are not moved by the reasonableness of an argument; they are moved by the power workers can bring to bear. Workplaces organised in this way recruit more members and retain them longer, because those members feel part of the union.

A vital role of the organisers is winning union recognition from companies. An early and very satisfying example concerned the airline Flybe. The company responded to our attempts to organise by bringing in the American union-busting firm the Burke Group, an outfit that had never been beaten in

Europe—which was hardly surprising given their level of commitment: one union buster to every 20 Flybe workers. Each union buster's job was to make sure those 20 workers voted against recognition using a whole range of tricks, from writing letters to the workers' partners to allegedly planting items in their lockers to get them disciplined. In our operation they met their match: 40 Unite organisers working for eight months defeated the Burke Group when more than 90 per cent of Flybe workers voted "Yes" to recognition. It was a sweet victory.

Real power comes when we are able to organise not just a company, but a whole sector. Unless the majority of companies in a sector are unionised, a dominant player that behaves badly will set the standard for the others, which can't afford to be undercut. Unite targets our resources at organising entire sectors simultaneously. We look at the top 10 employers in each sector, many of which may have no union recognition, and set about changing that. Once we have recognition across a sector, we connect the shop stewards and drive through the same terms in all the companies.

There is tremendous power in sectoral organising but there remains much work to do. Ideally, we would have a government that supports sectoral collective bargaining, but in the absence of that trade unions must do it themselves. If more of the economy had been organised by sector when the Covid-19 pandemic hit, bosses would have found it far more difficult to exploit the crisis and trade unions could have led the debates around financial assistance, rather than hoping a Tory government saw sense.

That kind of ambition is what I mean when I talk about trade unions getting on the front foot. When workers anywhere win, our whole class gains confidence. I have seen that play out within Unite. I have watched many capable, professional officers who saw their role as merely advisory—informing workers of their options but never saying, "We're not having this," and organising a strike ballot—gain in confidence as they embraced the 'fighting back' spirit that we embody. It's that psyche that I've sought to encourage as general secretary.

Confidence feeds off itself. Employers sense it too. The greatest sign of success for a 'fighting back' union is when we don't have to fight at all. In the vast majority of cases, our officers reach amicable agreements with companies on a whole range of individual and collective issues. When my personal involvement is called for, it's often to head off trouble rather than to go to war. Over the years I have met dozens of CEOs from every sector of the economy, forging relationships that have allowed me to promote our members' needs, concerns and aspirations. Many of those meetings resulted in positive outcomes. A way forward for one of our iconic companies, Jaguar Land Rover, was agreed when Cyrus Mistry, CEO of Tata, flew in from India for talks. My meetings with senior executives of Japanese car companies Nissan and Toyota helped secure investment. I flew out to Detroit to win commitments from General Motors to keep open the Vauxhall plants in Luton and Ellesmere Port. Unfortunately, General Motors then sold Vauxhall to Peugeot, prompting a number of trips to France to meet the CEO, Carlos Tavares, an impressive man. While we ensured significant investment for Luton with new models being produced there, it took longer to nail down the same for Ellesmere Port. I was delighted when it was announced in July 2021 that a new model had been secured and the future of the plant was safe. The workers there deserved that future—none more so than Unite's convenor, John Cooper, whose tireless work epitomises the thousands of dedicated convenors and shop stewards who make up our union.

Not all of my meetings have been successful. Discussions with Honda failed to stop the company announcing the closure of its Swindon site in 2019, inflicting devastation on the workers and the community there. And when, on a number of occasions, I met the European president of Ford, I received some indications that the company's Bridgend site in South Wales could be saved, but to no avail. Here was capitalism at its worst: decent, highly-skilled men and women who had created huge wealth for the company being cast aside because Ford could make bigger profits by moving its engine production to Mexico. In the cases of both Honda and Ford there was no help from central government—and people tell me politics doesn't matter.

The 'free market' is a myth. Capitalism relies on government intervention—the only question is in whose interests the intervention is made. When the

British steel industry was gravely threatened in 2015, a "Save Our Steel" campaign launched by Unite, together with our sister unions Community and the GMB, defied the predictions of media commentators by raising public awareness and forcing the government to get involved. Although my meetings with the business secretary, Sajid Javid, were painful due to his obstinate refusal to understand that a 'foundation industry' like steel was essential to a manufacturing economy, the government bowed to pressure and intervened.

I also recall the oil tanker dispute in 2012, when a potential strike by tanker drivers whose conditions were being eroded almost brought the country to a standstill with long queues at petrol stations. I met the cabinet office minister, Francis Maude, and persuaded him to work with us to create a government-approved driver's passport allowing oil tankers to be piloted only by skilled drivers who meet the appropriate standards.

It's the job of a general secretary, an officer or a shop steward to try to cut a deal for their members. The last thing most workers want you to do is come back and say, "I think we should go out on strike." From my earliest days in the union, I've been guided by the notion of 'principled pragmatism'—a determination to deliver an outcome without ever betraying the principle of solidarity. There are some in the trade union movement who would never cut a deal because, whatever was agreed, the terms wouldn't be good enough. Of course, there are situations where pragmatism has no role, such as when a company sacks a shop steward. Then it's purely about the principle. But, in my experience, workers want their trade union to battle hard for them and deliver concrete gains.

The fine judgement between cutting a deal and not selling out becomes most difficult in so-called concession bargaining and conditional pay offers, when a company agrees to a trade union demand in exchange for concessions from the workers in another area—for example a pay rise but only if the workers agree to change their working practices. Taking such an agreement back to the workers often results in a split workforce with all the accompanying anger and resentment. That's why I've always insisted—ever since the salutary lesson delivered by my mate Tony Corrigan when he accused me, as a new union officer, of having lost touch with the dockers—that it's up to the stewards to make those judgements themselves.

The workers are the ones risking their livelihoods if it comes to strike action, so it is they, through their shop stewards, who must make the final call. The job of the union's paid staff, its officers, is to support them. That doesn't mean there isn't room for disagreement and debate about tactics. There were occasions as a union officer when I doubted the wisdom of a particular strike. I would lay out my reasons to the shop stewards, but if the workers then said, "No, Len, thanks, but we're going out," I was with them 100 per cent.

That, above all else, is my core principle—I always back workers in struggle. It's not uncommon for unions to repudiate a strike to avoid being sued for damages by an employer. If any specific part of the strike regulations is not followed to the letter, the union can be liable. Given employers' eagerness to exploit every sub-clause and nuance in the deliberately complex legislation, and the tendency of judges to rule in their favour, mistakes can easily be made.

Over the years Unite has received dozens and dozens of solicitors' letters threatening legal action unless we repudiate a strike. As general secretary— aided by the brilliance of Assistant General Secretary for Legal Services Howard Beckett—I never have. I refuse to tell workers who have, in good conscience, and with a collective will, voted to take industrial action that they are wrong. When workers go on strike, to them it's the most important thing in the world. They want and expect the support of their union; they're not interested in excuses.

The biggest test of that philosophy came in 2012, when London bus workers decided to strike over the failure of their employers to award an Olympic bonus payment that had been received by other transport staff in the capital. Our officers and shop stewards worked hard to prepare co-ordinated action across a fragmented bus network in which 20 companies were busy undercutting each other. On the eve of the action, three of the companies were granted an injunction by the high court to stop the strike. The decision was an affront to democracy, flying in the face of a massive vote of the workers. With everyone assuming the other 17 companies would threaten legal action too, I had to decide whether to call off the strike. I knew that to do so would be a major setback, causing enormous disappointment to everyone involved and squandering our momentum. I'm not sure another general secretary would have given the green light, but I decided to take the risk. It paid off. Our members walked out and the companies were forced to concede. This sent the message we meant business, which made it slightly easier for us some years later when I sent in my troubleshooter, Assistant General Secretary Steve Turner, to conclude a fantastic agreement, with help from London Mayor Sadiq Khan, to stop the race to the bottom and create a forum enabling Unite to resolve concerns with the bus companies and Transport for London.

A commitment to never repudiate a strike has implications. What would I do if industrial action by Unite members put the union on the line for significant compensation? This is far from an academic question. There have been countless occasions when an employer has threatened to take us to court with every possibility of winning damages.

My view on this was crystallised by an incident back in 2005 when I was working for Tony Woodley, then the general secretary of the T&G. I visited his office one evening to find him worried sick. Catering workers at Gate Gourmet, which supplied aeroplane meals to British Airways, had walked out after 667 of them were summarily sacked. British Airways workers—many of them former colleagues from before catering had been outsourced—walked out in solidarity. That was 'secondary action,' illegal under Margaret Thatcher's anti-union laws. The walk out grounded British Airways' entire fleet at Heathrow for two days. The airline was threatening to hit us for £40 million damages by alleging that Tony had encouraged the solidarity strike at a meeting with shop stewards. They even set up a confidential hotline for workers to grass up the ringleaders, hoping people would tell them Tony told them to walk out.

At the time, £40 million would have bankrupted the union. (Unite's wealth has since risen from £50 million when I took over to £500 million in 2021, making us wealthier than all the other British unions put together.) I said: "Tony, stop worrying. What you should do now is get on the phone to British Airways and say, 'This hotline you've set up—let me make something crystal fucking clear to you: if you dare try to close down my union then I will personally make sure British Airways is destroyed as a company, not only here but around the world.'" If British Airways could persuade a judge to award them £40 million, my view was, "We won't pay it; let them sequestrate us, seize our assets, and we'll destroy them." I don't know if Tony followed my advice to the letter, but he made it clear to the airline that if they wanted a fight they would get one. They backed off.

When I became general secretary of Unite, I knew I had to be prepared to face a similar situation. If I was serious about never repudiating a strike, that might mean defying the laws that illegitimately shackle trade unions. Every four years Unite has a rules conference. As soon as I could, at the 2015 rules conference, I obtained a change to rule 2.1 of our rulebook, which sets out Unite's objectives with the qualifying words, "so far as may be lawful." The conference voted to delete that qualification—not because we were anarchists or bank robbers, but because we couldn't be bound by the commitment to stick within bad laws under all circumstances.

I announced the change in a speech to the Industrial Law Society. I argued that people have intrinsic rights which can sometimes be violated even by democratically-elected legislatures—and the right of working people to combine, to organise, is one. If a law violates an intrinsic right, there can be no duty to obey it. At the time, I pointed out, the Tories were threatening even more restrictive trade union laws that would have left the right to strike almost notional. But I was also thinking of the scenario Tony had found himself in. "If we are pushed outside the law," I said, "the moral argument will be with us and the consequences of our actions and any ensuing chaos will be the responsibility of the government."

I didn't spell out what those consequences would be, but I can reveal here that, if defending its members put Unite's existence under threat, I had a blueprint to bring the country to a halt.

It's not that I would have wanted a fight with the state. I certainly didn't see myself as an Earl Haig figure looking to send our people over the top to get mowed down—I'm not stupid. But from each defeat I've experienced over the years I have learned lessons, and none has been more important than this: if you say you'll stand by workers in struggle, you have to put your money where your mouth is.

The scenario I envisaged was a company taking legal action over a legitimate strike and a court ordering Unite to pay substantial damages. We would refuse to pay. The authorities would move to sequestrate our funds and buildings. We would see that as an attempt to shut us down and therefore we would resist using every means at our disposal.

I would move to TUC headquarters where we would form a war cabinet and work to a blueprint detailing what to hit. First, we would block vital transport arteries. Unite's road haulage branch would put at least 200 lorries at key locations to block the motorway network and roads into London. We would form picket lines outside rail and tube stations and trust the rail unions, who are great comrades, not to cross them. Having already been sequestrated, the restrictive trade union laws would no longer inhibit us, as we would have nothing left to lose.

In seven of the nine critical infrastructure sectors of the economy—things like energy, food and utilities—Unite is the leading trade union. Of course, one-and-a-half million Unite members would not come out on strike, but I know workers in key sectors and certain companies would defend their union. Quickly, employers all over the country would be wailing about their losses. The disruption to the public would be considerable.

We would launch a crisis leverage campaign the likes of which has never been seen, hitting vital national targets as well as the company we were in dispute with. We would mobilise on the streets with demonstrations organised by Unite Community. Anyone and everyone would be welcome to join us—anarchists, ulta-leftists, the lot.

Internationally, we would activate all the networks of global solidarity and call on our sister unions for help. If the dispute was with British Airways, for example, I know from discussions I've had that in various countries around the world planes would land and stay landed, with workers refusing to service them.

We would not go gently into the night. We would make the cost of our destruction unbearable. But, throughout, we would clearly communicate a simple way out of the crisis: if the company concerned would cease seeking damages, and our sequestrated assets were returned, we would all go back to work.

If all of that sounds romantic, gallant, and unrealistic, the blueprint I've described was developed because of a genuine belief it could be necessary. Many trade union officials' priority is to avoid legal confrontations in order to preserve the "fabric of the union." My view is different. The fabric of Unite is its members, not our buildings, our cars, or even our employees, as valuable as they are. If a union cannot stand up for its members at the workplace, if it cannot fight for them when they face injustice, then that infrastructure is not worth a damn. And in a situation where we are hamstrung to such a degree that we are unable to perform our duty as organised labour, then what's the point of the union?

Performing our duty as organised labour is what motivates me. As long as bosses can make more money by paying their employees less, or by sacking easily and then hiring cheaply, or by cutting corners on safety, then trade unions will need to exist. No one has come up with a better method of levelling the playing field at work. The obstacles facing us today may seem formidable, but they are far less imposing than those overcome by the first workers to band together more than two centuries ago. Our forerunners had to fight and sometimes die for the right to form unions. They did so because no one is going to protect workers but workers themselves. I believe Unite's 'fighting back' culture is true to that history and stands as an example for the trade unionism of the future.

I've often said that nothing we do as Unite stands in isolation. Every single element—from our schools programme to our strike fund, from Community to our leverage campaigns—is linked, tied together by the values of solidarity and community spirit. And it's to further those values that we proudly fly our flag in the political arena too.

History has taught us that the ideals of men and women, once sown, can never be destroyed. That is what frustrates the ruling elite, because they know that despite their wealth and power, they cannot defeat a united working class. So, in the words of that old labour slogan passed on by each generation:

Educate · Agitate · Organise

As a young man I read a pamphlet by the great T&G general secretary Jack Jones called "A World to Win." In it he evoked a future where bigotry, hatred and prejudice were no more and where the common good of humanity had triumphed.

It lit a flame in my heart that still burns brightly today and, as I enter the last few chapters of my life, I will still do all I can to fight for that world, to fight for workers everywhere, to fight for justice and equality, and to oppose oppression.

I commend to all those fabulous young men and women I see in our trade unions, at Labour Party conferences and beyond, to never despair, to always believe in your values and, in the face of injustice, to find the courage:

"To rise like lions"

"To always be on the side of the angels"

ACKNOWLEDGEMENTS

There have been so many people in my life to whom I owe my thanks for their support, encouragement and understanding. I have not been able to mention all of them in this book but I am content they will know how much I love and appreciate them. As I pass three score years and ten, I realise, in the words of the song by the Verve, that "I'm a lucky man."

I would like to give a special mention to Jo Fontana and Rita Kyriacou, my long-suffering secretaries, for their loyalty, professionalism and willingness to help with this book whenever I asked. I am thankful to Andrew Murray for reading the manuscript and offering his counsel. And I am grateful to Jennie Walsh for her able assistance.

Alex (or Alec, as I call him) Nunns helped me structure and shape the book and did an excellent job editing my handwritten manuscript. It is fair to say that without his involvement this project would never have been completed. Thank you, as well, to my publisher Colin Robinson and everybody at OR Books for being so understanding and encouraging.

It is my honour to be associated with such great comrades in my union. My senior team have been invaluable to me. I owe a lot to Pauline Doyle for valiantly trying to minimise my media controversies for more than a decade (I am not sure she has succeeded when it comes to this book), and to Howard Beckett for giving me the protection of his legal genius. Most importantly, I want to thank all the shop stewards and members of Unite and the T&G who have guided me throughout my life, and the dockers who inspired me as a young man and kept on inspiring me as I grew older.

I am grateful to Jeremy Corbyn for making possible the most exhilarating period of my political life, and to all the socialists who have spoken to me at political events or stopped me in the street, who fight on with heart and determination—you give me the energy to keep going.

To my children, Ian, Calum, Frankie and Victoria, you make me smile. And to all my family, I hope you know how much I value the care you have shown me throughout my life. To my friends, you keep my feet on the ground. Finally, thank you to Karie for persuading me to write this book and giving me the love and support to see it through.